BEA   MAR 1 7 '93

A11707 755022

D0572830

NOBEL PRIZE WINNERS
SUPPLEMENT 1987–1991

Biographical Dictionaries from The H. W. Wilson Company

Greek and Latin Authors 800 B.C.–A.D. 1000
European Authors 1000–1900
British Authors Before 1800
British Authors of the Nineteenth Century
American Authors 1600–1900
Twentieth Century Authors
Twentieth Century Authors: First Supplement
World Authors 1950–1970
World Authors 1970–1975
World Authors 1975–1980
World Authors 1980–1985

The Junior Book of Authors
More Junior Authors
Third Book of Junior Authors
Fourth Book of Junior Authors and Illustrators
Fifth Book of Junior Authors and Illustrators
Sixth Book of Junior Authors and Illustrators

Great Composers: 1300–1900
Composers Since 1900
Composers Since 1900: First Supplement
Musicians Since 1900
Popular American Composers
Popular American Composers: First Supplement
American Songwriters

World Artists 1950–1980
World Artists 1980–1990

American Reformers

World Film Directors

NOBEL PRIZE WINNERS
SUPPLEMENT 1987–1991

An H. W. Wilson Biographical Dictionary

Editor

Paula McGuire

Managing Editors

Debra Goldentyer
Mark Schaeffer

Consultants

Gert H. Brieger, M.D.
William H. Welch Professor of the History of Medicine
The Johns Hopkins University School of Medicine

Laurie M. Brown
Professor of Physics and Astronomy
Northwestern University

Erwin N. Hiebert
Professor Emeritus, History of Science
Harvard University

William McGuire
Former Editorial Manager, Bollingen Series
Bollingen Foundation and Princeton University Press

Peter Temin
Professor of Economics
Massachusetts Institute of Technology

The H. W. Wilson Company
New York
1992

Copyright © 1992 by The H. W. Wilson Company. All rights reserved. No part of this work may be reproduced or copied in any form or by any means, including but not restricted to graphic, electronic, and mechanical—for example, photo-copying, recording, taping, or information and retrieval systems—without the express written permission of the publisher, except that a reviewer may quote and a magazine or newspaper may print brief passages as part of a review written specifically for inclusion in that magazine or newspaper.

Library of Congress Cataloging-in-Publication Data

Nobel prize winners 1987–1991 supplement: an H. W. Wilson
   biographical dictionary / consultants, Gert H. Brieger . . . [et al.].
     p. cm.
   Summary: A biographical dictionary of Nobel Prize winners from 1987
to 1991.
     ISBN 0-8242-0834-X
     1. Nobel prizes. 2. Biography—20th century—Dictionaries.
   [1. Nobel prizes. 2. Biography—Dictionaries.] I. Brieger, Gert H.
   AS911.N9N59 1992
   001.4'4'0922—dc20
   [B]   92-12197
                                            CIP
                                            AC

Editorial development and production by
Visual Education Corporation, Princeton, N.J.

All photographs courtesy of the Nobel Foundation unless otherwise noted.

PRINTED IN THE UNITED STATES OF AMERICA

CONTENTS

———————————

LIST OF NOBEL PRIZE WINNERS,
1987–1991

Nobel Prize for Chemistry

1901	Jacobus van't Hoff
1902	Emil Fischer
1903	Svante Arrhenius
1904	William Ramsay
1905	Adolf von Baeyer
1906	Henri Moissan
1907	Eduard Buchner
1908	Ernest Rutherford
1909	Wilhelm Ostwald
1910	Otto Wallach
1911	Marie Curie
1912	Victor Grignard
	Paul Sabatier
1913	Alfred Werner
1914	Theodore W. Richards
1915	Richard Willstätter
1916	Not awarded
1917	Not awarded
1918	Fritz Haber
1919	Not awarded
1920	Walther Nernst
1921	Frederick Soddy
1922	Francis W. Aston
1923	Fritz Pregl
1924	Not awarded
1925	Richard Zsigmondy
1926	Teodor Svedberg
1927	Heinrich Wieland
1928	Adolf Windaus
1929	Hans von Euler-Chelpin
	Arthur Harden
1930	Hans Fischer
1931	Friedrich Bergius
	Carl Bosch
1932	Irving Langmuir
1933	Not awarded
1934	Harold C. Urey
1935	Frédéric Joliot
	Irène Joliot-Curie
1936	Peter Debye
1937	Walter N. Haworth
	Paul Karrer
1938	Richard Kuhn
1939	Adolf Butenandt
	Leopold Ružička
1940	Not awarded
1941	Not awarded
1942	Not awarded
1943	George de Hevesy
1944	Otto Hahn
1945	Artturi Virtanen
1946	John H. Northrop
	Wendell M. Stanley
	James B. Sumner
1947	Robert Robinson
1948	Arne Tiselius
1949	William F. Giauque
1950	Kurt Alder
	Otto Diels
1951	Edwin M. McMillan
	Glenn T. Seaborg
1952	Archer Martin
	Richard Synge
1953	Hermann Staudinger
1954	Linus C. Pauling
1955	Vincent du Vigneaud
1956	Cyril N. Hinshelwood
	Nikolay N. Semenov
1957	Alexander Todd
1958	Frederick Sanger
1959	Jaroslav Heyrovský
1960	Willard F. Libby
1961	Melvin Calvin
1962	John C. Kendrew
	Max Perutz
1963	Giulio Natta
	Karl Ziegler
1964	Dorothy C. Hodgkin
1965	R. B. Woodward
1966	Robert S. Mulliken
1967	Manfred Eigen
	Ronald Norrish
	George Porter
1968	Lars Onsager
1969	Derek Barton
	Odd Hassel
1970	Luis F. Leloir
1971	Gerhard Herzberg
1972	Christian Anfinsen

	Stanford Moore		W. Arthur Lewis
	William H. Stein	1979	
1973	Ernst Fischer		Theodore Schultz
	Geoffrey Wilkinson	1980	Lawrence Klein
1974	Paul J. Flory	1981	James Tobin
1975	John W. Cornforth	1982	George Stigler
	Vladimir Prelog	1983	Gerard Debreu
1976	William N. Lipscomb	1984	Richard Stone
1977	Ilya Prigogine	1985	Franco Modigliani
1978	Peter D. Mitchell	1986	James M. Buchanan
1979	Herbert C. Brown	1987	Robert M. Solow
	Georg Wittig	1988	Maurice Allais
1980	Paul Berg	1989	Trygve Haavelmo
	Walter Gilbert	1990	Harry M. Markowitz
	Frederick Sanger		Merton H. Miller
1981	Kenichi Fukui		William F. Sharpe
	Roald Hoffmann	1991	Ronald H. Coase
1982	Aaron Klug		
1983	Henry Taube		

1973 Ernst Fischer
    Geoffrey Wilkinson
1974 Paul J. Flory
1975 John W. Cornforth
    Vladimir Prelog
1976 William N. Lipscomb
1977 Ilya Prigogine
1978 Peter D. Mitchell
1979 Herbert C. Brown
    Georg Wittig
1980 Paul Berg
    Walter Gilbert
    Frederick Sanger
1981 Kenichi Fukui
    Roald Hoffmann
1982 Aaron Klug
1983 Henry Taube
1984 R. Bruce Merrifield
1985 Herbert A. Hauptman
    Jerome Karle
1986 Dudley R. Herschbach
    Yuan T. Lee
    John C. Polanyi
1987 Donald J. Cram
    Jean-Marie Lehn
    Charles J. Pedersen
1988 Johann Deisenhofer
    Robert Huber
    Harmut Michel
1989 Sidney Altman
    Thomas R. Cech
1990 Elias James Corey
1991 Richard R. Ernst

Nobel Memorial Prize in Economic Sciences
1969 Ragnar Frisch
    Jan Tinbergen
1970 Paul Samuelson
1971 Simon Kuznets
1972 Kenneth Arrow
    John Hicks
1973 Wassily Leontief
1974 Friedrich A. von Hayek
    Gunnar Myrdal
1975 Leonid Kantorovich
    Tjalling C. Koopmans
1976 Milton Friedman
1977 James Meade
    Bertil Ohlin
1978 Herbert Simon

1979 W. Arthur Lewis
    Theodore Schultz
1980 Lawrence Klein
1981 James Tobin
1982 George Stigler
1983 Gerard Debreu
1984 Richard Stone
1985 Franco Modigliani
1986 James M. Buchanan
1987 Robert M. Solow
1988 Maurice Allais
1989 Trygve Haavelmo
1990 Harry M. Markowitz
    Merton H. Miller
    William F. Sharpe
1991 Ronald H. Coase

Nobel Prize for Literature
1901 René Sully-Prudhomme
1902 Theodor Mommsen
1903 Bjørnstjerne Bjørnson
1904 José Echegaray
    Frédéric Mistral
1905 Henryk Sienkiewicz
1906 Giosuè Carducci
1907 Rudyard Kipling
1908 Rudolf Eucken
1909 Selma Lagerlöf
1910 Paul Heyse
1911 Maurice Maeterlinck
1912 Gerhart Hauptmann
1913 Rabindranath Tagore
1914 Not awarded
1915 Romain Rolland
1916 Verner von Heidenstam
1917 Karl Gjellerup
    Henrik Pontoppidan
1918 Not awarded
1919 Carl Spitteler
1920 Knut Hamsun
1921 Anatole France
1922 Jacinto Benavente y Martinez
1923 William Butler Yeats
1924 Władysław Reymont
1925 George Bernard Shaw
1926 Grazia Deledda
1927 Henri Bergson
1928 Sigrid Undset
1929 Thomas Mann
1930 Sinclair Lewis
1931 Erik Karlfeldt
1932 John Galsworthy

1933	Ivan Bunin	1984	Jaroslav Seifert
1934	Luigi Pirandello	1985	Claude Simon
1935	Not awarded	1986	Wole Soyinka
1936	Eugene O'Neill	1987	Joseph Brodsky
1937	Roger Martin du Gard	1988	Naguib Mahfouz
1938	Pearl S. Buck	1989	Camilo José Cela
1939	Frans Sillanpää	1990	Octavio Paz
1940	Not awarded	1991	Nadine Gordimer
1941	Not awarded		
1942	Not awarded		
1943	Not awarded	**Nobel Prize for Peace**	
1944	Johannes Jensen	1901	Henri Dunant
1945	Gabriela Mistral		Frédéric Passy
1946	Hermann Hesse	1902	Élie Ducommun
1947	André Gide		Albert Gobat
1948	T. S. Eliot	1903	William Cremer
1949	William Faulkner	1904	Institute of International Law
1950	Bertrand Russell	1905	Bertha von Suttner
1951	Pär Lagerkvist	1906	Theodore Roosevelt
1952	François Mauriac	1907	Ernesto Moneta
1953	Winston Churchill		Louis Renault
1954	Ernest Hemingway	1908	Klas Arnoldson
1955	Halldór Laxness		Fredrik Bajer
1956	Juan Jiménez	1909	Auguste Beernaert
1957	Albert Camus		Paul d'Estournelles de Constant
1958	Boris Pasternak	1910	International Peace Bureau
1959	Salvatore Quasimodo	1911	Tobias Asser
1960	Saint-John Perse		Alfred Fried
1961	Ivo Andrić	1912	Elihu Root
1962	John Steinbeck	1913	Henri La Fontaine
1963	George Seferis	1914	Not awarded
1964	Jean-Paul Sartre	1915	Not awarded
1965	Mikhail Sholokhov	1916	Not awarded
1966	S. Y. Agnon	1917	International Committee of the Red
	Nelly Sachs		Cross
1967	Miguel Asturias	1918	Not awarded
1968	Yasunari Kawabata	1919	Woodrow Wilson
1969	Samuel Beckett	1920	Léon Bourgeois
1970	Aleksandr Solzhenitsyn	1921	Karl Branting
1971	Pablo Neruda		Christian Lange
1972	Heinrich Böll	1922	Fridtjof Nansen
1973	Patrick White	1923	Not awarded
1974	Eyvind Johnson	1924	Not awarded
	Harry Martinson	1925	J. Austen Chamberlain
1975	Eugenio Montale		Charles Dawes
1976	Saul Bellow	1926	Aristide Briand
1977	Vicente Aleixandre		Gustav Stresemann
1978	Isaac Bashevis Singer	1927	Ferdinand Buisson
1979	Odysseus Elytis		Ludwig Quidde
1980	Czesław Miłosz	1928	Not awarded
1981	Elias Canetti	1929	Frank Kellogg
1982	Gabriel García Márquez	1930	Nathan Söderblom
1983	William Golding	1931	Jane Addams

11

	Nicholas Murray Butler
1932	Not awarded
1933	Norman Angell
1934	Arthur Henderson
1935	Carl von Ossietzky
1936	Carlos Saavedra Lamas
1937	Robert Cecil
1938	Nansen International Office for Refugees
1939	Not awarded
1940	Not awarded
1941	Not awarded
1942	Not awarded
1943	Not awarded
1944	International Committee of the Red Cross
1945	Cordell Hull
1946	Emily Greene Balch
	John Mott
1947	American Friends Service Committee
	Friends Service Council
1948	Not awarded
1949	John Boyd Orr
1950	Ralph Bunche
1951	Léon Jouhaux
1952	Albert Schweitzer
1953	George C. Marshall
1954	Office of the United Nations High Commissioner for Refugees
1955	Not awarded
1956	Not awarded
1957	Lester Pearson
1958	Georges Pire
1959	Philip Noel-Baker
1960	Albert Luthuli
1961	Dag Hammarskjöld
1962	Linus C. Pauling
1963	International Committee of the Red Cross
	League of Red Cross Societies
1964	Martin Luther King Jr.
1965	United Nations Children's Fund
1966	Not awarded
1967	Not awarded
1968	René Cassin
1969	International Labour Organization
1970	Norman Borlaug
1971	Willy Brandt
1972	Not awarded
1973	Henry Kissinger
	Le Duc Tho
1974	Sean MacBride
	Eisaku Sato

1975	Andrei Sakharov
1976	Mairead Corrigan
	Betty Williams
1977	Amnesty International
1978	Menachem Begin
	Anwar Sadat
1979	Mother Teresa
1980	Adolfo Pérez Esquivel
1981	Office of the United Nations High Commissioner for Refugees
1982	Alfonso García Robles
	Alva Myrdal
1983	Lech Wałesa
1984	Desmond Tutu
1985	International Physicians for the Prevention of Nuclear War
1986	Elie Wiesel
1987	Oscar Arias Sánchez
1988	United Nations Peacekeeping Forces
1989	Dalai Lama
1990	Mikhail Sergeyevich Gorbachev
1991	Aung San Suu Kyi

Nobel Prize for Physics

1901	Wilhelm Röntgen
1902	Hendrik Lorentz
	Pieter Zeeman
1903	Henri Becquerel
	Marie Curie
	Pierre Curie
1904	J. W. Strutt
1905	Philipp von Lenard
1906	J. J. Thomson
1907	Albert A. Michelson
1908	Gabriel Lippmann
1909	Ferdinand Braun
	Guglielmo Marconi
1910	Johannes van der Waals
1911	Wilhelm Wien
1912	Nils Dalén
1913	Heike Kamerlingh Onnes
1914	Max von Laue
1915	W. H. Bragg
	W. L. Bragg
1916	Not awarded
1917	Charles G. Barkla
1918	Max Planck
1919	Johannes Stark
1920	Charles Guillaume
1921	Albert Einstein
1922	Niels Bohr
1923	Robert A. Millikan

Year	Winner	Year	Winner
1924	Manne Siegbahn		Rudolf L. Mössbauer
1925	James Franck	1962	Lev Landau
	Gustav Hertz	1963	J. Hans D. Jensen
1926	Jean Perrin		Maria Goeppert Mayer
1927	Arthur H. Compton		Eugene P. Wigner
	C. T. R. Wilson	1964	Nikolai Basov
1928	Owen W. Richardson		Aleksandr Prokhorov
1929	Louis de Broglie		Charles H. Townes
1930	Venkata Raman	1965	Richard P. Feynman
1931	Not awarded		Julian S. Schwinger
1932	Werner Heisenberg		Sin-itiro Tomonaga
1933	P. A. M. Dirac	1966	Alfred Kastler
	Erwin Schrödinger	1967	Hans A. Bethe
1934	Not awarded	1968	Luis W. Alvarez
1935	James Chadwick	1969	Murray Gell-Mann
1936	Carl D. Anderson	1970	Hannes Alfvén
	Victor F. Hess		Louis Néel
1937	Clinton J. Davisson	1971	Dennis Gabor
	G. P. Thomson	1972	John Bardeen
1938	Enrico Fermi		Leon N. Cooper
1939	Ernest O. Lawrence		J. Robert Schrieffer
1940	Not awarded	1973	Leo Esaki
1941	Not awarded		Ivar Giaever
1942	Not awarded		Brian D. Josephson
1943	Otto Stern	1974	Antony Hewish
1944	I. I. Rabi		Martin Ryle
1945	Wolfgang Pauli	1975	Aage Bohr
1946	P. W. Bridgman		Ben R. Mottelson
1947	Edward Appleton		James Rainwater
1948	P. M. S. Blackett	1976	Burton Richter
1949	Hideki Yukawa		Samuel C. C. Ting
1950	Cecil F. Powell	1977	Philip W. Anderson
1951	John Cockcroft		Nevill Mott
	Ernest Walton		John H. Van Vleck
1952	Felix Bloch	1978	Pyotr Kapitza
	Edward M. Purcell		Arno A. Penzias
1953	Frits Zernike		Robert W. Wilson
1954	Max Born	1979	Sheldon L. Glashow
	Walther Bothe		Abdus Salam
1955	Polykarp Kusch		Steven Weinberg
	Willis E. Lamb Jr.	1980	James W. Cronin
1956	John Bardeen		Val L. Fitch
	Walter H. Brattain	1981	Nicolaas Bloembergen
	William Shockley		Arthur L. Schawlow
1957	Tsung-Dao Lee		Kai Siegbahn
	Chen Ning Yang	1982	Kenneth G. Wilson
1958	Pavel Cherenkov	1983	Subrahmanyan Chandrasekhar
	Ilya Frank		Willam A. Fowler
	Igor Tamm	1984	Simon van der Meer
1959	Owen Chamberlain		Carlo Rubbia
	Emilio Segrè	1985	Klaus von Klitzing
1960	Donald A. Glaser	1986	Gerd Binnig
1961	Robert Hofstadter		Heinrich Rohrer

	Ernst Ruska		Charles S. Sherrington
1987	J. Georg Bednorz	1933	Thomas Hunt Morgan
	K. Alex Müller	1934	George R. Minot
1988	Leon M. Lederman		William P. Murphy
	Melvin Schwartz		George H. Whipple
	Jack Steinberger	1935	Hans Spemann
1989	Hans G. Dehmelt	1936	Henry H. Dale
	Wolfgang Paul		Otto Loewi
	Norman F. Ramsey	1937	Albert Szent-Györgyi
1990	Jerome I. Friedman	1938	Corneille Heymans
	Henry W. Kendall	1939	Gerhard Domagk
	Richard E. Taylor	1940	Not awarded
1991	Pierre-Gilles de Gennes	1941	Not awarded
		1942	Not awarded
		1943	Henrik Dam
			Edward A. Doisy
Nobel Prize for Physiology or Medicine		1944	Joseph Erlanger
1901	Emil von Behring		Herbert S. Gasser
1902	Ronald Ross	1945	Ernst B. Chain
1903	Niels Finsen		Alexander Fleming
1904	Ivan Pavlov		Howard W. Florey
1905	Robert Koch	1946	Hermann J. Muller
1906	Camillo Golgi	1947	Carl F. Cori
	Santiago Ramón y Cajal		Gerty T. Cori
1907	Charles Laveran		Bernardo Houssay
1908	Paul Ehrlich	1948	Paul Müller
	Ilya Metchnikoff	1949	Walter R. Hess
1909	Theodor Kocher		Egas Moniz
1910	Albrecht Kossel	1950	Philip S. Hench
1911	Allvar Gullstrand		Edward C. Kendall
1912	Alexis Carrel		Tadeus Reichstein
1913	Charles Richet	1951	Max Theiler
1914	Robert Bárány	1952	Selman A. Waksman
1915	Not awarded	1953	Hans Krebs
1916	Not awarded		Fritz Lipmann
1917	Not awarded	1954	John F. Enders
1918	Not awarded		Frederick C. Robbins
1919	Jules Bordet		Thomas H. Weller
1920	August Krogh	1955	Hugo Theorell
1921	Not awarded	1956	André Cournand
1922	Archibald V. Hill		Werner Forssmann
	Otto Meyerhof		Dickinson W. Richards
1923	Frederick G. Banting	1957	Daniel Bovet
	John J. R. MacLeod	1958	George W. Beadle
1924	Willem Einthoven		Joshua Lederberg
1925	Not awarded		Edward L. Tatum
1926	Johannes Fibiger	1959	Arthur Kornberg
1927	Julius Wagner von Jauregg		Severo Ochoa
1928	Charles Nicolle	1960	Macfarlane Burnet
1929	Christiaan Eijkman		P. B. Medawar
	Frederick Gowland Hopkins	1961	Georg von Békésy
1930	Karl Landsteiner	1962	Francis Crick
1931	Otto Warburg		James D. Watson
1932	Edgar D. Adrian		

	Maurice H. F. Wilkins		D. Carleton Gajdusek
1963	John C. Eccles	1977	Roger Guillemin
	Alan Hodgkin		Andrew V. Schalley
	Andrew Huxley		Rosalyn S. Yalow
1964	Konrad Bloch	1978	Werner Arber
	Feodor Lynen		Daniel Nathans
1965	François Jacob		Hamilton O. Smith
	André Lwoff	1979	Allan Cormack
	Jacques Monod		Godfrey Hounsfield
1966	Charles B. Huggins	1980	Baruj Benacerraf
	Peyton Rous		Jean Dausset
1967	Ragnar Granit		George D. Snell
	H. Keffer Hartline	1981	David H. Hubel
	George Wald		Roger W. Sperry
1968	Robert W. Holley		Torsten Wiesel
	Har Gorbind Khorana	1982	Sune Bergström
	Marshall W. Nirenberg		Bengt Samuelsson
1969	Max Delbrück		John R. Vane
	Alfred Hershey	1983	Barbara McClintock
	Salvador Luria	1984	Niels K. Jerne
1970	Julius Axelrod		Georges Köhler
	Ulf von Euler		César Milstein
	Bernard Katz	1985	Michael S. Brown
1971	Earl W. Sutherland Jr.		Joseph L. Goldstein
1972	Gerald M. Edelman	1986	Stanley Cohen
	Rodney R. Porter		Rita Levi-Montalcini
1973	Karl von Frisch	1987	Susumu Tonegawa
	Konrad Lorenz	1988	James Black
	Niko Tinbergen		Gertrude B. Elion
1974	Albert Claude		George H. Hitchings Jr.
	Christian de Duve	1989	J. Michael Bishop
	George E. Palade		Harold E. Varmus
1975	David Baltimore	1990	Joseph E. Murray
	Renato Dulbecco		E. Donnall Thomas
	Howard M. Temin	1991	Erwin Neher
1976	Baruch S. Blumberg		Bert Sakmann

NOBEL PRIZE WINNERS BY
COUNTRY OF RESIDENCE, 1901–1991

Note: In this listing, the editors have attempted to reflect all recent geopolitical changes.

Argentina
Bernardo Houssay
Luis F. Leloir (Born in France)
César Milstein
Adolfo Pérez Esquivel
Carlos Saavedra Lamas

Australia
Macfarlane Burnet
John W. Cornforth
John C. Eccles
Patrick White (Born in England)

Austria
Robert Bárány
Alfred Fried
Karl von Frisch
Victor F. Hess
Richard Kuhn
Otto Loewi (Born in Germany)
Konrad Lorenz
Fritz Pregl
Erwin Schrödinger
Bertha von Suttner
Julius Wagner von Jauregg

Belgium
Auguste Beernaert
Jules Bordet
Christian de Duve (Born in England)
Corneille Heymans
Henri La Fontaine
Maurice Maeterlinck
Georges Pire
Ilya Prigogine (Born in Russia)

Bosnia
Ivo Andrić

Canada
Frederick G. Banting
Gerhard Herzberg (Born in Germany)
Lester Pearson

John C. Polanyi (Born in Germany)
Richard E. Taylor

Chile
Gabriela Mistral
Pablo Neruda

Colombia
Gabriel García Márquez

Costa Rica
Oscar Arias Sánchez

Czechoslovakia
Jaroslav Heyrovský
Jaroslav Seifert

Denmark
Fredrik Bajer
Aage Bohr
Niels Bohr
Henrik Dam
Johannes Fibiger
Niels Finsen
Karl Gjellerup
Johannes Jensen
August Krogh
Ben R. Mottelson (Born in United States)
Henrik Pontoppidan

Egypt
Naguib Mahfouz
Anwar Sadat

Finland
Frans Sillanpää
Artturi Virtanen

France
Maurice Allais
Henri Becquerel
Henri Bergson
Léon Bourgeois
Aristide Briand
Louis de Broglie
Ferdinand Buisson

NOBEL PRIZE WINNERS BY COUNTRY OF RESIDENCE, 1901–1991

Albert Camus (Born in Algeria)
Alexis Carrel
René Cassin
Marie Curie (Born in Poland)
Pierre Curie
Jean Dausset
Paul d'Estournelles de Constant
Anatole France
Pierre-Gilles de Gennes
André Gide
Victor Grignard
François Jacob
Frédéric Joliot
Irène Joliot-Curie
Léon Jouhaux
Alfred Kastler
Charles Laveran
Jean-Marie Lehn
Gabriel Lippmann (Born in Luxembourg)
André Lwoff
Roger Martin du Gard
François Mauriac
Frédéric Mistral
Henri Moissan
Jacques Monod
Louis Néel
Charles Nicolle
Frédéric Passy
Jean Perrin
Saint-John Perse
Louis Renault
Charles Richet
Romain Rolland
Paul Sabatier
Jean-Paul Sartre
Claude Simon (Born in Madagascar)
René Sully-Prudhomme

Germany
Kurt Alder
Adolf von Baeyer
Emil von Behring
Friedrich Bergius
Gerd Binnig
Heinrich Böll
Max Born
Carl Bosch
Walther Bothe
Willy Brandt
Ferdinand Braun
Eduard Buchner
Adolf Butenandt
Johann Deisenhofer

Otto Diels
Gerhard Domagk
Paul Ehrlich
Manfred Eigen
Rudolf Eucken
Emil Fischer
Ernst Fischer
Hans Fischer
Werner Forssmann
James Franck
Fritz Haber
Otto Hahn
Gerhart Hauptmann
Werner Heisenberg
Gustav Hertz
Hermann Hesse
Paul Heyse
Robert Huber
J. Hans D. Jensen
Klaus von Klitzing
Robert Koch
Georges Köhler
Albrecht Kossel
Max von Laue
Philipp von Lenard (Born in Austria-Hungary)
Feodor Lynen
Thomas Mann
Otto Meyerhof
Harmut Michel
Theodor Mommsen (Born in Denmark)
Rudolf L. Mössbauer
Erwin Neher
Walther Nernst (Born in West Prussia)
Carl von Ossietzky
Wilhelm Ostwald (Born in Latvia)
Wolfgang Paul
Max Planck
Ludwig Quidde
Wilhelm Röntgen
Ernst Ruska
Nelly Sachs
Bert Sakmann
Albert Schweitzer
Hans Spemann
Johannes Stark
Hermann Staudinger
Gustav Stresemann
Otto Wallach
Otto Warburg
Heinrich Wieland
Wilhelm Wien (Born in East Prussia)
Richard Willstätter
Adolf Windaus

Georg Wittig
Karl Ziegler
Richard Zsigmondy

Greece
Odysseus Elytis
George Seferis (Born in Turkey)

Guatemala
Miguel Asturias

Holland
Tobias Asser
Christiaan Eijkman
Willem Einthoven (Born in Dutch East Indies,
    now Indonesia)
Heike Kamerlingh Onnes
Hendrik Lorentz
Simon van der Meer
Jan Tinbergen
Jacobus van't Hoff
Johannes van der Waals
Pieter Zeeman
Frits Zernike

Iceland
Halldór Laxness

India
Venkata Raman
Rabindranath Tagore
Mother Teresa (Born in Ottoman Empire [now
    Macedonia])

Ireland
Samuel Beckett
Sean MacBride (Born in France)
George Bernard Shaw
Ernest Walton
William Butler Yeats

Israel
S. Y. Agnon (Born in Austria-Hungary)
Menachem Begin (Born in Poland)

Italy
Daniel Bovet (Born in Switzerland)
Giosuè Carducci
Grazia Deledda
Enrico Fermi
Camillo Golgi
Guglielmo Marconi
Ernesto Moneta

Eugenio Montale
Giulio Natta
Luigi Pirandello
Salvatore Quasimodo
Carlo Rubbia

Japan
Leo Esaki
Kenichi Fukui
Yasunari Kawabata
Eisaku Sato
Sin-itiro Tomonaga
Susumu Tonegawa
Hideki Yukawa

Mexico
Alfonso García Robles
Octavio Paz

Myanmar (formerly Burma)
Aung San Suu Kyi

Nigeria
Wole Soyinka

Northern Ireland
Mairead Corrigan
Betty Williams

Norway
Bjørnstjerne Bjørnson
Ragnar Frisch
Trygve Haavelmo
Knut Hamsun
Odd Hassel
Christian Lange
Fridtjof Nansen
Sigrid Undset (Born in Denmark)

Pakistan
Abdus Salam

Poland
Władysław Reymont
Henryk Sienkiewicz
Lech Wałesa

Portugal
Egas Moniz

Russia
Nikolai Basov
Ivan Bunin

NOBEL PRIZE WINNERS BY COUNTRY OF RESIDENCE, 1901–1991

Pavel Cherenkov
Ilya Frank
Mikhail Sergeyevich Gorbachev
Leonid Kantorovich
Pyotr Kapitza
Lev Landau
Boris Pasternak
Ivan Pavlov
Aleksandr Prokhorov
Andrei Sakharov
Nikolay N. Semenov
Mikhail Sholokhov
Aleksandr Solzhenitsyn
Igor Tamm

South Africa
Nadine Gordimer
Albert Luthuli (Born in Rhodesia [now Zimbabwe])
Max Theiler
Desmond Tutu

Spain
Vicente Aleixandre
Jacinto Benavente y Martinez
Camilo José Cela
José Echegaray
Juan Jiménez
Santiago Ramón y Cajal

Sweden
Hannes Alfvén
Klas Arnoldson
Svante Arrhenius
Sune Bergström
Karl Branting
Nils Dalén
Ulf von Euler
Hans von Euler-Chelpin (Born in Germany)
Ragnar Granit (Born in Finland)
Allvar Gullstrand
Dag Hammarskjöld
Verner von Heidenstam
George de Hevesy (Born in Austria-Hungary)
Eyvind Johnson
Erik Karlfeldt
Pär Lagerkvist
Selma Lagerlöf
Harry Martinson
Alva Myrdal
Gunnar Myrdal
Bertil Ohlin
Bengt Samuelsson

Kai Siegbahn
Manne Siegbahn
Nathan Söderblom
Teodor Svedberg
Hugo Theorell
Arne Tiselius
Torsten Wiesel

Switzerland
Werner Arber
J. Georg Bednorz (Born in Germany)
Élie Ducommun
Henri Dunant
Richard R. Ernst
Albert Gobat
Charles Guillaume
Walter R. Hess
Paul Karrer (Born in Russia)
Theodor Kocher
K. Alex Müller
Paul Müller
Wolfgang Pauli (Born in Austria)
Vladimir Prelog (Born in Bosnia)
Tadeus Reichstein (Born in Russia)
Heinrich Rohrer
Leopold Ružička (Born in Austria-Hungary)
Carl Spitteler
Alfred Werner

Tibet
Dalai Lama

Ukraine
Ilya Metchnikoff

United Kingdom
Edgar D. Adrian
Norman Angell
Edward Appleton
Francis W. Aston
Charles G. Barkla
Derek Barton
James Black
P. M. S. Blackett
John Boyd Orr
W. H. Bragg
W. L. Bragg (Born in Australia)
Elias Canetti (Born in Bulgaria)
Robert Cecil
James Chadwick
Ernst B. Chain (Born in Germany)
J. Austen Chamberlain
Winston Churchill

John Cockcroft
William Cremer
Francis Crick
Henry H. Dale
P. A. M. Dirac
Alexander Fleming
Howard W. Florey (Born in Australia)
Dennis Gabor (Born in Hungary)
John Galsworthy
William Golding
Arthur Harden
Walter N. Haworth
Friedrich A. von Hayek (Born in Austria)
Arthur Henderson
Antony Hewish
John Hicks
Archibald V. Hill
Cyril N. Hinshelwood
Alan Hodgkin
Dorothy C. Hodgkin (Born in Egypt)
Frederick Gowland Hopkins
Godfrey Hounsfield
Andrew Huxley
Niels K. Jerne
Brian D. Josephson
Bernard Katz (Born in Germany)
John C. Kendrew
Rudyard Kipling (Born in India)
Aaron Klug (Born in Lithuania)
Hans Krebs (Born in Germany)
W. Arthur Lewis
John J. R. MacLeod
Archer Martin
James Meade
P. B. Medawar (Born in Brazil)
Peter D. Mitchell
Nevill Mott
Philip Noel-Baker
Ronald Norrish
Max Perutz (Born in Austria)
George Porter
Rodney R. Porter
Cecil F. Powell
William Ramsay
Owen W. Richardson
Robert Robinson
Ronald Ross (Born in Nepal)
Bertrand Russell
Ernest Rutherford (Born in New Zealand)
Martin Ryle
Frederick Sanger
Charles S. Sherrington
Frederick Soddy

Richard Stone
J. W. Strutt
Richard Synge
G. P. Thomson
J. J. Thomson
Niko Tinbergen (Born in Holland)
Alexander Todd
John R. Vane
Maurice H. F. Wilkins (Born in New Zealand)
Geoffrey Wilkinson
C. T. R. Wilson

United States
Jane Addams
Sidney Altman (Born in Canada)
Luis W. Alvarez
Carl D. Anderson
Philip W. Anderson
Christian Anfinsen
Kenneth Arrow
Julius Axelrod
Emily Greene Balch
David Baltimore
John Bardeen
George W. Beadle
Georg von Békésy (Born in Hungary)
Saul Bellow (Born in Canada)
Baruj Benacerraf (Born in Venezuela)
Paul Berg
Hans A. Bethe (Born in Germany)
J. Michael Bishop
Felix Bloch (Born in Switzerland)
Konrad Bloch (Born in Germany)
Nicolaas Bloembergen (Born in Holland)
Baruch S. Blumberg
Norman Borlaug
Walter H. Brattain (Born in China)
P. W. Bridgman
Joseph Brodsky (Born in Russia)
Herbert C. Brown (Born in England)
Michael S. Brown
James M. Buchanan
Pearl S. Buck
Ralph Bunche
Nicholas Murray Butler
Melvin Calvin
Thomas R. Cech
Owen Chamberlain
Subrahmanyan Chandrasekhar (Born in India)
Albert Claude (Born in Belgium)
Ronald H. Coase (Born in England)
Stanley Cohen
Arthur H. Compton

NOBEL PRIZE WINNERS BY COUNTRY OF RESIDENCE, 1901–1991

Leon N. Cooper
Elias James Corey
Carl F. Cori (Born in Austria-Hungary)
Gerty T. Cori (Born in Austria-Hungary)
Allan Cormack (Born in South Africa)
André Cournand (Born in France)
Donald J. Cram
James W. Cronin
Clinton J. Davisson
Charles Dawes
Gerard Debreu (Born in France)
Peter Debye (Born in Holland)
Hans G. Dehmelt (Born in Germany)
Max Delbrück (Born in Germany)
Edward A. Doisy
Renato Dulbecco (Born in Italy)
Vincent du Vigneaud
Gerald M. Edelman
Albert Einstein (Born in Germany)
Gertrude B. Elion
T. S. Eliot
John F. Enders
Joseph Erlanger
William Faulkner
Richard P. Feynman
Val L. Fitch
Paul J. Flory
Willam A. Fowler
Jerome I. Friedman
Milton Friedman
D. Carleton Gajdusek
Herbert S. Gasser
Murray Gell-Mann
Ivar Giaever (Born in Norway)
William F. Giauque (Born in Canada)
Walter Gilbert
Donald A. Glaser
Sheldon L. Glashow
Joseph L. Goldstein
Roger Guillemin (Born in France)
H. Keffer Hartline
Herbert A. Hauptman
Ernest Hemingway
Philip S. Hench
Dudley R. Herschbach
Alfred Hershey
George H. Hitchings Jr.
Roald Hoffmann (Born in Poland)
Robert Hofstadter
Robert W. Holley
David H. Hubel (Born in Canada)
Charles B. Huggins (Born in Canada)
Cordell Hull

Jerome Karle
Frank Kellogg
Edward C. Kendall
Henry W. Kendall
Har Gorbind Khorana (Born in India)
Martin Luther King Jr.
Henry Kissinger (Born in Germany)
Lawrence Klein
Tjalling C. Koopmans (Born in Holland)
Arthur Kornberg
Polykarp Kusch (Born in Germany)
Simon Kuznets (Born in Ukraine)
Willis E. Lamb Jr.
Karl Landsteiner (Born in Austria)
Irving Langmuir
Ernest O. Lawrence
Joshua Lederberg
Leon M. Lederman
Tsung-Dao Lee (Born in China)
Yuan T. Lee (Born in Taiwan)
Wassily Leontief (Born in Russia)
Rita Levi-Montalcini (Born in Italy)
Sinclair Lewis
Willard F. Libby
Fritz Lipmann (Born in Germany)
William N. Lipscomb
Salvador Luria (Born in Italy)
Harry M. Markowitz
George C. Marshall
Maria Goeppert Mayer (Born in Germany)
Barbara McClintock
Edwin M. McMillan
R. Bruce Merrifield
Albert A. Michelson (Born in Germany)
Merton H. Miller
Robert A. Millikan
Czesław Miłosz (Born in Poland)
George R. Minot
Franco Modigliani (Born in Italy)
Stanford Moore
Thomas Hunt Morgan
John Mott
Hermann J. Muller
Robert S. Mulliken
William P. Murphy
Joseph E. Murray
Daniel Nathans
Marshall W. Nirenberg
John H. Northrop
Severo Ochoa (Born in Spain)
Eugene O'Neill
Lars Onsager (Born in Norway)
George E. Palade (Born in Romania)

Linus C. Pauling
Charles J. Pedersen (Born in Korea)
Arno A. Penzias (Born in Germany)
Edward M. Purcell
I. I. Rabi (Born in Austria-Hungary)
James Rainwater
Norman F. Ramsey
Dickinson W. Richards
Theodore W. Richards
Burton Richter
Frederick C. Robbins
Theodore Roosevelt
Elihu Root
Peyton Rous
Paul Samuelson
Andrew V. Schalley (Born in Poland)
Arthur L. Schawlow
J. Robert Schrieffer
Theodore Schultz
Melvin Schwartz
Julian S. Schwinger
Glenn T. Seaborg
Emilio Segrè (Born in Italy)
William F. Sharpe
William Shockley (Born in England)
Herbert Simon
Isaac Bashevis Singer (Born in Poland)
Hamilton O. Smith
George D. Snell
Robert M. Solow
Roger W. Sperry
Wendell M. Stanley
William H. Stein
John Steinbeck

Jack Steinberger (Born in Germany)
Otto Stern (Born in Germany)
George Stigler
James B. Sumner
Earl W. Sutherland Jr.
Albert Szent-Györgyi (Born in Hungary)
Edward L. Tatum
Henry Taube (Born in Canada)
Howard M. Temin
E. Donnall Thomas
Samuel C. C. Ting
James Tobin
Charles H. Townes
Harold C. Urey
Harold E. Varmus
John H. Van Vleck
Selman A. Waksman (Born in Ukraine)
George Wald
James D. Watson
Steven Weinberg
Thomas H. Weller
George H. Whipple
Elie Wiesel (Born in Romania)
Eugene P. Wigner (Born in Hungary)
Kenneth G. Wilson
Robert W. Wilson
Woodrow Wilson
R. B. Woodward
Rosalyn S. Yalow
Chen Ning Yang (Born in China)

Vietnam
Le Duc Tho

NOBEL PRIZE WINNERS
WHO HAVE DIED SINCE 1986

Luis W. Alvarez (*Physics, 1968*) d. August 31, 1988

Carl D. Anderson (*Physics, 1936*) d. January 11, 1991

John Bardeen (*Physics, 1956, 1972*) d. January 30, 1991

George W. Beadle (*Physiology or Medicine, 1958*) d. June 9, 1989

Samuel Beckett (*Literature, 1969*) d. December 22, 1989

Menachem Begin (*Peace, 1978*) d. March 9, 1992

Daniel Bovet (*Physiology or Medicine, 1957*) d. April 8, 1992

Walter H. Brattain (*Physics, 1956*) d. October 13, 1987

Louis de Broglie (*Physics, 1929*) d. March 19, 1987

André Cournand (*Physiology or Medicine, 1956*) d. February 19, 1988

Richard P. Feynman (*Physics, 1965*) d. February 15, 1988

Friedrich A. von Hayek (*Economics, 1974*) d. March 23, 1992

John Hicks (*Economics, 1972*) d. May 20, 1989

Robert Hofstadter (*Physics, 1961*) d. November 17, 1990

Le Duc Tho (*Peace, 1973*) d. October 13, 1990

Luis F. Leloir (*Chemistry, 1970*) d. December 2, 1987

W. Arthur Lewis (*Economics, 1979*) d. June 15, 1991

Konrad Lorenz (*Physiology or Medicine, 1973*) d. February 27, 1989

Sean MacBride (*Peace, 1974*) d. January 15, 1988

P. B. Medawar (*Physiology or Medicine, 1960*) d. October 2, 1987

William P. Murphy (*Physiology or Medicine, 1934*) d. October 9, 1987

Gunnar Myrdal (*Economics, 1974*) d. May 17, 1987

John H. Northrop (*Chemistry, 1946*) d. May 27, 1987

Charles J. Pedersen (*Chemistry, 1987*) d. October 26, 1989

I. I. Rabi (*Physics, 1944*) d. January 11, 1988

Ernst Ruska (*Physics, 1986*) d. May 30, 1988

Andrei Sakharov (*Peace, 1975*) d. December 14, 1989

Emilio Segrè (*Physics, 1959*) d. April 22, 1989

William Shockley (*Physics, 1956*) d. August 12, 1989

Isaac Bashevis Singer (*Literature, 1978*) d. July 24, 1991

George Stigler (*Economics, 1982*) d. December 1, 1991

Niko Tinbergen (*Physiology or Medicine, 1973*) d. December 21, 1988

Patrick White (*Literature, 1973*) d. September 30, 1990

Georg Wittig (*Chemistry, 1979*) d. August 26, 1987

CONTRIBUTORS TO *NOBEL PRIZE WINNERS*

Barbara Armstrong
Kathryn A. Barry
Don Bright
Cathy Castillo
Mary Ellen Curtin
Sheila Dent
Vivian Dent
Amy L. Einsohn
Debra Goldentyer
Amy Gottlieb
Devi Mathieu

Preface

The foundation volume of *Nobel Prize Winners* was published in 1987 and contained the biographies of all the 566 men, women, and institutions that won the Nobel Prize from 1901 through 1986. This supplement contains biographies of the 49 prize winners from 1987 through 1991. Like the earlier volume, it is intended for students and the general reader, introducing the lives and achievements of the laureates and placing special emphasis on the body of work for which they were awarded the Nobel Prize.

The biographical profiles are arranged alphabetically. Each sketch presents a narrative overview of a laureate's work and assesses its significance. Because the work is often highly technical and has not always been discussed in secondary sources, factual accuracy has been a particular concern. To ensure both correctness and clarity, we assembled a board of expert consultants to review each sketch. The consultants for this supplement were: for *physiology or medicine,* Gert H. Brieger, M.D., William H. Welch Professor of the History of Medicine, The Johns Hopkins University School of Medicine; for *physics,* Laurie M. Brown, professor of physics and astronomy, Northwestern University; for *chemistry,* Erwin N. Hiebert, professor of the history of science, Harvard University; for *literature,* William McGuire, former editorial manager, Bollingen Series, Bollingen Foundation and Princeton University Press; and for *economics,* Peter Temin, professor of economics, Massachusetts Institute of Technology.

Each laureate has been given a separate profile, even when a prize has been awarded jointly to two or three persons, as is often the case with the science prizes. While a certain amount of repetition therefore occurs in descriptions of joint work, the reader finds in one place a comprehensive account of an individual laureate's work. As leading members of the literary, scientific, and political community, the Nobel Prize winners shared in a wide network of mutual influence. As an aid to the reader in following these connections, the names of other laureates appear in capital and small-capital letters when first mentioned in a profile other than their own. This cross-referencing device encourages the reader to explore related profiles, thereby making it possible to trace the development of related ideas.

Bibliographies of works available in English supplement titles cited in the sketches. Works written by the subject appear chronologically by date of first publication in English; those about the subject are listed alphabetically by author or source.

In the text of sketches, foreign titles are given with an English translation of the title and a date. The English translation appears in italics if the work is a book that has been published under that title; in quotation marks if it is a poem, story, or essay published under that title; and in roman type if the editors have supplied the translation. The date is that of first publication of the original work.

By consulting the finding aids on pages 9–23, the reader can locate subjects (including those who appeared in the foundation volume) by prize and year of award and by country of residence. Winners who have died since 1986, when the first volume was concluded, are also listed. A short biography of Alfred Nobel and a history of the Nobel Prizes and Nobel institutions are also included.

The editor wishes to acknowledge the Nobel Foundation for its generous help in providing information and photographs. Special thanks are due to Debra Goldentyer and Mark Schaeffer, who led the team of writers and researchers in the development of this volume. For their efforts in evaluating the biographical sketches and generously providing helpful information and comments, the editor wishes to thank the board of consultants. Leon Gordenker is also owed thanks for his advice and assistance. Finally, the editor is indebted to her colleagues at Visual Education Corporation: Amy Lewis, assistant editor; Sheera Stern, production manager; Anita Crandall, production supervisor; Cindy Feldner, inputter; and Dale Anderson, helpful adviser.

—Paula McGuire
Princeton, N.J., 1992

ALFRED NOBEL
by Alden Whitman

Alfred Nobel, the Swedish chemical experimenter and businessman who invented dynamite and other explosive compounds and whose will established the prizes that have brought him lasting fame, was a person of many paradoxes and contradictions. His contemporaries in the last half of the nineteenth century often found him perplexing because he did not quite fit the mold of the successful capitalist of his expansionist era. For one thing, Nobel was fonder of seclusion and tranquility than of ostentation and urban life, although he lived in cities most of his life and traveled widely. Unlike many contemporary barons of business, Nobel was spartan in his habits; he neither smoked nor drank, and he eschewed cards and other games. While his heritage was Swedish, he was a cosmopolitan European, comfortable with the French, German, Russian, and English languages as well as with his native tongue. Despite the heavy demands of his business and industrial affairs, he managed to build a well-stocked library and was well acquainted with the works of such authors as Herbert Spencer, the British philosopher and exponent of social Darwinism; Voltaire; and Shakespeare. Of nineteenth-century men of letters, he most admired a number of French writers: the Romantic novelist and poet Victor Hugo; Guy de Maupassant, the short story craftsman; Honoré de Balzac, the novelist whose keen eye pierced the human comedy; and the poet Alphonse de Lamartine. He also liked to read the works of the Russian novelist Ivan Turgenev and the Norwegian playwright and poet Henrik Ibsen. The naturalism of the French novelist Émile Zola, however, left him cold. Above all, he loved the poetry of Percy Bysshe Shelley, whose works inspired in him an early resolve to embark on a literary career. To that end, he wrote a considerable number of plays, novels, and poems, only one of which was published. He then turned instead to a career in chemistry.

Likewise puzzling to his fellow entrepreneurs was Nobel's reputation for holding advanced social views. The notion that he was a socialist was, in fact, quite undeserved, for he was actually an economic and political conservative who opposed suffrage for women and expressed grave doubts about democracy. Nevertheless, as much as Nobel lacked confidence in the political wisdom of the masses, he despised despotism. As an employer of many hundreds of workers, he took a paternalistic interest in their welfare, without wishing to establish any personal contact. Shrewdly, he realized that a work force with high morale is more productive than a crudely exploited one, which may well have been the basis for Nobel's reputation as a socialist.

Nobel was quite unassuming and even reticent about himself. He had few confidants and never kept a diary. Yet at dinner parties and among friends, he was an attentive listener, always courteous and considerate. The dinners given at his home in one of the most fashionable neighborhoods of Paris were convivial and elegant, for he was a well-informed host able to call upon a fund of small talk. He could strike off words of incisive wit when the occasion arose, for instance once remarking, "All Frenchmen are under the blissful impression that the *brain* is a French organ."

He was a person of medium height, dark and slender, with deep-set blue eyes and a bearded face. In the custom of the time, he wore a pair of pince-nez (for nearsightedness) attached to a black cord.

Largely because his health was not robust, Nobel was sometimes capricious, lonely, and depressed. He would work intensely; then, finding it difficult to relax, he would often travel in search of the curative powers of various spas, at that time a popular and accepted part of a healthy regimen. One of Nobel's favorites was the spa at Ischl, Austria, where he kept a small yacht on a nearby lake. He was also fond of Baden bei Wien, not far from Vienna, where he met Sophie Hess. At their introduction in 1876, she was twenty years old, petite, and good-looking; he was forty-three. There appears to be no doubt that Nobel fell in love with "Sophie-chen," a clerk in a flower shop, for he took her to Paris with him and provided her with an apartment. The young woman called herself Madame Nobel, but with time she is said to have become financially demanding. The relationship ended around 1891, only a few years before Nobel's death.

Despite his physical frailty, Nobel was capable of bursts of concentrated work. He had an excellent scientific mind and loved to tackle problems in his chemistry laboratory. Nobel managed his decentralized industrial empire through the board of directors of his many companies, which operated independently of one another and in which Nobel typically owned a 20 to 30 percent interest. Despite his limited financial interest, Nobel personally oversaw many of the details of decision making in the companies that bore his name. According to one of his biographers, "Apart from his scientific and business activities, much of Nobel's time was taken up by voluminous correspondence and paperwork, every detail of which he coped with entirely alone, from duplicating to keeping his private accounts."

In early 1876 he attempted to engage a housekeeper and part-time secretary by advertising in an Austrian newspaper: "A wealthy and highly educated old gentleman living in Paris seeks to engage a mature lady with language proficiency as secretary and housekeeper." One respondent was thirty-three-year-old Bertha Kinsky, then working in Vienna as a governess. Daringly, she came to Paris for an interview and impressed Nobel by her personality and language fluency, but after a week or so, homesickness overtook her and she returned to Vienna to marry Baron Arthur von Suttner, the son of her former employer in Vienna. She and Nobel met again, and in his last ten years they corresponded about her projects for peace. Bertha von Suttner became a leading figure in the European peace movement and through her friendship with Nobel was able to gain from him substantial financial support for the cause. She received the 1905 Nobel Prize for Peace.

In his final three years, Nobel worked with a private assistant, Ragnar Sohlman, a Swedish chemist in his twenties and a person of great tact and patience. Sohlman functioned as both a secretary and a laboratory aide. Nobel liked and trusted the young man enough to name him chief executor of his will. "It was not always easy to be his assistant," Sohlman recalled. "He was exacting in demands, plainspoken, and always seemingly in a hurry. One had to be wide awake to follow his swiftly leaping thought and often amazing whims when he suddenly appeared and vanished as quickly."

During his lifetime, Nobel often exhibited uncommon generosity toward Sohlman and other employees. When the assistant got married, Nobel impulsively doubled his salary; and, earlier, when his French cook married, he gave her a gift of 40,000 francs, a large sum in those days. Nobel's generosity also often went beyond the realm of personal and professional contacts. For instance, although he was not a churchgoer, Nobel frequently gave money for the parish work of the Swedish church in Paris, whose pastor in the early 1890s was Nathan Soderblöm, later the Lutheran archbishop of Sweden and the recipient of the 1930 Nobel Prize for Peace.

Although he was often called the Lord of Dynamite, Nobel strongly opposed the military uses to which his inventions were frequently put. "For my part," he said three years before his death, "I wish all guns with their belongings and everything could be sent to hell, which is the proper place for their exhibition and use." On another occasion, he stated that war was "the horror of horrors and the greatest of crimes" and added, "I should like to invent a substance or a machine with such terrible power of mass destruction that war would thereby be impossible forever."

Alfred Nobel's distinguished career is all the more remarkable considering his humble origins. The Nobel family came of peasant stock, emerging from obscurity with the surname of

Nobelius only late in the seventeenth century. Alfred's grandfather, a barber-surgeon, shortened it to Nobel in 1775. His eldest son, Immanuel (1801–1872), was Alfred's father. Immanuel, an architect, builder, and inventor, had a precarious business life for several years until the family began to make its fortune in the oil fields of Baku, Russia. He married Caroline Andriette Ahlsell (1803–1879) in 1827; the couple had eight children, only three of whom survived to adulthood: Robert, Ludvig, and Alfred.

Born October 21, 1833, in Stockholm, Alfred Bernhard Nobel was the couple's fourth child. From his first days, he was weak and sickly, and his childhood was marked by chronic illness. Both as a young man and as an adult, Alfred enjoyed an especially close and warm relationship with his mother. No matter how busy he was as an older man, he managed a yearly visit and kept in frequent touch by letter.

After trying his hand at a business making elastic cloth, Immanuel fell on hard times and in 1837, leaving his family in Sweden, moved first to Finland and then to St. Petersburg, where he manufactured powder-charged explosive mines, lathes, and machine tools. In October 1842, when Alfred was nine, he and the rest of the family joined his father in Russia, where his now prosperous family was able to engage private tutors for him. He proved to be a diligent pupil, apt and eager to learn, with a special interest in chemistry.

In 1850, when he was seventeen years old, Alfred took an extended trip, traveling in Europe, where he visited Germany, France, and Italy, and the United States. He pursued his chemical studies in Paris, and in the United States he met John Ericsson, the Swedish inventor of the caloric engine who later designed the ironclad warship *Monitor*.

Returning to St. Petersburg three years later, Nobel was employed in his father's growing business, by then called Fonderies & Ateliers Mécaniques Nobel & Fils (Foundries and Machine Shops of Nobel and Sons), which was producing material for the Crimean War (1853–1856). At the end of the war, the company shifted to the manufacture of machinery for steamboats plying the Volga River and the Caspian Sea. Its peacetime production, however, was not enough to offset the loss of military orders, and by 1858 the company fell into financial trouble. Alfred and his parents returned to Stockholm while Robert and Ludvig remained in Russia to salvage what they could. Back in Sweden, Alfred became engrossed in mechanical and chemical experiments, obtaining three patents. This work sharpened his interest in further experimentation, which he conducted in a small laboratory his father had established on his estate near the capital.

At that time, the only usable explosive for powder-charged mines—either for military or for peaceful uses—was black gunpowder. It was known, though, that the substance nitroglycerin was an extraordinarily powerful explosive compound, which posed extraordinary risks because of its volatility. No one had yet figured out how to control its detonation. After several small experiments with nitroglycerin, Immanuel Nobel sent Alfred to Paris in search of financing in 1861; he succeeded in raising a 100,000-franc loan. Despite some initial failures by Immanuel, Alfred became actively involved in the project. In 1863 he invented a practical detonator, which used gunpowder to set off the nitroglycerin. This invention was one of the primary foundations of his reputation and his fortune.

One of Nobel's biographers, Erik Bergengren, has described the device in this fashion:

> In its first form, . . . [the detonator] is so constructed that initiation of the liquid nitroglycerin explosive charge, which is contained in a metal cap by itself or in a blocked-up borehole, is brought about by the explosion of a smaller charge let down into this, the smaller charge consisting of gunpowder in a wooden cap by itself, with a plug, into which a fuse has been inserted.

In order to increase the effect, the inventor altered various details of this construction several times, and as a final improvement in 1865 he replaced the original cap with a metal cap charged with detonating mercury. . . . With the invention of this so-called blasting cap, the Initial Ignition Principle was introduced into the technique of explosives, and this was fundamental to all later developments in this field. It was this principle which made possible the effective use of nitroglycerin and later other violent explosives as independent explosives; it also made it possible to study their explosive properties.

In the process of perfecting the invention, Immanuel Nobel's laboratory was blown up, an explosion that resulted in the loss of eight lives, including Immanuel's twenty-one-year-old son Emil. Shortly thereafter, the father suffered a stroke, and remained bedridden until his death eight years later in 1872.

Despite the setback caused by the explosion and the resulting public hostility to the manufacture and use of nitroglycerin, Nobel persevered, and in October 1864 he persuaded the Swedish State Railways to adopt his substance for the blasting of tunnels. In order to manufacture it, he won the financial backing of a Stockholm merchant; a company, Nitroglycerin, Ltd., was set up and a factory built in the Swedish countryside. In its first years, Nobel was the company's managing director, works engineer, correspondent, advertising manager, and treasurer. He also traveled extensively to demonstrate his blasting procedure. Among the company's customers was the Central Pacific Railroad in the American West, which used Nobel's nitroglycerin in blasting the line's way through the Sierra Nevadas. After obtaining patents in other countries for his device, Nobel established the first of his foreign companies—Alfred Nobel & Co. in Hamburg—in 1865.

Although Nobel was able to solve the major problems of manufacture, his explosives were sometimes carelessly handled by their purchasers. There were accidental explosions and deaths and even a ban or two on imports. Nonetheless, Nobel continued to expand his business. He won a United States patent in 1866 and spent three months there raising money for his Hamburg plant and demonstrating his blasting oil. Nobel also decided to found an American company that, after some maneuvering, became the Atlantic Giant Powder Company; following Nobel's death, it was acquired by E. I. du Pont de Nemours and Company. The inventor felt badly treated by American businessmen who were eager to float shares in his blasting oil companies. "In the long run I found life in America anything but agreeable," he later wrote. "The exaggerated chase after money is a pedantry which spoils much of the pleasure of meeting people and destroys a sense of honor in favor of imagined needs."

Although blasting oil, correctly used, was an effective explosive, it was nevertheless so often involved in accidents (including one that leveled the Hamburg plant) that Nobel sought some way to stabilize nitroglycerin. He hit upon the idea of mixing the liquid nitroglycerin with a chemically inert and porous substance. His first practical choice was kieselguhr, a chalklike, absorbent material. Mixed with nitroglycerin, it could be fashioned into sticks and placed into boreholes. Patented in 1867, it was called "Dynamite, or Nobel's safety blasting powder."

The new explosive not only established Alfred Nobel's lasting fame, but it also found such spectacular uses as in the blasting of the Alpine tunnel on the St. Gotthard rail line, the removal of underwater rocks at Hell Gate in New York City's East River, the clearing of the Danube River at the Iron Gate, and the cutting of the Corinth Canal in Greece. Dynamite was also a factor in oil drilling in the Baku fields of Russia, an enterprise in which Nobel's two brothers were so active and became so wealthy that they were known as the Russian Rockefellers. Alfred was the largest single stockholder in his brothers' companies.

Although Nobel held patent rights to dynamite and its later refinements in all the world's major countries, in the 1870s he was constantly harassed by competitors who stole his processes. In these years he refused to hire a secretary or a full-time lawyer, and he was forced to spend much time in patent litigation as his factories steadily increased production.

In the 1870s and 1880s, Nobel expanded his network of factories into the chief European countries, either besting his rivals or forming cartels with them to control prices and markets. Eventually, he established a worldwide web of corporations for the manufacture and sale of his explosives, which, in addition to an improved dynamite, by then included a blasting gelatin. The military uses of these substances began in the Franco-Prussian War of 1870–1871, but during his lifetime, the investments Nobel made in military inventions lost considerable amounts of money. The profits from his industrial ventures came from the use of dynamite in the construction of tunnels, canals, railways, and roads.

Describing the consequences to Nobel of the discovery of dynamite, Bergengren has written:

Not a day passed without his having to face vital problems: the financing and formation of companies; the procuring of trustworthy partners and assistants for managerial posts, and suitable foremen and skilled laborers for a manufacturing process that was extremely sensitive and contained very dangerous ingredients; the erection of new buildings on remote sites, with intricate security measures in accordance with the differing laws of each country. The inventor took part eagerly in the planning and starting of a new project, but he seldom lent his personal assistance to the detailed working of the various companies.

The biographer characterized Nobel's life in the ten years after the invention of dynamite as "restless and nerve-racking." After his move from Hamburg to Paris in 1873, he was sometimes able to escape to his private laboratories, one a part of his house. To help him there, he employed Georges D. Fehrenbach, a young French chemist, who remained with him for eighteen years.

Given a choice, Nobel would have preferred his laboratory to his business, but his companies always seemed to claim a priority as the trade in explosives increased and new factories were established to meet the demands. Indeed, at Nobel's death in 1896, some ninety-three factories were in operation producing 66,500 tons of explosives, including ammunition of all kinds as well as ballistite, a smokeless blasting powder that Nobel patented between 1887 and 1891. The new substance could be used as a substitute for black gunpowder and was relatively inexpensive to manufacture.

In marketing ballistite, Nobel sold his Italian patent to the government, an action that aroused the anger of the French. He was accused of stealing the idea for the substance from the French government's monopoly, and his laboratory was ransacked and shut down; his factory was also forbidden to make ballistite. Under these circumstances, in 1891, Nobel decided to close his Paris home and to leave France for a new residence in San Remo on the Italian Riviera. Apart from the uproar over ballistite, Nobel's last Paris years were not totally happy; his mother died in 1889, a year following the death of his older brother Ludvig. Moreover, his French business associate had involved his enterprises in dubious speculations in connection with an unsuccessful venture to build a Panama canal.

At his San Remo villa, which was set in an orange grove overlooking the Mediterranean, Nobel built a small chemical laboratory, where he worked as time permitted. Among other things, he experimented in the production of synthetic rubber and silk. However much he liked San Remo for its climate, Nobel had warm thoughts of his homeland, and in 1894 he bought the Bofors ironworks in Värmland, where he fitted out a nearby manor house for private quarters and built a new laboratory. He spent the last two summers of his life at the Värmland manor house. During the second summer, his brother Robert died, and Nobel himself began to feel unwell.

Examined by specialists in Paris, he was warned that he had angina pectoris, a lack of oxygen supply to the heart, and was advised to rest. He then returned to San Remo, where he worked on a play he hoped to complete and where he drew up a remarkable will in his own hand. Shortly after midnight on December 10, 1896, he suffered a cerebral hemorrhage and died. Except for Italian servants who could not understand him, Nobel was alone at his death, and his final words went unrecorded.

The origins of Nobel's will, with its provisions for awards in a number of fields of human endeavor, are imprecise. The final document is a revision of earlier testaments. Its bequests for science and literature awards, it is generally agreed, are extensions of Nobel's lifelong concern with those fields—physics, physiology, chemistry, and the elevation of the art of writing. Evidence suggests that the award for peace may well have been the fruition of the inventor's long-standing aversion to violence. Early in 1886, for example, he told a British acquaintance that he had "a more and more earnest wish to see a rose red peace sprout in this explosive world."

As an inventor with a fertile imagination and as a businessman with a robust eagerness to exploit the industrial and commercial aspects of his brainchildren, Alfred Nobel was typical of his times. Paradoxically, he was a reclusive and lonely person whose worldly success failed to bring him the consolations of life for which he so avidly yearned.

THE NOBEL PRIZES AND NOBEL INSTITUTIONS
by Carl Gustaf Bernhard

Alfred Nobel died on December 10, 1896. In his remarkable will, written in Paris on November 27, 1895, Nobel stated:

The whole of my remaining realizable estate shall be dealt with in the following way:

The capital shall be invested by my executors in safe securities and shall constitute a fund, the interest on which shall be annually distributed in the form of prizes to those who, during the preceding year, shall have conferred the greatest benefit on mankind. The said interest shall be divided into five equal parts, which shall be apportioned as follows: one part to the person who shall have made the most important discovery or invention within the field of physics; one part to the person who shall have made the most important chemical discovery or improvement; one part to the person who shall have made the most important discovery within the domain of physiology or medicine; one part to the person who shall have produced in the field of literature the most outstanding work of an idealistic tendency; and one part to the person who shall have done the most or the best work for fraternity among nations, for the abolition or reduction of standing armies, and for the holding and promotion of peace congresses.

The prizes for physics and chemistry shall be awarded by the [Royal] Swedish Academy of Sciences; that for physiological or medical works by the Karolinska Institute in Stockholm; that for literature by the [Swedish] Academy in Stockholm; and that for champions of peace by a committee of five persons to be elected by the Norwegian Storting [Parliament]. It is my express wish that in awarding the prizes no consideration whatever shall be given to the nationality of the candidates, so that the most worthy shall receive the prize, whether he be a Scandinavian or not.

The invitation to assume the responsibility of selecting laureates was accepted by the awarding bodies designated in Nobel's will only after considerable discussion. Several members of these organizations were doubtful and, referring to the vague formulation of the will, claimed that it would be difficult to implement. In spite of these reservations, in 1900 the Nobel Foundation was established and statutes were worked out by a special committee on the basis of the will's stipulations.

The foundation, an independent, nongovernment organization, has the responsibility of administering the funds in a manner "destined to safeguard the financial basis for the prizes, and for the activities associated with the selection of prizewinners." The foundation also protects the common interests of the prize-awarding institutions and represents the Nobel institutions externally. In this capacity the foundation arranges the annual Nobel Prize ceremonies on behalf of the awarding institutions. The Nobel Foundation itself is not involved in proposing candidates, in the evaluation process, or in the final selections. These functions are all performed independently by the prize-awarding assemblies. Today, the Nobel Foundation also administers the Nobel Symposia, which since 1966 have been supported mainly through grants to the foundation from the Bank of Sweden's Tercentenary Foundation.

The statutes for the Nobel Foundation and the special regulations of the awarding institutions were promulgated by the King in Council on June 29, 1900. The first Nobel Prizes were awarded on December 10, 1901. The political union between Norway and Sweden came to a peaceful end in 1905. As a result, the current special regulations for the body awarding the peace prize, the Norwegian Nobel Committee, are dated April 10, 1905.

THE NOBEL PRIZES AND NOBEL INSTITUTIONS

In 1968 the Bank of Sweden at its tercentenary made a donation for a prize in the economic sciences. After some hesitation, the Royal Swedish Academy of Sciences accepted the role of prize-awarding institution in this field, in accordance with the same rules and principles that apply to the original Nobel Prizes. This prize, which was established in memory of Alfred Nobel, is also awarded on December 10, following the presentation of the other Nobel Prizes. Officially known as the Prize in Economic Sciences in Memory of Alfred Nobel, it was awarded for the first time in 1969.

Today, the Nobel Prize—independent of the monetary award which at present exceeds 2 million Swedish kronor ($225,000)—is widely regarded as the highest recognition of intellect that can be bestowed on a man or woman. It is also one of the few prizes known by name to a great part of the nonscientific public, and probably the only prize about which almost every scientist knows. According to the statutes, the Nobel Prize cannot be given jointly to more than three persons. As a consequence, relatively few, however distinguished, can hope to receive the award.

The prestige of the Nobel Prizes depends on the serious work devoted to the selection of the prizewinners and on the effective mechanisms for this procedure, which were instituted from the very outset. It was felt desirable to obtain properly documented proposals from qualified experts in different countries, thereby also emphasizing the international character of the prizes.

For each prize there is a Nobel committee. The Royal Swedish Academy of Sciences appoints three committees, one each for physics, chemistry, and the economic sciences. The Karolinska Institute names a committee for physiology or medicine, and the Swedish Academy chooses a committee for literature. In addition, the Norwegian Parliament, the Storting, appoints a peace prize committee. The Nobel committees play a central role in the selection process. Each consists of five members but may also request temporary assistance from additional specialists in relevant fields.

Nominations of candidates for the prizes can be made only upon invitation, and these invitations are distributed in the fall of the year preceding the award. The recipients are invited to submit a written proposal stating the reasons for their choice. For each prize, more than 1,000 individuals in different parts of the world are invited to submit nominations. Invitations for the science prizes are sent out to active scholars at universities and research institutions. For the literature prize, submissions are invited from academic representatives in the fields of literature and languages as well as from members of distinguished academies and societies of the same character as the Swedish Academy. In order to obtain proposals for the peace prize, representatives from the fields of philosophy, history, and the legal and political sciences, as well as those active in various peace activities, are contacted. Some individuals always receive invitations to submit nominations; among them are previous Nobel laureates and members of the Royal Swedish Academy of Sciences, the Nobel Assembly of the Karolinska Institute, and the Swedish Academy, as well as permanent and active professors in the respective fields from all the Scandinavian countries. Invitations to propose names are confidential, as are the nominations.

Nominations must be received by February 1 of the award year. At that date, the work of the Nobel committees begins, and from then until September committee members and consultants evaluate the qualifications of the nominees. Committees meet several times, with proposals assigned to different committee members as well as to outside experts, all of whom attempt to determine the originality and significance of the nominee's contributions. Several committee members or outside experts may report on various aspects of a single proposal. Every year several thousand persons are involved in the preparatory work. After this work is completed, the committees submit their secret reports and recommendations to the respective prize-awarding bodies, which have the sole right to make the final decisions.

By September or the beginning of October, the Nobel committees are ready with their work. In physics, chemistry, and the economic sciences, they submit their reports to the respective "classes" of the Royal Swedish Academy of Sciences, each of which has about twenty-five members. The classes then send their recommendations to the academy for the final decision. The procedure for the prize in physiology or medicine is similar, except that the recommendation of the Nobel committee goes directly to the fifty-member Nobel Assembly of the Karolinska Institute. In deciding the literature prize, the eighteen members of the Swedish Academy make the decision on the basis of the proposal from the Nobel committee. The decision for the peace prize is made by the Norwegian Nobel Committee itself.

In October, final votes are cast in the various assemblies. The laureates are immediately notified of the decisions, which are then announced internationally at a press conference held in Stockholm and attended by representatives of the international news media. The messages contain the names of the laureates and a short statement describing the reasons for the awards. At this occasion, specialists in the various fields are also present to give a more comprehensive explanation of the winners' achievements and their significance.

Subsequently, the Nobel Foundation invites the laureates and their families to the Nobel ceremonies held in Stockholm and Oslo on December 10. In Stockholm the prize ceremony takes place in the Concert Hall and is attended by about 1,200 persons. The prizes in physics, chemistry, physiology or medicine, literature, and the economic sciences are presented by the King of Sweden following a short résumé of the laureates' achievements presented by representatives of the prize-awarding assemblies. The celebration continues at a foundation banquet in the Town Hall.

In Oslo the peace prize ceremony takes place in the Assembly Hall of the University of Oslo in the presence of the King of Norway and the royal family. The laureate receives the prize from the chairman of the Norwegian Nobel Committee. In connection with the ceremonies in Stockholm and Oslo, the laureates present their Nobel lectures, which are later published in the volume *Les Prix Nobel*.

Obviously, a considerable amount of work is devoted to the sifting process by which laureates are selected. In the sciences, the distribution of more than 1,000 invitations for each prize results in 200 to 250 nominations. Since the same scientists are often proposed by several nominators, the number of actual candidates is somewhat less. In literature the Swedish Academy makes the choice from 100 to 150 candidates. Generally, most of the strong candidates are proposed over several years, and very rarely is a laureate selected after having been proposed only once.

The Nobel selections have often been criticized in the international press, as has the secrecy of the selection procedure. As to the complaints about the secrecy, suffice it to say that the statutes mandate that the deliberations, opinions, and proposals of the Nobel committees in connection with the awarding of prizes may not be made public or otherwise revealed. They direct that no protest shall be laid against the award of an adjudicating body and that if conflicts of opinion have arisen, they shall not be recorded in the minutes or otherwise revealed.

As to the singularity of the prizes, it is certainly true that there are many more worthy candidates than prizes. The 1948 Swedish Nobel laureate in chemistry, Arne Tiselius, who served as chairman of the Nobel Foundation for several years, described the situation in the following way: "You cannot in practice apply the principle that the Nobel Prize should be given to the person who is best; you cannot define who is best. Therefore, you are left with the only alternative: to try to find a particularly worthy candidate."

Naturally, the handling of the prizes is based on the principles delineated in the will of Alfred Nobel. In physics, chemistry, and physiology or medicine, the will speaks of an important discovery, improvement, or invention within these fields. Thus, the science prizes are awarded not for the work of a lifetime, but for a specific achievement or a particular discovery. As an experimenter and inventor, Nobel knew very well what a discovery was. Concepts are extremely useful, but concepts change; what remains are the experimental facts—the discoveries. The contributions of some scientists may be of great importance in the development of their fields, but they may not fulfill the specific requirements stipulated by the Nobel Prize rules.

The performance of scientific work and the conditions under which scientists now labor are quite different from those in effect during Alfred Nobel's lifetime, a fact that complicates the selection of laureates. Today, teamwork is common and often results in significant discoveries. The prizes, however, are meant for individuals and not for large groups. This contemporary situation has resulted in a dilemma with which the prize-awarding juries have had to deal in their efforts to fulfill Nobel's intentions.

In his will, Nobel declares that "an idealistic tendency" should be an essential qualification for the prize in literature. This vague expression has caused endless arguments. In *Nobel, The Man and His Prizes* (1962), Anders Österling, a past secretary of the Swedish Academy, writes: "What he really meant by this term was probably works of a humanitarian and constructive character which, like scientific discoveries, could be regarded as of benefit to mankind." Today the Swedish Academy by and large refrains from trying to find guidance from this expression.

To appraise achievements in widely different fields with reference to the phrase "for the benefit of mankind" is, of course, extremely difficult. A glance at the lengthy list of Nobel Prize winners in all fields shows, however, that serious efforts have been made to pay respect to a great variety of claims. For instance, the science prizes have been given for discoveries in pure sciences as well as for advances in applied fields. Lars Gyllensten, a former secretary of the Swedish Academy, has noted, "One has to adopt some sort of pragmatic procedure and take into consideration the basic view in Alfred Nobel's will to promote science and poetry and to distribute prizes in an international perspective to the benefit of mankind, not to distribute empty status awards."

At an early point, it became clear that the stipulation that the prizes be awarded for literary or scientific achievements made during the preceding year could not be observed in practice while at the same time maintaining a high standard. To resolve this difficulty, the following rule was inserted in the regulations: "The provision in the will that the annual award of prizes shall refer to works during the preceding year shall be understood in the sense that the award shall be made for the most recent achievements and for the older works only if their significance has not become apparent until recently." The discovery of penicillin, for instance, took place in 1928, but the prize was not given until 1945 when the drug's value had been established by practical use. Likewise, the importance of literary contributions may not be fully appreciated until they can be seen in the context of an entire body of work. Therefore, many laureates in literature have received their prizes late in their careers.

That the choice of laureates for the peace and literature prizes often arouses controversy is self-evident; that there are some unfortunate mistakes in the list of the science prizes must also be admitted. These circumstances reflect the difficulties that the prize juries encounter. It is, however, surprising that criticism is so relatively scarce in the extensive literature that has been written about the Nobel Prizes and the Nobel work.

Very often the Nobel Foundation is criticized for not awarding prizes in other fields. The reason is simply that it was Nobel's wish that only the five specific areas he designated be taken into account. The single exception is the Nobel Prize in Economic Sciences, also administered by the foundation. Nonetheless, contemporary juries are in fact acting within successively widening frameworks. In 1973, for instance, the medicine prize was given to three ethologists for their discoveries concerning organization and elicitation of individual and social behavior patterns, and in 1974 pioneering research in radio astrophysics was honored. The physics prize in 1978, given for the discovery of cosmic microwave background radiation, also provides an example of the increasingly liberal interpretation of the prize field.

For twenty-five years, while a professor of physiology at the Karolinska Institute, I served as a member and chairman of its Nobel committee. Subsequently, as president and later secretary-general of the Royal Swedish Academy of Sciences, I also had the pleasure of taking part in the Nobel work in physics, chemistry, and the economic sciences for ten years. During this thirty-five-year period, I saw firsthand the diligence with which the members of the science prize juries fulfilled their delicate mission and witnessed the painstaking work of the specialists in various fields when adjudicating the prize proposals.

While engaged in work relating to the Nobel Prizes, I was often asked by representatives of organizations around the world to discuss the Nobel selection process when some new international prize was going to be created. I usually gave three pieces of advice. First, define the topics carefully so that a proper assessment can be made. We know how extremely difficult it is to make a selection, even in a "hard science" like physics. Second, allow enough time for the selection process. Third, ask for sufficient funds to cover the costs of the selection process, one which may involve a great many specialists and consist of several steps. Actually, the magnitude of the costs of selecting the Nobel laureates and of organizing and conducting the prize ceremonies is more or less the same as that of the Nobel Prizes themselves.

The Nobel Prizes are unique and carry with them considerable prestige. It is frequently wondered why the prizes attract more attention than any other twentieth-century award. One reason may be that they were created at the right time and that they epitomize some of the principal historical transformations of the age. Alfred Nobel was a true internationalist, and from the very beginning, the international character of the prizes made an important impression on society. The strict rules of the selection process, which were implemented from the outset, have also been crucial in establishing the importance of the awards. As soon as the prizes are awarded in December, the task of selecting the next year's Nobel laureates begins. This year-round activity, in which so many of the world's intellectuals are engaged, plays a decisive role in directing the interest of society to the importance of the work that is proceeding in the various fields covered by the prizes, for "the benefit of mankind."

KEY TO PRONUNCIATION

ā   āle
â   câre
a   add
ä   ärm

ē   ēve
e   end

g   go

ī   īce
i   ill

ᴋ   German ch as in *ich* (iᴋ)

ɴ   not pronounced, but indicates
    the nasal tone of the preceding
    vowel, as in the French *bon*
    (bôɴ)

ō   ōld
ô   ôrb
o   odd
oi oil
o͞o o͞oze
o͝o fo͝ot
ou out

th *th*en
th thin

ū   cūbe
û   ûrn; French eu, as in *jeu* (zhû),
    German ö, oe, as in *schön*
    (shûn), Goethe (gû′ tə)
u   tub

ü   pronounced approximately as
    ē, with rounded lips: French u,
    as in *vu* (vü); German ü, as in
    Gefühl (gə fül′)

ə   the schwa, an unstressed vowel
    representing the sound that is
    spelled
    a as in sofa
    e as in fitted
    i as in edible
    o as in melon
    u as in circus

zh azure

ALLAIS, MAURICE
(May 31, 1911–)
Nobel Memorial Prize in Economic Sciences,
1988

The French economist Maurice Félix Charles
Allais (ä lä′) was born in Paris, where his parents,
Maurice and Louise (Caubet) Allais, ran a small
cheese shop. In 1914 his father left to fight in
World War I; in 1915 he died in captivity in Ger-
many. Of his father's death, Allais later wrote,
"My youth, indeed my entire life, was deeply
marked by this, directly and indirectly."

Despite circumstances he later described as "often difficult," Allais completed primary and secondary school, where he studied Latin, science,
mathematics, and philosophy. He initially wanted
to pursue an interest in history, but a mathematics
teacher convinced him to attend the École Poly-
technique, one of the most prestigious science institutes in France. Allais began studying there in
1931 and graduated first in his class in 1933. The
summer after his graduation, he visited the United
States and observed the effects of the Great Depression, which he later called "a very astonishing
phenomenon for which no generally acceptable
explanation could be found." When he returned
home, the scene was scarcely better. For France,
also in the grip of the depression, the 1930s were
an era of almost constant financial and political in-
stability. The acute social discontent of these
pre–World War II days had a profound impact on
his life's work.

After a year's military service and two years at
the École Nationale Supérieure des Mines in Paris,
Allais was hired as an engineer at the national
mines administration in Nantes. His work, however, did not reflect his interests. He occupied himself by reading and writing about physics and
probability theory.

These pursuits were interrupted in 1939, when
Allais was called to fight in World War II. As he
later recounted in his Nobel lecture, he was a different person when, after the French defeat in 1940,
he returned to a German-occupied Nantes. "My
prewar concerns had completely changed. . . . It
was clear that the best I could do was to contribute
to prepare for the postwar period." He recalled pon-
dering the social and economic problems he had
seen in the United States and France and thinking,
"What could be a better way of preparing for the aftermath of the war than to try to find a solution to
the fundamental problem of any economy, namely
*how to promote the greatest feasible economic effi-
ciency while ensuring a distribution of income that
would be generally acceptable?*" In this way, he
said, he discovered his "vocation as an economist."
His goal was "to endeavor to lay the foundations on

MAURICE ALLAIS

which an economic and social policy could be
validly built."

Beginning in 1940, Allais began reading whatever economic works he could find in French. He
was especially interested in the works of Léon
Walras, Vilfredo Pareto, and Irving Fisher. While
these men "had the deepest influence" on his
thought, Allais remained unsatisfied. Though economics claimed to be a science, Allais found that
it lacked scientific rigor. It relied on too many
untested assumptions and lacked the mathematical
precision of the natural sciences in which he had
been trained.

Allais took it upon himself to find a remedy for
these deficiencies. In 1941, while continuing to
work at his government job, he began to write *In
Quest of an Economic Discipline*. He finished the
manuscript in 1943 and submitted it to several
publishers, every one of which turned it down. Allais ended up publishing the book himself.

Unlike previous economics texts, Allais's book
used rigorous, detailed mathematical proofs to
show how the opposing forces of supply and demand can achieve a state of equilibrium within a
market. (Equilibrium is the point at which demand
for an item precisely matches the supply of that
item.) Allais dispensed with the idea of "the market" as a single entity. Instead, he devised a far
more realistic model that assumed a large number
of interacting markets. He showed how changes in
one market (shoe production, for example) can affect related markets (such as cattle, nails, and labor) and ultimately the economy as a whole.

Allais believed that the goal of any economic
system should be to achieve a state of maximum
efficiency. Maximum efficiency exists when re-

41

sources are allocated in a way that most nearly satisfies everyone's needs—that is, when one person cannot become better off without making someone else worse off. Through a series of complex mathematical proofs, he demonstrated that maximum efficiency is the natural outcome of any perfectly competitive free-market economy. "To a large extent," he wrote later, "[my book] focused on the proof of *two fundamental propositions:* any state of equilibrium of a market economy is a state of maximum efficiency, and, vice versa, any state of maximum efficiency is a state of equilibrium of a market economy."

Contrary to the beliefs of many economists of the time, Allais also demonstrated that the forces of supply and demand can lead to maximum efficiency even in state-run monopolies. Even though a monopoly has the power to set prices higher or lower than they would be in a competitive market, the monopoly would not benefit by doing so. (If the price is set too high, demand will drop and there will be insufficient sales; if the price is set too low, the monopoly will lose money with each sale.) Therefore, if government regulators set prices arbitrarily—for example, to achieve certain political goals—the economy as a whole will suffer.

Remarkably, despite Allais's lack of formal training in economics, *In Quest of an Economic Discipline* won the 1943 Charles Dupin Prize of the Academy of Moral and Political Sciences. It was later described as "fundamental" by Ingemar Ståhl of the Royal Swedish Academy of Sciences.

In 1944 Allais became a professor at the École Nationale Supérieure des Mines, and in 1946 he accepted the directorship of a research unit at the Centre National de la Recherche Scientifique. Despite this workload, Allais managed to publish a second fundamental work, *Economy and Interest,* in 1947. In this book, Allais used his ideas about maximum efficiency to formulate new theories of capital. (*Capital* refers to produced goods that are used to produce other goods.) Earlier, the economist Stanley Jevons had hypothesized that a nation's total income is a function of the nation's past investment in capital. Allais applied his usual rigorous techniques to Jevons's hypothesis, converting it into a series of mathematical statements.

Expanding on Jevons's work, Allais explored the relationship between capital investment and interest rates, interest being the price of borrowing money. Like other prices, interest rates are controlled by the forces of supply and demand—specifically, the supply of and the demand for money. In *Economy and Interest,* Allais examined the effects of these forces on a no-growth economy—an economy in which, among other things, the supply of money remains constant. He demonstrated that if capital is allocated with maximum efficiency in such an economy, no producer will have reason to invest in additional capital. There will, therefore, be no demand to borrow money, and, as a result, the optimal interest rate will be zero. Although Allais's conclusions do not hold true in real-world economies (in which there is always some degree of positive or negative growth), his model provided a solid base on which more-comprehensive models could be built.

Allais gave up his administrative duties at the Centre National in 1948 in order to be able to devote his time to research and teaching. Throughout the following decades, Allais published pioneering works about money, inflation, business cycles, and risk analysis (how a person evaluates risk and benefit when making an economic decision). In 1960 Allais married Jacqueline Bouteloup, with whom he has one daughter. He remained a member of the French civil service until his retirement in 1980.

Despite Allais's prodigious output throughout his career, his early works—specifically, *In Quest of an Economic Discipline* and *Economy and Interest*—represent his most influential contributions. The principles in these books, which resemble ideas developed independently by economists such as PAUL SAMUELSON and JOHN HICKS, reflect Allais's commitment "to the search for the conditions of the greatest possible economic efficiency and to the analysis of the income distribution it implies." Allais consistently stressed the need to support theories with empirical data, and he developed mathematical models that allowed such data to be analyzed with the necessary precision. As a result, according to Ingemar Ståhl, Allais made it possible "to investigate the conditions under which social efficiency, equilibrium, and stability can be attained in an economy with decentralized decisions made by independent consumers and producers"—that is, in a market economy. Allais's models have inspired further analysis of markets and social efficiency by economists such as GERARD DEBREU and KENNETH ARROW.

Not surprisingly, given his interest in the social effects of economic theories, Allais has always worked to apply his ideas to real economies. He sees his job not as making policy but as testing the feasibility of policies devised politically. He has written, "The ends to pursue belong to the field of politics, and it is in fact the essential task of political systems to define them through overall compromises. But . . . the economist's role is to examine whether the ends defined through such compromises are actually compatible with each other and whether the means used to reach them are really the most appropriate."

Allais has done economic studies for private and government-owned businesses and for the European Economic Community (now the European Community), in whose organization he played an active role. His ideas have been used to provide a practical framework for investment and pricing in nationalized industries—particularly in his native France, where railroads, utilities, and other industries came under state control in the years following World War II. By following Allais's principles about free-market pricing, the French government was able to keep these state-owned monopolies viable well into the 1980s.

In presenting Maurice Allais with the 1988 Nobel Memorial Prize in Economic Sciences, Ståhl emphasized Allais's "pioneering contributions to the theory of markets and efficient resource allocation." He added, however, that Allais had shown the need for this "mathematical line of research . . . to be supplemented by other analytical approaches such as comparative and empirical studies of economies."

Allais has contributed some of this supplementary work himself. His abiding interest in history has led him to study the growth and decline of civilizations in relation to economic factors. A second field of interest, physics, has also occupied his attention. Indeed, his experiments on gravitation received the 1959 Galabert Prize of the French Astronautical Society and made him a laureate of the United States Gravity Research Foundation. He does not see his scientific work as separate from his work as an economist. "These researches," he has written, ". . . have led me to reflect on the nature of our knowledge, the nature of experience and theory, the difficulties of experimentation and the interpretation of results, and the scientific method in general. . . . *Nothing has been more instructive for me than this confrontation* between two apparently so dissimilar sciences."

This desire to bring together apparently disparate ideas above all characterizes Allais's thought and efforts. As he stated succinctly in his Nobel lecture, "Throughout my work, my dominant concern has been with synthesis." Since receiving the Nobel Prize, Allais has continued to "work actively in teaching, research, and writing."

Allais has received many honors. The International Econometric Society, the New York Academy of Sciences, and the Operations Research Society of America have all named him a fellow; he is also a member of the International Statistical Institute and an honorary member of the American Economic Association. He has served on the editorial boards of the *Revue d'Économie Politique* and *Econometrica,* on the Council of the Econometric Society, and as chair of the French Association of Economic Sciences. Allais is an officer in l'Ordre des Palmes Académiques, a Chevalier in l'Ordre de l'Économie Nationale, and an officer in the Legion of Honor.

Organizations that have given him prizes include the Academy of Moral and Political Sciences (1954), Johns Hopkins University (1958), the Operations Research Society of America (1958), the Atlantic Community (1960), the Association for Economic Liberty and Social Progress (1968), and the Society for the Promotion of National Industry (1970). In 1978 his lifetime work achievements were honored with the Gold Medal of the National Center for Scientific Research, which Allais has called "the most distinguished honor in French science." As of that time, he was the only economist ever to receive the award.

ADDITIONAL WORKS IN ENGLISH TRANSLATION: General Theory of Surpluses, 1981.

ABOUT: International Who's Who, 1989; Markets and Risk: Essays in Honour of Maurice Allais, 1989; New Palgrave Dictionary, 1987; New York Times October 19, 1988; Who's Who in Economics, 1986.

ALTMAN, SIDNEY
(May 7, 1939–)
Nobel Prize for Chemistry, 1989
(shared with Thomas R. Cech)

The Canadian-American molecular biologist Sidney Altman was born in Montreal, Quebec. His parents were both immigrants; his father was a grocer and his mother, before her marriage, worked in a textile mill. "It was from them," Altman recalled, "that I learned that hard work in stable surroundings could yield rewards, even if only in infinitesimally small increments."

Altman, the family's second son, showed an early interest in science. He enrolled as a physics major at the Massachusetts Institute of Technology, where he received his bachelor's degree in 1960. He spent a year and a half as a graduate student in physics at Columbia University, "waiting unhappily for an opportunity to work in a laboratory and wondering if I should continue in physics." In the end, he decided to move to the newly emerging field of molecular biology.

Molecular biology is an interdisciplinary pursuit that combines biochemistry, genetics, and structural chemistry to study the molecular basis of form, function, and evolutionary theory of living organisms. The revolution in molecular biology began in 1954, when JAMES D. WATSON and FRANCIS CRICK discovered the structure of the amino acid deoxyribonucleic acid (DNA). Work by many scientists during the 1950s and 1960s established that genetic information is almost always carried

SIDNEY ALTMAN

by DNA, in the nucleus of the cell, transcribed (copied) into ribonucleic acid (RNA), in the cytoplasm, or nonnuclear portion of the cell, and then translated from RNA into proteins. Proteins make up much of the substance of living things and, in their role as biological catalysts (enzymes), perform many functions within living organisms.

In the fall of 1962, Altman entered the University of Colorado to work with Leonard Lerman on the replication of the T4 bacteriophage. (A bacteriophage infects bacterial cells as viruses infect human cells.) He obtained his Ph.D. in 1967 and then spent two years at Harvard University as a postdoctoral fellow for the biochemist Matthew Meselson, performing further studies of the DNA of the T4 bacteriophage.

In 1969 Altman moved to the Medical Research Council Laboratory of Molecular Biology in Cambridge, England, to work with Francis Crick, the molecular biologist Sydney Brenner, and their colleagues. His intention was to study the three-dimensional structure of transfer RNA. Transfer RNA, or tRNA, is the RNA that carries amino acids into the translation process. Altman soon found that his plans were largely superseded by the studies of AARON KLUG, among others. "Although some of my colleagues remember me as being upset," Altman later recalled, "the feeling must have passed quickly because I only recall being presented with a marvelous opportunity to follow my own ideas."

Altman decided to change his focus from the structure of tRNA to its transcription from DNA. Normally, the DNA that produces tRNA is transcribed not directly into tRNA but into a long "precursor RNA." Precursor RNA is made up of a

tRNA strand with additional sequences on each end of the strand. Altman began working with the tRNA genes of the bacterium *Escherichia coli*. By combining the *E. coli* with toxic chemicals, Altman produced mutations in the tRNA genes. Production of these mutations helped Altman to develop the first method for isolating precursor tRNA from bacterial cells.

Altman and his colleagues found that the additional sequences found on each end of precursor RNA were "edited" away by something in the bacterial cells, presumably an enzyme, which they called ribonuclease P (RNase P). RNase P would cut RNA only at a very precise point; it was the most specific ribonuclease known at the time. "The novelty of [the specificity of] this reaction assured our continuing interest in it," Altman wrote, so they began to try purifying the enzyme.

Altman continued working on RNase P after he was hired as an assistant professor at Yale University in 1971. In 1978 he published the results of an experiment by his graduate student, Benjamin Stark, showing that RNase P included an RNA component, which demonstrated that this RNA molecule had an essential role in the enzymatic activity.

Altman recalled, "When Stark's experiments were published, we did not have the temerity to suggest, nor did we suspect, that the RNA component alone of RNase P could be responsible for the enzyme's catalytic activity. The fact that an enzyme had an essential RNA subunit, in itself, seemed heretical enough." Ever since JAMES B. SUMNER's and JOHN H. NORTHROP's work studying enzymes, it had been axiomatic that enzymes are made of protein but not of nucleic acids.

In 1981, while Altman and his colleagues were working to characterize the RNA and protein components of RNase P at Yale, THOMAS R. CECH and his associate Arthur Zaug were doing related work at the University of Colorado. Cech and Zaug reported that precursor RNA from the protozoan *Tetrahymena* were edited down to their final size without the assistance of protein. Cech's suggestion that the precursor RNA itself catalyzed this reaction was startling, but biochemists soon accepted his results. "Tom's work was done so convincingly," noted Ohio State University biochemist Philip S. Perlman, "that within a few months, everyone was sure it was true."

What was not so readily accepted was Cech's referring to the RNA as a type of biological catalyst. The traditional definition of a catalyst specified that it accelerates a reaction without itself being affected, yet Cech's RNA used itself up in the course of the reaction.

In 1983 Altman's colleague Cecilia Guerrier-Takada was engaged in testing the catalytic activity of RNase P. She was surprised to observe catalysis even in the control experiments that used the RNA subunit of RNase P (called the M1 RNA) but contained no protein.

Altman and his associates quickly showed that the M1 RNA fulfilled all the classical requirements for a catalyst: it was stable, needed only in small amounts, and (in contrast to the RNA Cech studied) was unchanged by the reaction. By 1984 there was no longer any doubt that RNA could act as an enzyme.

"Who could ever have suspected that scientists, as recently as in our own decade, were missing such a fundamental component in their understanding of the molecular prerequisites of life?" said Bertil Andersson of the Royal Swedish Academy of Sciences in presenting Cech and Altman the 1989 Nobel Prize for Chemistry. "Altman's and Cech's discoveries not only mean that the introductory chapters of our chemistry and biology textbooks will have to be rewritten, they also herald a new way of thinking and are a call to new biochemical research."

Catalytic RNA had an immediate, shattering impact on theories of the origin of life. Chemists had long debated whether proteins—which catalyze biological reactions—or nucleic acids such as RNA—which carry genetic information to make proteins—were the first elements of life. It seemed that whichever came first would have intractable problems without the other. In the late 1960s Francis Crick, Leslie Orgel of the Salk Institute, and Carl Woese of the University of Illinois had pointed out that many of these difficulties could be reduced if RNA acted as a catalyst, but the suggestion had never been more than a curiosity. Altman's and Cech's discoveries convinced researchers that the earth's original biological system was indeed an "RNA world," in which, as Andersson stated, RNA was "both genetic code and enzyme at one and the same time."

The practical applications of catalytic RNA were also potentially enormous. "RNA is at the heart of all viral and many other diseases in man," Cech noted, and RNA enzymes, or ribozymes, "have the ability to act as a sort of molecular scissors" to cut RNA from an infectious virus. "There are tens of millions of dollars being invested right now in programs to find out whether there are ways to cut up infectious RNA," he said. "This will either be a passing fad or a central therapy that allows us to cure everything from the common cold to AIDS."

Altman married Ann Korner in 1972; they have a son and a daughter. He became a United States citizen in 1984 but retains his Canadian citizenship. Altman has remained at Yale since 1971. He became a full professor in 1980, was chairman of the biology department from 1983 to 1985, and was dean of Yale College from 1985 to 1989, "an experience that not only provided me with the opportunity to make many new friends, mostly outside the sciences, but also revealed to me the full panorama of human and academic problems that exist in a university community," he wrote.

ABOUT: American Men and Women of Science, 1989–90; New York Times October 13, 1989; Science October 20, 1989; Scientific American December 1989; U.S. News and World Report October 23, 1989; Wall Street Journal October 13, 1989; Washington Post October 13, 1989.

ARIAS SÁNCHEZ, OSCAR
(September 13, 1940–   )
Nobel Prize for Peace, 1987

The Costa Rican economist, lawyer, and politician Oscar Arias Sánchez (är′ ē äs sän′ chez) was born in the city of Heredia, the oldest child of Juan Rafael Arias Trejos and the former Lillian Sánchez Cortés. Arias's father was a prominent coffee grower and banker, and several members of his family held government positions. After early schooling in Costa Rica, Arias attended Boston University in the United States, where he planned to study medicine. The 1960 United States presidential campaign between John F. Kennedy and Richard M. Nixon deepened his already strong interest in politics. Taking Kennedy, whom he had met, as a role model, Arias decided in 1961 to return to Costa Rica to study law and economics and, eventually, to enter politics himself.

During his six years at the University of Costa Rica, Arias began organizing student support for the Partido Liberación Nacional (PLN), the social democratic party founded by José "Don Pepe" Figueres Ferrer. (Figueres had been a popular leader in the 1948 War of National Liberation, a civil war that led to the overthrow of Costa Rica's dictatorship. From 1953 to 1958, he had served as the country's president.)

After Arias completed his degree in 1967, he received a British government grant that enabled him to study at the University of Essex and the London School of Economics and Political Science. He returned to Costa Rica in 1969 and accepted a position as professor of political science at the University of Costa Rica. A year later, he published an award-winning book on Costa Rican interest groups. He received his Ph.D. from the University of Essex in 1974, with a dissertation on the socioeconomic backgrounds of Costa Rican political leaders.

Meanwhile, in 1970, Figueres had been re-elected to the presidency of Costa Rica after

OSCAR ARIAS SÁNCHEZ

twelve years out of office. He asked Arias to join his economic council and, two years later, made Arias his minister of planning and economics (a post that Arias held into the next president's term). In 1973 Arias married the biochemist Margarita Penón Góngora, with whom he eventually had two children, Sylvia Eugenia and Oscar Felipe.

In 1978 the PLN lost the presidency, but Arias was elected to represent Heredia in the national assembly. He became his party's general secretary in 1979, and through this position he helped the party regain the presidency in 1983. In 1986 the PLN made Arias its presidential candidate.

Arias and his major opponent had similar platforms, differing primarily in their positions on the web of Central American conflicts. Especially important were troubles related to the government of Nicaragua, Costa Rica's northern neighbor.

Until 1978 Nicaragua had been ruled by a dictatorship under Anastasio Somoza. A national uprising in that year culminated in a civil war led by Marxist guerrillas of the Sandinista party. When the war was over, the Sandinistas took power. The new government allied itself with the communist countries of Cuba and the Soviet Union, thereby earning the distrust of the anticommunist United States government.

The years that followed were difficult for Central America. Soon after the Sandinistas took power, the United States actively backed a group of anti-Sandinista rebels known as the contras, while the Soviet Union threw its weight behind the Nicaraguan government. In the meantime, the Sandinistas, in an effort to topple the right-wing government of neighboring El Salvador, had begun to offer military aid to leftist insurgents in that country. The United States, a supporter of the Salvadoran government, threatened retaliatory action.

The governments of other Central American countries resented the involvement of the United States and the Soviet Union in their regional affairs. Nevertheless, because of their fear of the Sandinistas and their economic dependence on the United States, the governments of Honduras, Guatemala, and Costa Rica were forced to support the United States' position. Honduras let the contras establish bases within its borders, and agents of the United States flew supplies to the contras from a secret airfield in Costa Rica.

Four other regional governments, however—Mexico, Venezuela, Colombia, and Panama—took it upon themselves to develop a solution without the help of outsiders. In 1983 they agreed on a peace plan (called the Contadora plan, after the Panamanian island where it was developed) that outlined general methods for handling conflicts within the region. The plan provided for the cessation of arms sales and the withdrawal of foreign powers and advisers from Central America. The four sponsoring countries succeeded in getting representatives of Nicaragua, El Salvador, Honduras, Guatemala, and Costa Rica to sign preliminary versions of the plan but failed to bring about final agreements. The Contadora plan continued to be negotiated, but its implementation seemed less and less likely.

Against this background, the appropriate role of Costa Rica in Central American affairs became the most important issue of Arias's 1986 presidential campaign. His conservative opponent suggested sending Costa Rican border guards to fight if Nicaragua attacked the contra stronghold in Honduras. Arias's commitment to diplomacy and to keeping Costa Rica out of the struggle won popular support. He was elected president with 52 percent of the vote.

The nation's acceptance of Arias's position is not surprising, given Costa Rica's longstanding commitment to neutrality. A small, mountainous country, it has neither exploitable natural resources nor large farming areas. As a result, unlike many of its Latin American neighbors, it never developed a plantation economy, in which a few powerful landholders rule over a landless majority. Instead, Costa Rica became a nation of small, self-sufficient, landowning farmers.

Historically, Costa Rica's lack of riches resulted in little interference from Spain, which allowed the country to become independent peacefully in the 1830s. As citizens of a free republic with a relatively stable political system, Costa Ricans have developed a strong sense of independence. Since 1869 mass public education, essential to a democratic society, has been free and compulsory. The constitution that the nation adopted after a brief insurrection in 1948 eliminated Costa Rica's armed forces. As Arias said in his Nobel lecture, "Mine is an unarmed people, whose children have never seen a fighter or a tank or a warship . . . . Because my country is a country of teachers, we believe in convincing our opponents, not defeating them. We prefer raising the fallen to crushing them, because we believe that no one possesses the absolute truth. Because mine is a country of teachers, we seek an economy in which men cooperate in the spirit of solidarity, not an economy in which they compete to their own extinction."

When he took office on May 8, 1986, Arias vowed to keep Costa Rica out of armed conflict and to "prevent Central American brothers from killing each other." He moved quickly and firmly to close the secret United States air base and to discourage any thought that Costa Rica would help the contras. At the end of May, he met with the presidents of Honduras, El Salvador, Guatemala, and Nicaragua to discuss the Contadora peace plan. This meeting failed to achieve an agreement, but by the following February, Arias had unveiled his own plan.

Arias's peace plan was both broader and more detailed than the Contadora plan. It specifically barred outside aid to guerrillas and their use of foreign territory. Most significantly, it set an immediate deadline for cease-fires in all regional conflicts. It called on the governments to open discussions with "unarmed oppositions." (The contras, in other words, would have to disarm; in return, the Sandinistas would have to agree to negotiate with them.) The plan also called for free elections and guarantees of improved human and civil rights in all Central American nations.

Politicians in Central America, western Europe, and the United States responded enthusiastically to Arias's plan; indeed, the United States Senate endorsed it (with only one dissenting vote) despite the objections of Ronald Reagan's administration. (Reagan believed that the plan did not make strong enough demands on Nicaragua's government and that it contained too many loopholes.) Finally, on August 7, 1987, the five Central American presidents signed the Procedure for the Establishment of the Firm and Lasting Peace in Central America. They had achieved what many had considered impossible—agreement on a strategy for bringing peace to their region.

Two months later, Arias was awarded the 1987 Nobel Prize for Peace. The Norwegian Nobel Committee expressed the "hope that the award will help to speed up the process of peace in Central America." Egil Aarvik of the committee described Arias's peace plan as impressive in two ways. First, the five nations had themselves developed and agreed upon the plan, without superpower involvement. Second, the plan showed a clear commitment to linking peace with democracy. The signatory nations had recognized that their difficulties stemmed from longstanding internal social and economic injustices, and they had acknowledged that they must look to themselves, not to outside powers, to address these issues.

Arias accepted the prize as a tribute to his country and his region. He told a jubilant Costa Rican crowd, "This prize is a recognition of Costa Rica. . . . It has been given to a magnificent country and to the values we share: freedom, peace, and democracy." In his Nobel lecture, he said that he received the prize "as one of 400 million Latin Americans who, in the return to liberty, in the exercise of democracy, are seeking the way to overcome so much misery and so much injustice."

Reiterating his lifelong position that "peace can only be achieved through its own instruments: dialogue and understanding; tolerance and forgiveness; freedom and democracy," Arias said, "Let Central Americans decide the future of Central America. Leave the interpretation and implementation of our peace plan to us. Support the efforts of peace instead of the forces of war in our region. Send our people ploughshares instead of swords, pruning hooks instead of spears." Arias pledged to use his $340,000 prize money to start a foundation "to meet the needs of the poorest, humblest, and neediest" of Costa Rica's people.

Awarding Arias the Nobel Prize did not solve Central America's problems, but it did have an influence. Soon after the award, the United States Congress voted to end military aid to the Nicaraguan contras. Unfortunately, the peace plan's cease-fire agreements were never implemented, and the United States continued to support the contras secretly. Nevertheless, Central America had made a stand for resolving its own political difficulties without outside interference. Arias's peace plan and negotiating stance remain a model for current and future efforts. In Nicaragua, in 1990, the plan led the way to open elections, a peaceful transfer of power from the Sandinista ruling party, and the disbanding of the contras.

Arias's presidential term ended in 1990; the constitution forbade his reelection. Turning down a teaching fellowship at Harvard University, he has established the Arias Foundation for Peace and Human Progress and continues to work and speak worldwide to promote his vision of peace, stability, and justice.

WORKS IN ENGLISH TRANSLATION: Pressure Groups in Costa Rica, 1970; Who Governs Costa Rica? 1976; Latin Democracy, Independence and Society, 1977; Roads for Costa

Rica's Development, 1977; New Ways for Costa Rican Development, 1980.

ABOUT: Abrams, I. The Nobel Peace Prize and the Laureates, 1988; Ameringer, C. D. Democracy in Nicaragua, 1982; Bell, J. P. Crisis in Costa Rica: The 1948 Revolution, 1971; Biesanz, R. The Costa Ricans, 1982; Current Biography Yearbook, 1987.

AUNG SAN SUU KYI

AUNG SAN SUU KYI
(June 19, 1945–   )
Nobel Prize for Peace, 1991

Burmese political activist Aung San Suu Kyi (äng sän sōo chē) was born in Rangoon to U Aung San, the political founder of modern Burma, and his wife Khin Kyi.

Since the thirteenth century Burma had been ruled by a succession of foreign powers. After a series of wars between 1824 and 1886, Great Britain annexed the country, making it a province of British India. By 1920, however, Burmese nationalism had become pronounced. Student strikes and peasant uprisings for independence forced the British to give the Burmese more power over their own affairs. In 1923 Britain established in Burma a dyarchy consisting of an appointed British governor and elected Burmese representatives. In 1937, after further protests, Great Britain separated Burma from India.

U Aung San (the U is a Burmese honorific; it becomes part of the name of men of status) was a student at the University of Rangoon and was one of the leaders of Burma's nationalist movement. In 1936 he and former student U Nu led a student strike; in the 1940s they enlisted the aid of Japan to build the Burma Independence Army and force the British out. The alliance with Japan backfired: With the British gone, the Japanese occupied the country. The Burmese found themselves in the middle of World War II, allying themselves with the British again to free themselves of Japanese rule. General Aung San, determined to rid Burma of all foreign influence, formed a new political party called the Anti-Fascist People's Freedom League.

After the war, as U Aung San's party increased in strength and popularity, Great Britain acquiesced to Burma's demand for independence. In January 1947 U Aung San was appointed the leader of an interim government. In elections held in April the Anti-Fascist People's Freedom League won decisively. U Aung San was hailed as the architect of the new democracy.

Three months after the elections and just before he was to take office, U Aung San and all the members of his cabinet were assassinated by a political rival. The British government appointed U Nu, the second in command of the league, interim leader. Burma became a formally independent nation under the leadership of U Nu in January 1948.

Aung San Suu Kyi, whose name translates as "a bright collection of strange victories," was two years old when her father was killed. In 1960 her mother was appointed the Burmese ambassador to India. Living in New Delhi with her mother, Suu Kyi studied at an exclusive secondary school where she encountered Mohandas K. Gandhi's philosophy of nonviolence. She then went to Oxford University in England in 1964 to study politics, philosophy, and economics. After graduation she worked as a teacher in England and for a while at the United Nations in New York City. While at Oxford she had met a British professor, Michael Aris, who was a scholar of Tibetan anthropology, and they married in 1972, but not before she warned him that she might have to return to her homeland someday. "I only ask one thing," she wrote him, "that should my people need me, you would help me to do my duty by them."

After their marriage Suu Kyi and Aris spent time in Bhutan, where Aris was a tutor to the royal family. They returned to Oxford in 1974, where Aris accepted a teaching position and where the couple's two sons were born. In 1988, when her mother became ill, Suu Kyi returned home.

Burma had undergone many changes during the years she had been away. In 1962 the military leader U Ne Win launched a coup that overthrew U Nu and replaced the young democracy with a military regime. As dictator, U Ne Win began what he termed the "Burmese way to socialism," but his socialist innovations devastated the nation. His attempts to set up a state marketing system and to regiment agriculture, in combination with the government's new isolationist policy and general mismanagement of affairs, quickly ruined Burma's economy. In twenty-five years Burma went from Asia's main rice exporter and a country rich in oil, grain, gems, and timber to one of the poorest nations in the world.

U Ne Win's policies included the use of the military to suppress all political dissent. Nevertheless, in 1987, when his decision to devalue the Burmese dollar brought instant poverty to the populace, violence and protests grew to such an extent that he was forced to resign in July 1988. Appointing a hard-line general to head the government, he continued to control the military regime from the background. When student strikes and civilian protests reached a climax in August and September, a military junta called the State Law and Order Restoration Council (SLORC) began a crackdown on the protesters. Some 3,000 were killed.

What she witnessed upon her return compelled Suu Kyi to become politically active. As she later explained, "My instinct was, 'This is not a time when anyone who cares can stay out.' As my father's daughter, I felt I had a duty to get involved."

With a goal that mirrors her father's—a democratic system of government in which all regions and ethnic groups are represented—Suu Kyi founded the National League for Democracy (NLD) and began speaking out against Ne Win and the military government. "The people of Burma are like prisoners in their own country, deprived of all freedom under military rule," she said in an interview. She led peaceful rallies, ignoring martial law regulations and facing down armed soldiers. At one NLD rally soldiers pointed rifles into the crowd, prompting Suu Kyi to comment, "We are grateful to those who are giving the people practice in being brave."

In an effort to appease the people, the ruling SLORC promised to hold elections in May 1990 and to gradually restore democracy. However, to ensure that it would not face opposition in the elections, the junta ordered the arrest of the NLD's leaders and hundreds of its members. On July 20, 1989, Suu Kyi was placed under house arrest and disqualified from the election; later she was denied visits from and communication with her family. The detention was supposed to last up to one year, but in the spring of 1992 she was still detained in her mother's home.

Finally, in May 1990, after it had silenced all opposition to the government-backed National Unity Party, SLORC allowed elections in which Suu Kyi's party won 82 percent of the local races. Frustrated by their inability to control the outcome of the elections, the military government refused to turn over control to the civilian government, as

it had promised to do earlier. All winning candidates from the NLD have since been arrested or disqualified.

Aung San Suu Kyi received the 1991 Nobel Prize for Peace for her "nonviolent struggle for democracy and human rights." In announcing the prize, the Norwegian Nobel Committee said that it wanted to show its support "for the many people throughout the world who are striving to attain democracy, human rights, and ethnic conciliation by peaceful means." Suu Kyi's struggle, the committee noted, "is one of the most extraordinary examples of civil courage in Asia in recent decades."

Unable to make contact with the award winner, the committee called her husband at Harvard University, where he is a visiting professor. Describing his feelings, Aris said, "It was not surprise. It was great emotion, great joy and pride, and also sadness and continued apprehension about her situation." Aris and their two sons had not been allowed contact with Suu Kyi since Christmas 1989. In November 1991 the government permitted her to receive unsealed letters from her family, but she still is not permitted contact with anyone else.

The military government of Burma (which in 1979 changed the name of the country to Myanmar) has offered to free Suu Kyi if she leaves the country immediately and does not return. She has agreed to leave, but only under four conditions: The military must release all political prisoners, turn power over to the civilians, give her five minutes to address the country over television and radio to explain the conditions under which she is leaving, and allow her to make a public procession to the airport. The government has refused these conditions.

Even in captivity and although she had only eleven months of vocal political activity, Aung San Suu Kyi has become a symbol for Burmese citizens. They often wear pins displaying her picture or T-shirts with the symbol of her party, a peasant's hat. Although her stance has not swayed the Burmese rulers, it has had an effect internationally. Six weeks after the Nobel Prize was announced, the United Nations issued a resolution protesting the military leadership's refusal to yield power and denouncing its human rights abuses. Member nations moved more quickly on this resolution than they had moved on any other before it. Speaking of Suu Kyi, Czechoslovakian president Vaclav Havel commented, "She has refused to be bribed into silence by permanent exile. . . . She is an outstanding example of the power of the powerless."

On December 10, 1991, Aris and their sons accepted the Nobel Prize on behalf of Aung San Suu Kyi. At the same time, students and others staged two days of demonstrations in Burma, protesting the continued imprisonment of Suu Kyi. The demonstrations were the largest in the country since the arrest of the NLD leaders.

Since accepting the award, Aris has compiled Suu Kyi's writings and speeches into a book, *Freedom from Fear and Other Writings* (1991), in order to publicize her fate and "liberate her voice." In 1991 Suu Kyi also won the Sakharov Prize for Freedom and Thought by the European Parliament.

ADDITIONAL WORKS: Aung San of Burma, 1991.

ABOUT: Christian Science Monitor July 20, 1990; Current Biography, February 1992; Economist July 21, 1990; International Who's Who, 1992; Newsweek June 11, 1990; New York Times October 15, 1991; November 24, 1991; Time August 21, 1989; June 11, 1990; October 28, 1991.

J. GEORG BEDNORZ

BEDNORZ, J. GEORG
(May 16, 1950–)
Nobel Prize for Physics, 1987
(shared with K. Alex Müller)

The German physicist and mineralogist Johannes Georg Bednorz (bet′ norz) was born in Neuenkirchen, North-Rhine Westphalia, the youngest child of Anton Bednorz and the former Elisabeth Jeziorowski. As Bednorz later recounted in an autobiographical essay, "My parents . . . had lost sight of each other during the turbulences of World War II, when my sister and two brothers had to leave home. . . . I was a latecomer completing our family after its joyous reunion in 1949."

Bednorz's parents both taught—his father, primary school, and his mother, piano. They tried hard throughout his early years to interest him in classical music. Yet, he wrote, "I was more practical-minded and preferred to assist my brothers in fixing their motorcycles and cars." Only later did an art teacher help him discover that an enjoyment of the arts could coexist with his pragmatism. This teacher "cultivated that practical sense and helped to develop creativity and team spirit within the class community, inspiring us to theater and artistic performances even outside school hours." At age thirteen, he wrote, "I even discovered my interest in classical music." He went on to play violin and trumpet in the school orchestra.

Bednorz's interest in the natural sciences developed during his high school years, though initially he preferred chemistry to physics. "The latter," he wrote, "was taught in a more theoretical way, whereas in chemistry, the opportunity to conduct experiments on our own, sometimes even with unexpected results, was addressing my practical sense." As a result, he enrolled as a chemistry major at the University of Münster in 1968. He found,

however, that the department's size created an impersonal atmosphere that left him feeling lost. "Thus I soon changed my major to crystallography, that field of mineralogy which is located between chemistry and physics."

In 1972 Bednorz went to the IBM Zurich Research Laboratory as a summer student, a decision that "set the course for my future." He joined a department headed by K. ALEX MÜLLER, a physicist whose many accomplishments included years of studying the oxides, compounds of metallic elements and oxygen. Bednorz found his summer in Zurich extremely stimulating. "I was . . . learning about different methods of crystal growth, materials characterization, and solid-state chemistry. I soon was impressed by the freedom even I as a student was given to work on my own, learning from mistakes and thus losing the fear of approaching new problems in my own way."

Having enjoyed his experience so deeply, he visited the laboratory again the next year. In 1974 he returned again—this time for six months—to do experimentation for his diploma (the equivalent of a master's degree). His experiments involved "work on crystal growth and characterization" of a particular oxide that Müller had studied extensively. With Müller's encouragement, Bednorz moved to Zurich permanently after finishing his diploma in 1976. He joined the Laboratory of Solid State Physics at the Swiss Federal Institute of Technology, where he pursued his Ph.D. under the supervision of Müller and Professor Heini Granicher. In 1978 he was joined by a new Ph.D. student, Mechthild Wennemer, whom he had met at the University of Münster in 1974. The couple married a few months after her arrival.

During this period, Bednorz has written, "I began to interact more closely with Alex [Müller] and learned about his intuitive way of thinking and his capability of combining ideas to form a new concept." The two formed a strong bond, and on completing his doctorate in 1982, Bednorz joined Müller at the IBM laboratory. They began an "intense collaboration," in which, roughly, Bednorz provided the talent for experimentation and Müller the capacity for original, intuitive thinking.

In 1983 the two physicists became interested in the problem of high-temperature superconductivity. Superconductivity had first been observed in 1911, when the Dutch physicist HEIKE KAMER-LINGH ONNES cooled mercury to an extremely low temperature and found that electricity would flow through it with no loss of energy to resistance. This discovery immediately excited scientific thinkers. With zero resistance, the costs of generating and transmitting electricity would plummet; thus, the discovery offered the possibility of cheap and almost limitless electrical power. Furthermore, superconductors have the curious property of floating above a magnetic field. As a result, engineers imagined that investigations in superconductivity could bring about the invention of low-cost, low-friction, high-speed trains.

Unfortunately, cooling mercury to $4°K$, the temperature necessary to make it a superconductor, required too much effort and expense to make superconductivity practical for most applications. (Absolute zero—$0°K$—is the point at which atomic motion effectively ceases; $0°K$ is equivalent to $-459.67°F$.) Nevertheless, because superconductivity offered such extraordinary promise, researchers began a long and arduous search for substances that would superconduct at higher temperatures. By 1973 the maximum temperature for superconductivity had reached $23°K$.

At this point, however, all progress stopped. By the 1980s, many scientists believed that they had discovered nature's own upper limit on superconductivity, yet $23°K$ remained far too cold for most practical applications.

High-temperature superconductivity research was therefore considered almost quixotic by the time Bednorz and Müller began their work. Their research was particularly unusual in that it concerned oxides—materials that normally do not conduct at all—rather than the metals that previous researchers had examined. Inspired by the knowledge that some oxides do become conductors at very low temperatures, Bednorz and Müller began a painstaking process of synthesizing various compounds, cooling them, and measuring their conductivity. Sometimes they discovered that a minor change in a molecule's structure created a conductor where none had existed before, but their efforts to achieve superconductivity went unrewarded.

Then, after years of trial and failure, Bednorz read a French paper describing a newly synthesized oxide of copper mixed with barium and lanthanum. The French researchers had thoroughly examined the material, but they had not tested it for superconductivity. Bednorz and Müller decided to do so. On January 27, 1986, they observed what they had sought—a sharp drop in resistance as the substance cooled, but at a temperature far higher than ever before measured. By April, they had raised the record for a superconductor to $35°K$. This temperature was still too low for practical applicability, but it surpassed by $12°K$ the limit that for thirteen years had seemed insurmountable.

The two scientists, hoping to stay out of the limelight for a year or two while they improved on their discovery, published a modest article on "possible" high-temperature superconductivity in the lesser-known German journal *Zeitschrift für Physik*. Nevertheless, word of their discovery spread rapidly through the physics community. Laboratories almost immediately began competing to build on their work, and within a year, the American researcher Paul Chu had raised the base temperature for superconductivity to $90°K$. This temperature is a full $13°K$ warmer than the temperature of liquid nitrogen, a common laboratory coolant. The dream of practical superconductivity had become a reality.

Bednorz's and Müller's superconductivity research earned them a Nobel Prize in 1987. Although the entire physics community acknowledged the importance of their work, the swiftness with which Bednorz and Müller received the award—just one year after they had published their research—surprised some observers. Yet, as Gösta Ekspong of the Royal Swedish Academy of Sciences noted in presenting the award, Bednorz's and Müller's discovery had "already stimulated research and development throughout the world to an unprecedented extent." Ekspong credited the team with having "reopened and revitalized" scientific discussion in superconductivity, and with having inspired the explosion in research that had finally produced a practical superconductor. Finally, he noted, their discovery had provoked a new theoretical interest in superconductivity. No one yet understands how oxides, which in some ways resemble common ceramics, can become superconductors. Therefore, no one can say what factors might limit the temperatures at which they do so. Indeed, some scientists have even entertained the possibility of eventual room-temperature superconductivity.

Bednorz's work has earned him many honors in addition to the Nobel Prize. The German Mineralogical Society awarded him its Viktor Moritz Goldschmidt Prize (1987), and the Free University of Berlin its Otto-Klung Prize (1987). Bednorz has shared with Müller such awards as the German Physical Society's Robert Wichard Pohl Prize (1987), the Hewlett-Packard Europhysics Prize (1988), and the American Physical Society's International Prize for New Materials Research (1988).

ABOUT: International Who's Who, 1990; New York Times October 15, 1987; New York Times Magazine August 16, 1987; Physics Today December 1987; Science October 25, 1987.

BISHOP, J. MICHAEL
(February 22, 1936–   )
Nobel Prize for Physiology or Medicine, 1989
(shared with Harold E. Varmus)

J. MICHAEL BISHOP

The American virologist and biochemist John Michael Bishop was born in York, Pennsylvania, the son of John S. and Carrie (Grey) Bishop. Bishop and his brother and sister grew up in a rural area. He later wrote, "My youth was permeated with the concerns of my father's occupation as a Lutheran minister, tending to two small parishes. My most tangible legacy from then is a passion for music." His early education came in very small public schools, where "I heard little of science," he recalled. "My aspirations for the future were formed outside the classroom," particularly by his friendship with the family physician. He entered nearby Gettysburg College in 1953 "intent on preparing for medical school. But my ambition was far from resolute." He graduated in 1957 with a chemistry degree, but "still knowing nothing of original research in science." Thinking to become a teacher of medicine, he entered Harvard Medical School, where he "discovered that the path to an academic career in the biomedical sciences lay through research, not through teaching, and I was probably least among my peers at Harvard in my preparation to travel that path."

Bishop was "rescued," as he put it, by pathologists at Massachusetts General Hospital, who offered him a year of independent study in the middle of his medical training. "There was little hope that I could do any investigation of substance during that year, and I did not. But I became a practiced pathologist. . . . And I was riotously free to read and think, which led me to a new passion: molecular biology," Bishop recalled.

Molecular biology, the study of the large molecules that perform biological functions, had only recently been established by FRANCIS CRICK's and JAMES D. WATSON's discovery of the structure of the nucleic acid DNA, the genetic material. During the 1950s and 1960s many scientists worked to show that DNA molecules are made up of a chain of variable subunits, known as bases. They found that the order of the bases in a particular piece of DNA (a gene) can be translated, mostly by another nucleic acid called RNA, to produce a chain of amino acids making up a protein. Proteins make up most of the substance of and perform most of the functions within living organisms.

Much of this early molecular biology research was summarized by Crick in the "central dogma" that genetic information flows from DNA to RNA to protein, but not back. The central dogma was a useful unifying concept, but there were clearly some exceptions. One of the most important involved viruses. Viruses are organisms so small that they consist only of nucleic acid and a shell of protein. In order to reproduce, a virus must invade a cell from a more complex organism and commandeer the cell's genetic machinery, forcing it to make more viruses instead of more cells. A virus composed of DNA would introduce its DNA in place of the cell's. However, some viruses are made of RNA; clearly, without possessing DNA, their reproduction via cellular systems that normally follow the central dogma presented interesting problems.

Bishop became aware of these problems through one of his teachers, the virologist Elmer Pfefferkorn. He was excused from most of his fourth-year medical courses to work in Pfefferkorn's laboratory, where he studied the reproduction of RNA viruses. Bishop received his M.D. in 1962, spent two years as an intern and resident at Massachusetts General Hospital, and then for three years was a postdoctoral fellow at the United States National Institutes of Health, in "a program designed to train mere physicians like myself in fundamental research." He studied the replication of the RNA virus that causes polio, working under the virologists Leon Levintow and Gebhard Koch. Koch then persuaded Bishop to work with him in Hamburg, Germany, for a year.

In 1968 Bishop joined Levintow on the faculty at the University of California, San Francisco. There the microbiologist Warren Levinson had set up a program to study Rous sarcoma virus (RSV). RSV, discovered by PEYTON ROUS, is an RNA virus that causes tumors in chickens. HOWARD M. TEMIN's studies of this process led him to propose that RSV was a retrovirus, that is, a virus that copies its RNA into DNA (the reverse of the usual process and contrary to the central dogma). This DNA, he proposed, somehow both induces cancers (uncontrolled cell growth) and produces copies of the original RNA virus. Bishop and his colleagues had barely begun studying how RSV accomplishes these tasks when Temin and DAVID BALTIMORE announced that they had independently isolated an enzyme called reverse transcriptase, which copies RNA into DNA.

"The discovery of reverse transcriptase was sobering for me: a momentous secret of nature, mine for the taking, had eluded me," Bishop recollected. "But I was also exhilarated because reverse transcriptase offered new handles on the replication of retroviruses, handles that I seized and deployed with a vengeance." He started studying viral DNA in 1970. One of his co-workers was a new postdoctoral fellow, HAROLD E. VARMUS. "Harold's arrival changed my life and career," Bishop recalled. "Our relationship evolved rapidly to one of co-equals, and the result was surely greater than the sum of the two parts."

In 1970 G. Steven Martin of the University of California, Berkeley, showed that a certain RSV gene, named *src,* determined the virus's ability to cause cancers; genes with this property are called oncogenes. Peter K. Vogt of the University of Southern California soon found an RSV mutant in which the *src* gene was left out, or deleted (*src⁻*). Bishop and Varmus reasoned that by matching up (hybridizing) DNA from "normal" type (*src⁺*) virus with RNA from *src⁻* virus, they could isolate the *src* gene. Dominique Stehelin, a postdoctoral fellow in Varmus's and Bishop's laboratory, eventually performed the work, and in 1976 they developed an *src* gene "probe" that could locate the *src* gene in organisms. Stehelin then used the probe and found that *src*-like genes were present not only in RSV but also in normal chicken DNA.

This result had been predicted by Robert J. Huebner and George J. Todaro of the National Cancer Institute in 1969 in their popular "virogene-oncogene hypothesis." They theorized that the DNA of normal cells contains silent oncogenes, descended from virus infections in their ancestors, that can be activated by carcinogens to cause new cancers.

When Bishop and his colleagues used the *src* with other species, however, they saw startling results. Stehelin found the *src* gene was present in every other bird he studied, even those distantly related to the chicken. Another postdoctoral fellow, Deborah Specter, even found *src*-like sequences in mammals. These findings led the group to conclude that the cancer-causing gene was not from a viral infection but was a normal, cellular gene carried by the host. Bishop and his associates suggested that cellular oncogenes are present in all the animals because they have some normal, necessary function in animal cells, and probably "normally influenced those processes gone awry in tumorigenesis, control of cell growth or development."

The discovery of cellular oncogenes caused great excitement and controversy in the scientific community. By 1981 evidence from numerous laboratories confirmed the conclusions Bishop and his co-workers had formed.

Bishop and Varmus were jointly awarded the 1989 Nobel Prize in Physiology or Medicine for their discoveries. Erling Norrby of the Karolinska Institute stated when presenting the Nobel Prizes, "Through your discovery of the cellular origin of retroviral oncogenes you set in motion an avalanche of research on factors that govern the normal growth of cells. This research has given us a new perspective on one of the most fundamental phenomena in biology and as a consequence also new insights into the complex group of diseases that we call cancer."

When the award was announced, Dominique Stehelin, by then a researcher at the Pasteur Institute, complained that the narrowly worded citation could refer only to the 1976 *src* experiments for which he claimed to have done "all the work from A to Z." Some other French scientists and government officials joined in his protest.

In 1959 Bishop married Kathryn Ione Putnam; they have two sons. "If offered reincarnation, I would choose the career of a performing musician with exceptional talent, preferably in a string quartet," Bishop has written. "One lifetime as a scientist is enough—great fun, but enough." He is an outstanding teacher and an avid reader and is noted for a scientific writing style far above what he calls "the dreadful prose that afflicts much of the contemporary scientific literature."

Bishop is a member of the National Academy of Sciences, the American Academy of Arts and Sciences, and numerous other scientific societies. His awards include the Albert Lasker Basic Medical Research Award (1982), an honorary doctorate from Gettysburg College (1983), the Passano Foundation Award (1983), the Armand Hammer Cancer Prize (1984), the Gairdner Foundation International Award (1984), the American Cancer Society National Medal of Honor (1985), and the American College of Physicians Award (1987).

ABOUT: American Men and Women of Science, 1989–90; New York Times October 10, 1989; Science October 20, 1989; Washington Post October 10, 1989; Who's Who in America, 1989.

BLACK, JAMES
(June 14, 1924–   )
Nobel Prize for Physiology or Medicine, 1988
(shared with Gertrude B. Elion and George H. Hitchings Jr.)

JAMES BLACK

The British pharmacologist James Whyte Black was born in Uddingston, Scotland, the fourth of five sons of a mining engineer. As a child, Black was enamored of music and mathematics, but the example of an older brother influenced him to study medicine. He attended the University of St. Andrews, Scotland, and graduated with degrees in chemistry and medicine in 1946. That same year, he married the biochemist Hilary Vaughan, with whom he later had a daughter, Stephanie.

Black spent the year 1947 working at St. Andrews under the physiologist R. C. Garry, studying the effects of certain drugs on blood pressure. He then spent three years teaching at the University of Singapore and eight years on the faculty of the University of Glasgow Veterinary School.

"As I slowly learned, like a primitive painter, how to be an effective experimenter," Black wrote later, "ideas began to ferment." One idea was for a new approach to the treatment of heart disease. People whose coronary arteries have been narrowed because of arteriosclerosis or other problems experience pain (angina) during exercise or emotional stress. Their hearts demand more oxygen, yet their damaged arteries cannot handle the extra blood. The traditional approach of the pharmaceutical industry was to look for drugs that could dilate the coronary arteries and increase the blood supply to the heart. Such drugs had been found, but they did not work as well against angina as had been expected. Black believed that a more effective approach might be to lower the heart rate and thus decrease the heart's demand for additional blood.

Black's investigation began with the hormone adrenaline. Adrenaline is released by the body at times of physical or emotional stress, and among its effects is an increase in the heart rate. For some reason, however, drugs that were known to counteract the general effects of adrenaline did not lower the pulse. In 1948 Raymond Ahlquist of the University of Georgia offered a possible explanation. He proposed that there are two kinds of molecular locks to which adrenaline is the key: alpha-receptors, which enable adrenaline to stimulate most organs, and beta-receptors, which allow adrenaline to stimulate the heart. Black decided to look for drugs that would specifically interfere with the beta-receptors; such drugs are now called beta-blockers. By preventing the beta-receptors from being influenced by adrenaline, it was possible to minimize adrenaline's effect on heart rate. Without the higher heart rate, patients suffered less angina.

Black took his ideas about beta-blockers to Imperial Chemical Industries (ICI), a major British pharmaceutical firm, and began working for the firm in 1958. "My whole experience at ICI was an educational tour de force," he later wrote. "I had to learn how to collaborate across disciplines, how to change gears when changing from research to development, how to make industry work—in short, how to be both effective and productive." Much of Black's labor went to develop a new bioassay system (a system to compare effects of a new drug against those of a known preparation) that would test drugs for their effects on cardiac beta-receptors. This step was critical, he said, because "what we are allowed to see of a new molecule's properties is totally dependent on the techniques of bioassay we use." Black, working with the chemist John Stephenson and others, used isoprenaline as his starting point. Isoprenaline is a relative of adrenaline that was known to stimulate beta-receptors but did not have as many side effects as adrenaline. If isoprenaline can be thought of as a key that turned the beta-receptor lock, Black's team was looking for another key that was similar enough to fit the lock but dissimilar enough to jam it.

In 1960 Stephenson synthesized the first effective beta-blocker, pronethalol. "Pronethalol always seemed to us to be a prototype drug, good enough to answer questions of principle but not good enough to be marketable," Black wrote later. The ICI chemical team, under the lead of Bert Crowther, soon made a safer, more effective variant—propranolol—which was marketed in 1964 under the brand name Inderal. Propranolol was first employed as a treatment for angina, but it was later used to treat high blood pressure as well. In the late 1970s, it was discovered that propranolol decreases the death rate for heart attack survivors. At that time, it was the only drug known to do so. Propranolol, and the family of beta-blockers to which it gave rise, now form a large and vital part of the treatment for heart disease.

"By 1963," Black later stated, "I faced opposing pressures. I saw that the success of the beta-receptor antagonist program would suck me more and more into the role of giving the young propranolol technical support and promotion—just as I was itching to start a new program."

Black had been interested in ulcer treatments since 1953. Stomach ulcers are caused by excessive production of gastric acid, which HENRY H. DALE had shown was stimulated by histamines. Available antihistamines, however—such as those developed by DANIEL BOVET—did not affect the stomach. Black saw that the situation was parallel to that for antiadrenaline drugs: the known antihistamines acted on the equivalent of alpha-receptors (called H_1), while gastric acid was controlled by the equivalent of beta-receptors (H_2). The histamine equivalent of beta-blockers should therefore stop overproduction of gastric acid.

Smith, Kline and French Laboratories hired Black in 1964 as head of biological research, and he began to search for H_2 blockers. This was a significant departure from the standard approach at the time, which was to focus on the acid-inducing hormone gastrin as the target for antiulcer drugs. After developing bioassays specifically to track the production of histamine-stimulated acid, Black began to search for inhibiting compounds.

Normally—as with the search for beta-blockers—such efforts begin with a known compound that has some of the desired effects. Researchers then test chemical variants of the compound until they find a useful drug. In this case, however, no appropriate starting compound was known. Therefore, Black and his co-workers had to start with the structure of histamine itself, modifying it to find a substance similar enough to bind to the histamine receptors without activating them.

In the first four years of the project, Black's colleagues, led by C. Robin Ganellin, synthesized over 200 compounds without success. Just when the pharmaceutical company had decided to cancel the project altogether, Black suggested using a more sophisticated bioassay to reexamine certain of the earlier compounds they had made. One of these compounds, guanylhistamine, led to the discovery of burimamide, the first compound with a clear H_2-blocking effect. Further modification of burimamide led to cimetidine, which was introduced in 1976 under the brand name Tagamet. Cimetidine marked a new era in the treatment of ulcers, which previously could often be cured only by surgery.

In 1973, when cimetidine was clearly on the way to a commercial launch, Black was once again looking for a new project. "I was now totally committed to arranging marriages between bioassay and medicinal chemistry. . . . The potential freedom from commercial constraints in academia was looking more and more attractive." He agreed to head the pharmacology department of University College, London, and tried to form a new discipline that linked medicinal chemistry and bioassays. This new field, he wrote later, would be "as exciting to the imagination as astrophysics or molecular biology." This effort, and Black's endeavors to reform pharmacology teaching, met with only limited success. In 1977 he gladly accepted an offer to become director of the therapeutic research division of the Wellcome Foundation.

Although Black found his experience as a manager at Wellcome to be less than fully satisfying, he had much success with his own research on the structure and dynamics of drug receptors. In 1984 he became professor of analytical pharmacology at the King's College School of Medicine. In 1987, in order to allow Black and his colleagues to pursue their research without constraint, the Johnson & Johnson Company set up the James Black Foundation at King's College.

Black shared the 1988 Nobel Prize for Physiology or Medicine with two other pharmacologists, GERTRUDE B. ELION and GEORGE H. HITCHINGS JR. Though the work of Elion and Hitchings was unrelated to Black's, the Nobel committee cited all three scientists "for their discoveries of important principles for drug treatment." In presenting the award, Folke Sjöqvist of the Karolinska Institute said, "While drug development had earlier mainly been built on chemical modification of natural products, [Black and his co-winners] introduced a more rational approach based on the understanding of basic biochemical and physiological processes."

The pharmacologist Stanley Glick has called Black "the greatest and most important . . . pharmacologist of our time." Other colleagues have described him as a modest and exceptionally hard-working scientist and a dedicated teacher.

Black was knighted in 1981 for his services to medical research. His numerous other awards include the Albert Lasker Clinical Medical Research Award (1976), the Artois-Baillet Latour Health Prize (1979), the Gairdner Foundation International Award (1979), the Wolf Prize in Medicine (1982), and almost twenty honorary degrees. He is a member of the Royal Society of London, the Royal College of Physicians, the Royal Society of Edinburgh, and the Royal Academy of Medicine, Belgium.

ABOUT: New Scientist October 22, 1988; New York Times October 18, 1988; Science October 28, 1988; Who's Who, 1990.

JOSEPH BRODSKY

BRODSKY, JOSEPH
(May 24, 1940–   )
Nobel Prize for Literature, 1987

The Russian-American poet and essayist Joseph Alexandrovich Brodsky (brôt' ski) was born in Leningrad, the only child of Jewish parents. His father, Alexander I. Brodsky, was an officer in the Soviet navy. When blocked from promotion by anti-Semitism, he resigned and became a professional photographer. Finding regular work proved difficult, and the family often depended on the earnings of Joseph's mother, Maria M. (Volpert) Brodsky, who worked variously as a German-Russian interpreter, a clerk, and a bookkeeper.

In school, Brodsky endured both anti-Semitism and communist indoctrination. He found the latter particularly oppressive. He recalls feeling disgusted even in the first grade with the ubiquitous images of Lenin, and at the age of fifteen he dramatically walked out of his classroom, never to return to formal schooling. He worked briefly as a milling machine operator, then at a hospital morgue. He later was a metalworker, a laborer on geological expeditions, and a merchant seaman.

At the same time, Brodsky continued his education on his own, reading widely in Russian and Western literature and in classical mythology, history, and poetry. His study of Polish introduced him to the works of the great Polish poets and of several Western writers not then available in Russian translation, including WILLIAM FAULKNER, Joseph Conrad, Franz Kafka, and Virginia Woolf.

Brodsky began writing poetry himself in the late 1950s. His lyric works, simultaneously metaphysical, erudite, and evocative of the details of day-to-day life, soon attracted the attention of important Soviet poets, especially Anna Akhmatova, who dedicated a volume of her work to him in 1963. The state, however, did not officially recognize

Brodsky as a poet, and it expected him to devote himself to officially sanctioned activities. Though not a political dissident by nature, Brodsky refused to hold any job that would interfere with his writing. When a Leningrad newspaper denounced him in November 1963, his official harassment began. Brodsky was several times brought in for questioning, his papers were seized, he was twice committed to mental institutions, and finally, in early 1964, he was put on trial for "social parasitism." He was convicted in March and sentenced to five years at hard labor at an Arctic work camp near Archangelsk.

Although the intense physical work of a state farm taxed him, northern Russia's harsh climate and long winter nights left Brodsky with time for reading and writing, much of which he used to master English. Meanwhile, the circumstances of his trial had drawn criticism from Western intellectuals and protest from prominent Soviet writers and artists. In November 1965 the government responded by freeing Brodsky and allowing him to return to Leningrad.

At this time, Brodsky's work began to be published in the West. A Russian-language volume of his poetry was printed in New York in 1965, and a French and two German translations appeared in 1966. The first volume of English translations of his poems, *Elegy to John Donne and Other Poems,* was issued in London in 1967. The Soviet government refused to allow Brodsky to attend international poetry festivals, however, and eventually all publication of his work within the Soviet Union was banned.

In late 1971 Brodsky received two invitations to emigrate to Israel. The Soviet Ministry of the Interior advised him that he should accept the invitations or be prepared to face increasing persecution. Brodsky left the Soviet Union on June 4, 1972, an involuntary exile.

Brodsky never made it to Israel. Stopping in Vienna on the way, he was befriended by the poet W. H. Auden, who had a summer home nearby, at Kirchstetten, and who introduced Brodsky to many Western writers and intellectuals. One of these new acquaintances helped him secure an appointment as poet-in-residence at the University of Michigan. Brodsky retained this position until 1980, when he moved to New York to teach at Columbia University and New York University. In 1981 he became the Five-College Professor of Literature at Mount Holyoke College in Massachusetts; in 1986 Mount Holyoke named him Andrew Mellon Professor of Literature. Brodsky has been a visiting professor at numerous schools in the United States and England, including Queens College, Smith College, and Cambridge University. He became a United States citizen in 1977.

Further translation, publication, and mass distribution of Brodsky's works in the West followed his departure from the Soviet Union. In 1973 Harper & Row published an American edition of *Selected Poems,* with a foreword by Auden, the first major collection of his work to appear in English. Although some critics raised doubts about the quality of the translations, the collection received a generally enthusiastic response. Indeed, the *New York Times Book Review* lauded Brodsky as "the greatest poet of his generation." *A Part of Speech,* published in 1980, brought together thirty-seven poems written between 1965 and 1978 and translated by several different writers, including Brodsky himself. Though again some critics questioned the adequacy of the translations, this volume led CZESŁAW MIŁOSZ, among others, to hail Brodsky as a poet of world stature. The publication in 1986 of *Less Than One,* a collection of essays written in English, added to his reputation as a writer who drew effectively upon distinct languages and traditions. The critic Fernanda Eberstadt wrote about this collection, "Unlike the majority of Russian and Eastern European writers living in the West, Brodsky has adopted the English language as his own and brought to it an independence of thought, a thickness and subtlety of texture, and an omnivorous appetite for idiom that are uniquely his." The book received the 1986 National Book Critics' Circle Award for Criticism in the United States.

Brodsky also achieved renown for his work as a translator, especially for his Russian translations of the English metaphysical poets and of Miłosz and other Polish poets. Thus when Joseph Brodsky received the Nobel Prize for Literature in 1987, the choice received almost universal approval. The *New York Times* stated, "Rarely have the Swedes displayed as much wit and sense as in bestowing the Nobel Prize in literature on Joseph Brodsky." Susan Sontag described Brodsky as a "serious, committed, great writer," one of a "small number . . . who are going to be a part of literature."

Brodsky's broad and deep reading of the literature of Russia, Poland, and the West, including classical and biblical sources, has deeply affected his poetry, both aesthetically and thematically. He insists on the importance of enduring aesthetic values, and he sees the rediscovery, rejuvenation, and perpetuation of these values as one of the great tasks of his generation—the generation born in the shadow of Auschwitz and the Stalinist camps. As he stated in his Nobel Prize lecture, "Looking back, I can say again that we were beginning in an empty—indeed, a terrifyingly wasted—place, and that intuitively rather than consciously, we aspired precisely to the recreation of the effect of culture's continuity, to the reconstruction of its forms and tropes, toward filling its few surviving, and often totally compromised, forms, with our own . . . content."

Thus his careful attention to form takes on an ultimately moral end. For, despite his frequently voiced pessimism about the world as a whole, he holds that aesthetic experience can redeem the individual: "I'll just say that I believe—not empirically, alas, but only theoretically—that, for someone who has read a lot of Dickens, to shoot his like in the name of some idea is more problematic than for someone who has read no Dickens."

After Brodsky received the Nobel Prize, six of his poems, the first to appear legally in the Soviet Union since the 1960s, were published in the monthly *Novy Mir.* In the United States, he has published an additional volume of poetry, *To Urania,* which he himself translated into English.

Brodsky has not returned to Russia since his exile. The authorities of the former Soviet Union refused his requests to visit his parents before their deaths in the early 1980s. After the Soviet political climate changed in the late 1980s, Brodsky expressed conflicting attitudes toward visiting his native land. Although he wanted to see his son, Andrei, who was only five when he left, he also said, "I find it hard to imagine myself a visitor and performer touring the country in which I was born and grew up. That will be one more of the absurdities which my existence, as it is, already has in abundance. While it may still make some sense for a criminal to return to the scene of the crime . . . it's basically senseless to return to the scene of love."

Brodsky has received other honors and awards in addition to the Nobel Prize, including a John Simon Guggenheim Memorial Fellowship (1977) and honorary degrees from several universities, including Yale University (1978) and Oxford University (1991). He was inducted into the American Academy and Institute of Arts and Letters in 1979 but resigned in 1987 after the organization awarded honorary membership to Yevgeny Yevtushenko, a Soviet poet whom Brodsky accused of political opportunism. In 1981 the John D. and Catherine T. MacArthur Foundation awarded Brodsky one of the first five-year MacArthur fellowships. In May 1991 the Librarian of Congress appointed Brodsky the fifth Poet Laureate (Consultant in Poetry) of the United States, effective September 1991.

ADDITIONAL WORKS: Poems by Joseph Brodsky, 1972; Verses on the Winter Campaign, 1981; Roman Elegies, 1984; History of the Twentieth Century, 1986; Marbles, 1989.

ABOUT: American Poetry Review July–August 1981; Carlisle, O. Poets on Street Corners, 1968; Contemporary Authors, 1979; Contemporary Literary Criticism, 1975; Modern Encyclopedia of Russian and Soviet Literature, 1979; The New Russian Poets 1953–1966, 1966; New York Times October 23, 1987; New York Times Book Review November 8, 1987; Who's Who in America, 1990.

THOMAS R. CECH

CECH, THOMAS R.

(December 8, 1947–)
Nobel Prize for Chemistry, 1989
(shared with Sidney Altman)

The American biochemist Thomas Robert Cech (chek) was born in Chicago, the son of a physician, Robert Franklin Cech, and his wife, the former Annette Marie Cerveny. Both parents were of Czechoslovakian descent. Cech and his younger sister and brother grew up in Iowa City, Iowa. "My father, who loved physics as much as medicine, interjected a scientific approach and point of view into most every family discussion," Cech recalled. Cech entered Grinnell College in 1966 and graduated with a degree in chemistry in 1970. He was "attracted to biological chemistry because of the almost daily interplay of experimental design, observation, and interpretation," he later wrote, as well as for "the realization that one might be able to contribute to the revolution in molecular biology at the level of chemistry."

Molecular biology is an interdisciplinary pursuit that combines biochemistry, genetics, and structural chemistry to study the molecular basis of form, function, and evolutionary theory of living organisms. The revolution in molecular biology began in 1954, when JAMES D. WATSON and FRANCIS CRICK discovered the structure of the amino acid deoxyribonucleic acid (DNA). Work by many scientists during the 1950s and 1960s established

that genetic information is almost always carried by DNA in the nucleus of the cell, transcribed (copied) into ribonucleic acid (RNA) in the cytoplasm, or nonnuclear portion of the cell, and then translated from RNA into proteins. Proteins make up much of the substance of living things and, in their role as biological catalysts (enzymes), perform many functions within living organisms.

Cech attended graduate school at the University of California, Berkeley, where he studied the structure of chromosomes (bundles of DNA) under the biochemist John Hearst. After receiving his Ph.D. in chemistry in 1975, he moved to the Massachusetts Institute of Technology (MIT) to work with biologist Mary Lou Pardue as a postdoctoral fellow. Cech's research with Hearst and Pardue was on features of DNA organization in the mouse. He recalled, "I began to be dissatisfied with this global approach and became interested in the prospect of being able to dissect the structure and expression of some particular gene." As assistant professor at the University of Colorado in 1978, he decided to concentrate on the genes for ribosomal RNA in Tetrahymena thermophila, a ciliated protozoan similar to Paramecium.

Ribosomal RNA (rRNA) is one of three types of RNA manufactured by DNA transcription. Cech chose to study Tetrahymena rRNA genes. He explained, "Unlike most nuclear genes, which are embedded in giant chromosomes, the genes for rRNA in Tetrahymena are located on small [extra-chromosomal] DNA molecules." Tetrahymena rDNA molecules (the name rDNA indicates that it is transcribed to make rRNA) may be copied 10,000 times over in active cells, much faster than other molecules. These properties, isolation and speed of replication, made it possible for Cech to purify a significant amount of rDNA. He reasonably could hope to be the first to isolate a gene's DNA together with whatever molecular material was necessary to make the RNA copy. This material was expected to be made largely of proteins, because the reactions involved are chemically difficult and require catalysts. Biochemical catalysts (called enzymes) were thought invariably to be proteins, and not nucleic acids.

Cech's first work on rDNA from *Tetrahymena* showed that much of the length of the rDNA matched the rRNA, but there also existed additional pieces of rDNA that were not found in the rRNA. These intervening pieces, or introns, had been discovered first in 1977 by Phillip Sharp and his colleagues at MIT and by researchers at Cold Spring Harbor Laboratory. Apparently, the DNA was initially fully copied or transcribed into a precursor RNA (pre-RNA); from this precursor RNA the introns were edited out to produce a final RNA. Though no mechanism for removing introns (called splicing) yet had been found, biochemists assumed that normal enzymes (i.e., those consisting of protein) were responsible. By 1979 introns had been found in many genes, including rDNA from other species of *Tetrahymena*, and Cech's discovery seemed in no way remarkable.

His next experiment was remarkable. In order to locate and isolate the splicing enzyme, Cech and his colleague Arthur Zaug transcribed *Tetrahymena* rDNA into pre-RNA in a test tube in the absence of all cell material except for the cell nuclei. Cech included the cell nuclei on the assumption that the nuclei contained the splicing enzyme. Their experiments indicated that the intron in this precursor RNA was being removed as it would have been in the living organism. "This was a finding of considerable excitement," Cech wrote; it was only the second time that RNA splicing had been done in the test tube. Because *Tetrahymena* cells contain so many rDNA copies and hence make so much RNA that needs splicing, Cech reasoned that they would find an unusually high concentration of the splicing enzyme in the nuclei.

"Our strategy for purifying the splicing enzyme was conventional," Cech recalled. They planned to treat pre-rRNA with extracts of cell nuclei, gradually modifying the extracts to determine which nuclear component was responsible for the splicing reaction.

The experiment seemed successful from the start. The RNA in the tubes containing nuclear extract was properly spliced. The only surprise was that the control RNA without nuclear extract was spliced, too. Cech's reaction was, "Well, Art, this looks very encouraging, except you must have made some mistake making up the control sample."

Cech and Zaug reran the experiment several times and obtained the same results. They looked at the chemistry of the spliced rRNA and the excised intron. They altered the various experimental conditions. All their results indicated that they were tracking a highly specific example of chemical bond breakage and formation. "Such a chemically difficult reaction between very unreactive molecules certainly had to be catalyzed," Cech theorized. "But what was the catalyst?

"Our first hypothesis was that the splicing activity was a protein tightly bound to the pre-rRNA isolated from *Tetrahymena* nuclei. This would have to be a very unusual protein-RNA complex to survive the multiple forms of abuse to which we had subjected it," Cech noted.

The only alternative was that the protein was not involved and the RNA itself was acting as a biological catalyst, an enzyme. As succeeding experiments made the earlier hypothesis more and more unlikely, Cech and his co-workers began to consider the "RNA only" theory more favorably.

This theory was certain to be strongly opposed as it conflicted with the biochemical rule—almost a dogma—that only proteins could be enzymes. To eliminate the first hypothesis completely before their idea could be widely accepted, Cech and his colleagues knew they would have to find catalytic activity in RNA which had never been in contact with *Tetrahymena* cells.

In 1982 Cech and his co-workers showed that pre-rRNA prepared from bacteria genetically engineered to carry a *Tetrahymena* rDNA gene was indeed a catalyst. They named their find a "ribozyme," an RNA-enzyme. As they had expected, the discovery (and naming) of ribozymes was at first quite controversial. It was not until 1984, when SIDNEY ALTMAN and his colleagues demonstrated that an RNA could catalyze a reaction involving something other than itself, that the resistance to calling a nucleic acid an enzyme ended.

"Who could ever have suspected that scientists, as recently as in our own decade, were missing such a fundamental component in their understanding of the molecular prerequisites of life?" said Bertil Andersson of the Royal Swedish Academy of Sciences in presenting Cech and Altman the 1989 Nobel Prize for Chemistry.

Catalytic RNA had an immediate, shattering impact on theories of the origin of life. Chemists had long debated whether proteins—which can catalyze biological reactions—or nucleic acids—which can carry genetic information—were the first elements of life. Cech's and Altman's discoveries convinced researchers that Earth's original biological system was an "RNA world," in which, as Andersson stated, RNA was "both genetic code and enzyme at one and the same time."

"Ribozymes have the ability to act as a sort of molecular scissors" to cut RNA, Cech noted, and "RNA is at the heart of all viral and many other diseases in man." Ribozymes possibly might be designed, for instance, selectively to inactivate the RNA virus that causes AIDS. Cech's and Altman's discoveries established the field of RNA engineering, in which Cech and the University of Colorado were granted the most important patent.

Cech married the biochemist Carol L. Martinson, a classmate at Grinnell, in 1970; they have two daughters. Cech is an active skier, hiker, and cook.

He is a member of the U.S. National Academy of Sciences, the American Academy of Arts and Sciences, the American Society of Biochemistry and Molecular Biology, and the American Association for the Advancement of Science, and an honorary member of the Japanese Biochemical Society. His awards include the Harrison Howe Award (1984), the Pfizer Award in Enzyme Chemistry (1985), an honorary doctorate from Grinnell College (1987), the Gairdner Foundation International Award (1988), the Louisa Gross Horwitz Prize (1988), the Albert Lasker Basic Medical Research Award (1988), and the Bonfils-Stanton Award for Science (1990).

ABOUT: American Men and Women of Science, 1989–90; New York Times October 13, 1989; Science October 20, 1989; Scientific American December 1989; U.S. News and World Report October 23, 1989; Wall Street Journal October 13, 1989; Washington Post October 13, 1989.

CELA, CAMILO JOSÉ
(May 11, 1916–   )
Nobel Prize for Literature, 1989

The Spanish novelist, travel writer, and poet Camilo José Cela (thä´ lä) Trulock was born in Iria Flavia in the northwestern province of La Coruña. His father, Camilo Cela Fernandez, was a customs official who worked part-time as a writer. His mother, Camila Trulock, was an English immigrant. Cela later credited his childhood experiences in Galicia with helping him develop as a writer. He would eventually use Galicia as the locale of some of his fiction.

Cela attended the University of Madrid from 1933 to 1936 and again from 1939 to 1943, studying medicine, the arts, and law. In 1935 he published an autobiographical sketch and some poems in the Argentinean magazine El Argentino. Cela's first book of poems, Pisando la dudosa luz del día (Treading the Dubious Daylight), was written in 1936 and published in 1945.

The 1930s were a tumultuous time in Spanish history. The dictator Miguel Primo de Rivera was

CAMILO JOSÉ CELA

forced out in 1930, and in 1931, the monarchy was replaced by a republic. In the years that followed, the liberals, the church, landowners, and the working class struggled for political power. The struggle became violent and eventually erupted into the Spanish Civil War, which lasted from 1936 to 1939. It pitted the mainly liberal and leftist supporters of the republic against an array of conservative elements, known as the Nationalists, led by the army and determined to overthrow the Republican government.

When the war ended, the leader of the victorious Nationalists, Generalissimo Francisco Franco, took power, becoming chief of state and sole legislator. He established a totalitarian government and invalidated all laws of which he disapproved. He imposed strict censorship rules, banned public meetings, and outlawed all groups and associations not approved by his government.

During the civil war, Cela had served as a foot soldier in the Nationalist army. "It was after serving in the trenches, being wounded and lying awhile in field hospitals, after the war was over and he had come home and Spain had embarked on her many dreary years under the new regime that he made his debut—as a prose writer," Knut Ahnlund of the Swedish Academy said in his presentation speech. His first novel, La familia de Pascual Duarte (The Family of Pascual Duarte, 1942), is filled with images of the squalor, misery, brutality, and violence he had witnessed.

The novel is narrated by a multiple murderer who relates his life story while awaiting execution. The narrative describes the protagonist's life of poverty and his upbringing by a loveless, abusive, and bitter mother. It goes on to describe his violent killings in a manner both grotesque and surreal. Critics have called the book an allegory about the internal sufferings of Spain and a moral statement about the repressive nature of Spanish society. "It is difficult to find in Spanish literature a novel which approaches *La familia de Pascual Duarte* in its sustained atmosphere of impending catastrophe, its powerful portrayal of human malevolence, and in nightmarish effects," wrote critics Jacob Ornstein and James Y. Causey.

To avoid the censors, who would surely ban the novel, Cela had it secretly printed in a garage. By the time the book was noticed by the Spanish authorities, the edition was almost sold out. In the barren years of literary production during the Franco regime, Cela's novel was hailed as a landmark work. *La familia de Pascual Duarte* was a critical and commercial success and was considered by critics to have established the tone of the postwar Spanish novel. It was translated for American readers by Anthony Kerrigan in 1964.

In 1944, Cela married María del Rosario Conde Picavea, and in 1946 their son, Camilo José, was born. During this time, Cela experimented with various literary styles. His novel *Pabellón de reposo* (*Rest Home*, 1943) takes the form of letters and reflections by seven inmates dying in a tuberculosis sanatorium. Ornstein and Causey note that Cela "dips his pen in blood to portray the anguished and tortured soul-states of his protagonists, in the last stages of consumption." Another critically acclaimed novel of that period was *Nuevas andanzas y desventuras de Lazarillo de Tormes* (New Wanderings and Misfortunes of Lazarillo de Tormes, 1944), which revives the Spanish tradition of the picaresque narrative by extending the adventures of the sixteenth-century rogue Lazarillo.

In 1951, Cela published his most respected work, *La colmena*, translated by J. M. Cohen and Arturo Barea as *The Hive*. As with many of Cela's works, the novel was banned in Spain because of its scathing social critique. It was first published in Buenos Aires; censorship prevented it from reaching a wide Spanish readership until 1963.

La colmena is a novel without a plot. It has no theme and no direction, offering only brief sketches of the scores of characters who frequent a lower-class café in postwar Madrid. This novel, which Cela calls "a slice of life . . . without charity," gives the reader a view of the bleak, sordid lives of working-class families and a taste of the atmosphere of Madrid in the 1940s. Writing in the common, often racy slang typical of his characters, Cela illustrates the political repression, poverty, hunger, and boredom that followed the civil war.

Cela continued to experiment with the novel form in the 1950s. The best known of his novels

from this period is *Mrs. Caldwell habla con su hijo* (*Mrs. Caldwell Speaks to Her Son*, 1953). It takes the form of excerpts from the letters of a mentally disturbed English woman with strong incestuous feelings. The 200-page novel is made up of 212 chapters with virtually no connection between them. Critic D. W. McPheeters says of *Mrs. Caldwell,* "The work is about as much an antinovel as has yet been conceived in Spain."

During this period, Cela also produced travel books, sketches, reminiscences, and various other pieces. His 1969 novel *Vísperas, festividad y octava de San Camilo del año 1936 en Madrid* (translated as *San Camilo, 1936,* 1991) expresses the thoughts of a young student in stream-of-consciousness style. Again, in form and content, the work is far from a traditional novel. It uses interior monologue and extracts from newspaper and radio bulletins to create a portrait of a city about to be irrevocably altered by the civil war. As a backdrop, Cela provides a detailed description of brothel life, including the actual names and addresses of Madrid's brothels.

Cela's travel books are remarkable for their detail as well. About his first travel book, *Viaje a la Alcarria* (*Journey to the Alcarria,* 1948), the critic Paul Ilie noted, "There is a poetic purity to be found in the magic naming of the thistles and sprigs, in following the minute movements of insect life, and in tracing the scents and sound of a countryside trembling with sensation. The beauty of these descriptions is beyond praise." Woven through these books is a search for the true Spanish identity, which Cela has not been able to find in the corrupt, isolating, artificial cities of Spain.

Cela's literary technique is most often labeled as *tremendismo,* a Spanish style that dwells on the darker side of life and emphasizes the grotesque and vulgar. This style is not evident in all of Cela's work, though a critic in the *Times Literary Supplement* wrote that Cela's work is "perversely restricted to a pathology of human decay and loneliness." It is Cela's range of experimentation within the form of the novel, however, that has placed him at the forefront of contemporary trends. This is apparent in Cela's lack of emphasis on plot and on a traditional sequencing of events. As critic David W. Foster has noted, Cela "has chosen to make his career one of a complete reexamination and reconsideration of the novel as an art form."

In the 1960s, Cela left Madrid and settled in Palma de Mallorca, where he founded the literary review *Papeles de Son Armadans,* which he still edits. The magazine began as the only major literary review in Spain that published work by writers opposing the Franco regime. In addition to novels and travel writings, Cela's body of work includes poetry and humorous and serious essays. He has published the four-volume *Enciclopedia del erotismo* (Encyclopedia of Eroticism, 1976–1986) and the two-volume *Diccionario secreto* (Secret Dictionary, 1968, 1972), a compendium of Spanish slang and vulgar words. These works again reflect Cela's mocking defiance of the moral concerns of traditional Spanish society.

Franco died in 1975. In 1977, his successor, King Juan Carlos, appointed Cela to a Senate seat in the first post-Franco parliament, and Cela participated in the writing of a new constitution. In 1984 Cela won Spain's National Prize for Literature for his novel *Mazurca para dos muertos* (Mazurka for Two Dead People, 1983). The novel combines Cela's graphic, *tremendismo* style with myth and regional superstition. It is a dreamlike story of murder taking place in Galicia, where Cela was born.

Cela was awarded the 1989 Nobel Prize for Literature. In his presentation speech, Knut Ahnlund of the Swedish Academy said of Cela's work, "What we have before us is an extraordinarily rich, weighty, and substantial body of writings that possess great wildness, license, and violence, but which nonetheless in no way lack sympathy or common human feeling, unless we demand that these sentiments should be expressed in the simplest possible way. Cela has renewed and revitalized the Spanish language as few others have done in our modern age."

The announcement of Cela as the recipient for the prize was met with some skepticism. Critics said that though Cela produced some highly significant works until the mid-1950s, he has failed to write anything of major importance since then. However, specialists in Spanish literature recognize Cela as the dominant figure in Spanish writing in the period after the civil war, when under Franco the emphasis was on conformism and conservative tradition. According to critic D. W. McPheeters, in the early 1940s "the Spanish novel . . . had virtually ceased to exist. . . . Almost singlehandedly, Cela gave the genre new life and international significance."

Since winning the Nobel Prize, Cela has been much in the public eye, appearing on numerous television programs and even in commercials. He left Palma for mainland Spain, near Guadalajara. In 1991 he divorced his wife and married Marina Castaño, a journalist. Cela has explored every part of Spain and has visited most European countries, Africa, South America, and the United States.

Cela was awarded the Premio de la Critica for his 1955 book, *Historias del Venezuela: La catira* (Stories of Venezuela: The Blonde). He is a member of the Royal Spanish Academy and holds honorary doctorates from Syracuse University, University of Birmingham (Great Britain), John F. Kennedy University (Buenos Aires), University of Palma de Mallorca, University of Santiago de Compostela, Interamericana University (Puerto Rico), and the Hebrew University of Jerusalem. An edition of Cela's *Obra completa* (Complete Works), which began in 1962, now comprises seventeen volumes.

ADDITIONAL WORKS IN ENGLISH TRANSLATION: Avila, 1956.

ABOUT: Chandler, R., and Schwartz, K. A New History of Spanish Literature, 1961; Contemporary Authors, 1990; Contemporary Literary Criticism Yearbook, 1990; Current Biography Yearbook, 1990; Foster, D. W. Forms of the Novel in the Work of Camilo José Cela, 1967; Jones, M. E. W. The Contemporary Spanish Novel, 1939–1975, 1985; Kirsner, R. The Novels and Travels of Camilo José Cela, 1964; McPheeters, D. W. Camilo José Cela, 1969; World Authors, 1950–1970; Ornstein, J., and Causey, J. Y. "Camilo José Cela: Spain's New Novelist," Books Abroad, volume 27, 1953.

COASE, RONALD H.

(December 29, 1910–)
Nobel Memorial Prize in Economic Sciences, 1991

The American economist and law professor Ronald H. Coase (kōs) was born in Willesden, near London, England. He entered the London School of Economics in 1929, planning a career in commerce, "a choice of occupation for which I was singularly ill suited," he later wrote. In 1931, five months before he was to take his final examinations in commerce, he attended a seminar taught by the economist Arnold Plant. "It was a revelation," he recalled. "Before being exposed to Plant's teaching, my notions on how the economy worked were extremely woolly. After Plant's seminar I had a coherent view of the economic system." Having received a scholarship awarded by the University of London, Coase spent a year traveling and studying industries in the United States. In 1932 he received his bachelor's degree and joined the faculty of the London School of Economics.

In the summer of 1932 Coase presented a lecture that was to become the basis of his first important paper. In the lecture he posed a very simple question: Why do companies exist? A producer who needs a certain service can simply buy it on the market each time it is needed. The problem with doing that, Coase explained, is that every time the producer goes to the market, he or she must expend time and energy negotiating a contract for that service. Even finding appropriate individuals with whom to negotiate carries a certain cost, as does monitoring an individual's work in progress. All these transaction costs affect the efficiency of going to the market for services.

RONALD H. COASE

Journal of Law and Economics. At a time when government regulation was considered the only way to settle disputes between individuals or firms, Coase argued that regulation actually impeded economically sound dispute resolution.

In his paper, called "The Problem of Social Cost," Coase focused on externalities. Externalities are the outside costs of an enterprise. Pollution, for example, is an externality caused by many types of manufacturing. Conventional wisdom had long held that the only way to control externalities was to regulate them. As Coase later explained, most economists reasoned that "some kind of government action (usually the imposition of taxes) was required to restrain those whose actions had harmful effects on others." Coase, by contrast, theorized that if there were no transaction costs, the parties involved—the polluter and the person suffering from the effects of pollution—could develop a sensible way to settle matters on their own, without the need for regulation or other legal intervention. By signing a voluntary contract, both parties could gain something.

Coase introduced the idea of buying and selling legal entitlements, or "property rights"—the rights to use (rather than own) goods and factors of production. Property rights might include the right to use something (such as a public waterway), to make decisions about something (such as whether to pollute the air), or to dispose of something. To illustrate his point, Coase described the conflict that arose when sparks from a steam train set fire to farmers' fields as the train passed. Rather than seek government regulation, Coase argued, the farmers and the railroad could settle this problem themselves on the basis of their respective property rights. If farmers, for example, were by law granted the right to have the area around their fields free from fire and sparks, railroads would have three choices. They could make a wide berth around the fields, equip their trains with spark arresters, or negotiate with the farmers to purchase the property right to emit sparks. Whichever method they chose would settle the matter to the benefit of both parties. If the railroad had the right to emit sparks, a similar process would yield the same mutual benefit, although with a different distribution of income.

Of course, Coase went on, society does not have zero transaction costs and never will, but looking at legislation in this way can serve as a stepping-stone. It can help economists and lawyers seek more sensible, market-based alternatives to regulation and encourage negotiation rather than legislation. His argument that "the appropriate role of government is to establish the laws that make it possible for markets to operate" became known as the Coase theorem.

If the producer were instead to organize a company that employed service providers, he or she could reduce the transaction costs considerably and thus increase efficiency. In this way the producer can create ongoing contracts to have work done rather than having to negotiate a contract each time. Belonging to a company is also advantageous to the service providers: While they might have greater flexibility or the opportunity to earn more by working independently, they would still have to face the transaction costs of continually seeking work and negotiating with each producer. As a member of a company, a service provider can concentrate on his or her particular service rather than on developing skills in marketing and contract negotiation. Therefore, Coase concluded, producers organize companies because the cost of organizing activities within a company is lower than the cost of market exchange.

Looking at firms in this way was unprecedented. The existence of firms had always been taken for granted; studying why they existed had seemed unnecessary. Economists tended to focus instead on how firms determined pricing. As Coase later noted, "I have made no innovations in high theory. My contribution to economics has been to urge the inclusion in our analysis of features of the economic system so obvious that . . . they have tended to be overlooked." Coase published his theories in "The Nature of the Firm" in the journal *Economica* in 1937.

In 1951 Coase moved to the United States and took a position at the University of Buffalo. He moved from there in 1958 to the University of Virginia. In 1960 he submitted a revolutionary paper to the University of Chicago's recently founded

When Coase's paper became known in Chicago, it touched off a heated debate among members of the university's economics faculty. Coase was invited to speak at the school to defend his idea. Twenty-one economists, including MILTON FRIEDMAN and GEORGE STIGLER, debated with Coase for hours until all eventually agreed with Coase's logic. Stigler later wrote, "In the course of two hours of argument, the vote went from twenty against and one for Coase to twenty-one for Coase. What an exhilarating event!"

"The Problem of Social Cost" was published in the *Journal of Law and Economics* in October 1960. It has been cited since in arguments against government regulation and more recently as a model for eastern European countries to follow as they move toward capitalism. The paper has also had a marked effect on the teaching of law. After the paper was published, lawyers "began thinking about legal rules from an economic perspective," Harvard law professor Stephen Shavell remembers. This spurred the growth of a new field called law and economics. In 1964 Coase accepted the University of Chicago's invitation to join its law school faculty as a leader in this new field.

In 1974 Coase published a paper titled "The Lighthouse in Economics." It questioned the widespread belief that there were some services that the government had to provide because there was no way of extracting payment from everyone who would use those services. A frequently cited example was the lighthouse. Scholars argued that all ships could see the light from a lighthouse regardless of whether they had paid for the facility and that the operation of lighthouses by private firms was therefore unrealistic.

Coase pointed out that this conclusion was erroneous. Britain's lighthouse system began in the seventeenth century as a private enterprise. Fees were collected in port, not by taxation. Enough people were willing to pay to make the operation profitable, even though there were others who were freeloaders. If the transaction costs are low enough that the private operator can realize a profit, there is no need to have the government step in. As Coase explained, "Government regulation or centralized planning [is] not necessary to make an economic system function in an orderly way." His idea has stimulated an investigation of the possibility of privatizing airports, air traffic control, and highways to improve their efficiency. On a much smaller scale it has been credited for the success of private protection programs in which residents of city neighborhoods pool their funds to pay for extra police protection. Even though these programs benefit some people who do not contribute to the fund, contributors find funding the program sufficiently beneficial to make the expenditure worthwhile.

Coase became professor emeritus at the University of Chicago Law School in 1981 but remains active in the school's academic life and in his research. In a speech delivered at a Yale University conference after his retirement, Coase said that he felt the paper called "The Nature of the Firm" had gone only halfway; his dream, he said, was to develop a comprehensive theory of the structures of firms.

The Royal Swedish Academy of Sciences awarded Coase the 1991 Nobel Memorial Prize in Economic Sciences for his "breakthrough in understanding the institutional structure of the economy." The academy described Coase's work on transaction costs as the identification of "a new set of 'elementary particles' in the economic system." The academy noted, "His achievements have provided legal science, economic history, and organization theory with powerful impulses and are therefore also highly significant in an interdisciplinary context."

Paul Craig Roberts, chairman of the Institute for Political Economy, applauded the academy's decision. The award "shows how much economics has changed in the past thirty years," he wrote. In the 1960s Coase was "raising fundamental challenges to an economics that was little more than a ramp for government intervention, and this did not sit well with those who saw more government as the hallmark of progress. . . . [But the work] has stood the test of time and achieved world recognition."

In his Nobel Prize lecture Coase distinguished his work from that of other economists: "What is studied [by others] is a system which lives in the minds of economists but not on earth. I have called the result 'blackboard economics.' The firm and the market appear by name, but they lack any substance. . . . As these institutional arrangements determine to a large extent what is produced, what we have is a very incomplete theory. All this is beginning to change, and in this process I am glad to have played my part." He acknowledged that unlike previous winners of the prize, he is not very mathematical. However, he noted that "once we begin to uncover the real factors affecting the performance of the economic system, the complicated interrelations between them will clearly necessitate a mathematical treatment . . . and economists like myself, who write in prose, will take their bow."

Coase is the first law professor to be awarded the economics prize. In addition to his research at the University of Chicago, he helped to establish the Center for the Study of Contracts and the Structure of Enterprise at the Business School of the University of Pittsburgh, where he is pursuing a number of projects on contracts, data research, and the activities of firms.

ADDITIONAL WORKS: The Firm, the Market, and the Law, 1988.

ABOUT: Barron's October 28, 1991; Business Week October 28, 1991; November 25, 1991; Economist February 23, 1991; New York Times October 16, 1991; October 20, 1991; Science October 25, 1991; Wall Street Journal October 17, 1991; Washington Post October 30, 1991.

COREY, ELIAS JAMES
(July 12, 1928–)
Nobel Prize for Chemistry, 1990

The American chemist Elias James Corey was born in Methuen, Massachusetts, to Elias and Fatina (Hasham) Corey. He was named William at birth, but when his father died eighteen months later, his mother renamed him Elias. He was raised with the help of his mother's sister and her husband, who came to live with the family, which included a brother and two sisters.

Corey was an active and independent child who preferred baseball and football to work; nevertheless, his aunt, "who was much stricter than my mother," taught him a strong work ethic. He attended a Catholic elementary school and graduated from Lawrence Public High School in 1945 at age sixteen. He entered the Massachusetts Institute of Technology (MIT) with no career plans except for the notion that he might study electronic engineering because he enjoyed mathematics. In his first year, however, he took a chemistry course. He later recalled, "I became a convert to chemistry before even taking an engineering course because of the excellence and enthusiasm of my teachers, the central position of chemistry in the sciences, and the joy of solving problems in the laboratory. Organic chemistry was especially fascinating with its intrinsic beauty and its great relevance to human health."

Corey quickly mastered the basic reactions necessary for simple organic syntheses. Organic synthesis is the process of building a specific complex carbon-based compound in the laboratory from simpler compounds. In the late 1940s scientists were just learning how to create complex molecules such as vitamin A and cortisone.

After graduating Corey remained at MIT as a graduate student to work on the organic synthesis of penicillin with one of his professors, John Sheehan. He was only twenty-two in 1950 when he completed his Ph.D. in chemistry and took a position as an instructor at the University of Illinois at Urbana-Champaign. By 1954 he was promoted to assistant professor, and in 1956 to professor of chemistry.

In 1957 Corey received a Guggenheim fellowship and took a sabbatical, part of which he spent

ELIAS JAMES COREY

at Harvard working with R. B. WOODWARD on chemical synthesis. He soon conceived a systematic approach for planning syntheses of organic chemicals, an approach that was to form the basis of his future work.

Traditionally, the process of organic synthesis had always begun with a scientist's selection of a relatively simple compound that had a molecular structure resembling the target compound he or she wished to synthesize. From a basic knowledge of molecular reactions, the scientist would choose the proper sequence of steps for the synthesis while using a largely intuitive strategy to construct the target organic molecule. "Asking a chemist why he chose precisely the starting materials and reactions that so elegantly led to the desired result would probably be as meaningless as asking Picasso why he painted as he did," commented Salo Gronowitz of the Royal Swedish Academy of Sciences.

At Woodward's lab and in the years that followed Corey examined the intuitive process conventionally used by organic chemists to develop a formalized system for logically selecting an appropriate sequence of reactions. He then developed a very different approach, which he called retrosynthetic analysis. Rather than assuming a starting chemical, retrosynthetic analysis begins with the structure of the finished synthesized molecule and works backward. The molecule is conceptually dissected into progressively simpler structures. The result is an analytic "tree" that branches from the target molecule back to several possible compounds; by analyzing the pathways represented by the branches, the chemist can select the appropriate process and materials for the synthesis. With this approach, over the next decade

Corey simplified the planning of syntheses into a logical, repeatable process.

Because Corey created a simplified process that is logical and repeatable, it later became possible to develop computer-assisted retrosynthetic analysis. Now, with the aid of computers, a scientist can generate many possible synthetic routes from which to choose.

In addition to his work at Harvard, Corey spent part of his 1957 sabbatical in Europe. In Lund, Sweden, Corey visited SUNE BERGSTRÖM and became intrigued with his work with prostaglandins. Prostaglandins are a group of hormonelike chemicals that regulate a wide range of biological processes, including blood pressure, uterine contractions, immune responses, and fertility. Prostaglandins are produced by most mammalian tissues, but only in very small quantities. Corey set out to synthesize prostaglandins in order to make these important compounds available for research and medical applications. His research was complicated by the unstable nature of the chemicals and the existence of three different families of prostaglandins, each with a slightly different structure.

In 1959 Corey accepted a professorship at Harvard, where he continued his research. He performed the first successful synthesis of one of three prostaglandin families in 1967. He eventually developed a single intermediate, commonly known as the Corey lactone aldehyde, from which prostaglandins in all three families could be synthesized. Prostaglandins and related chemicals are now used widely in pharmaceutical products.

Corey received the 1990 Nobel Prize for Chemistry "for masterly development of organic synthesis." When announcing the award, Salo Gronowitz noted, "Corey has contributed in high degree to his own and other researchers' being able . . . to complete total syntheses, hitherto impossible, of complicated, naturally occurring, biologically active compounds, according to simple logical principles." Using retrosynthetic analysis, Corey and his students have synthesized over 100 important natural products, including the complex extract from the ginkgo tree, ginkgolide B, which is used to treat disturbances of blood circulation and asthma. Corey's most important syntheses are pharmaceuticals derived from cell-regulating chemicals such as prostaglandins, prostacyclins, thromboxanes, and leukotrienes. As part of his research, Corey also developed fifty new or improved synthetic reactions. "No other chemist has developed such a comprehensive and varied assortment of methods, often showing the simplicity of genius, which have become commonplace in organic synthesis laboratories," Gronowitz said in his presentation speech.

Corey is still at Harvard, where he heads an organic synthesis laboratory that supports dozens of graduate students. He continues to work on the synthesis of complex bioactive molecules, the logic of chemical synthesis, new methods of synthesis, the relevance of prostaglandins to medicine, and the application of computers to organic chemical problems, especially to retrosynthetic analysis. Corey summarizes his professional goals as follows: "to be creative over a broad range of the chemical sciences, to sustain that creativity over many years, to raise the power of research in chemistry to a qualitatively higher level, and to develop new generations of outstanding chemists." He is proud that "the Corey research family now includes about 150 university professors and an even larger number of research scientists in the pharmaceutical and chemical industry."

Corey married Claire Higham in September 1961. They have three children. He has eleven honorary degrees, including doctorates from the University of Chicago (1968), Oxford University (1982), the University of Liège (1985), and Hokkaido University (1990). He has received numerous awards, including the Award in Pure Chemistry (1960), the Award for Creative Work in Synthetic Organic Chemistry (1971), and the Arthur C. Cope Award (1976), all from the American Chemical Society, and the Robert Robinson Medal (1988) from the Royal Society of Chemistry. He has received awards from over a dozen universities and is on the editorial board of several scientific journals.

SELECTED WORKS: The Logic of Chemical Synthesis, 1989, with X.-M. Cheng.

ABOUT: American Men and Women of Science, 1990; Binder, J. Creativity in Organic Synthesis, 1975; International Who's Who, 1991–92; Science October 26, 1990; Science News October 27, 1990; Time October 29, 1990.

CRAM, DONALD J.

(April 22, 1919–)
Nobel Prize for Chemistry, 1987
(shared with Jean-Marie Lehn and Charles J.
  Pedersen)

The American chemist Donald James Cram was born in Chester, Vermont, to William and Joanna (Shelley) Cram. His father, a lawyer, died of pneumonia when Cram was four. Cram's early education took place in a series of one-room schoolhouses in Brattleboro, Vermont, and outside the classroom, where he pored over literary works, explored the natural world, and was engaged in a variety of jobs for neighbors. When Cram was

DONALD J. CRAM

sixteen, his family dispersed, and he briefly continued his secondary education in Lake Worth, Florida. He spent his last year of high school at Winwood, a small private school on Long Island, New York, where he took his first chemistry course. He graduated in 1937.

With the aid of a four-year scholarship, Cram attended Rollins College in Winter Park, Florida. While studying chemistry and philosophy, he pursued a variety of extracurricular activities such as acting, radio production, singing in a barbershop quartet, and obtaining a pilot's license. During the summers he worked for the National Biscuit Company in New York City—first as a salesman and later in a laboratory, where he analyzed cheeses for moisture and fat content. Cram later credited these summer jobs with teaching him self-discipline but also with giving him "an overwhelming dislike of repetitive activities." When he graduated from college in 1941, he decided to pursue a research career in chemistry because he believed that such a career would allow him the most freedom.

Cram took a graduate teaching assistantship at the University of Nebraska and earned a master's degree in organic chemistry in 1942. By that time, the United States had entered World War II. For the duration of the war, he worked for Merck & Company, a pharmaceutical firm, where he helped develop a practical process for manufacturing penicillin. In 1945 Cram enrolled at Harvard University on a National Research Council Fellowship. With the help and inspiration of Professors L. F. Fieser, Paul D. Bartlett, and R. B. WOODWARD, he completed his Ph.D. in organic chemistry in 1947.

That same year, Cram went to the University of California at Los Angeles to teach and do research.

He has remained there ever since, rising from instructor and assistant professor in 1947, to associate professor in 1952, and to full professor in 1956. In 1984, Cram was named the Saul Winstein Professor of Chemistry.

During the late 1950s, Cram and his colleagues were attempting to synthesize enzymes. Enzymes are proteins that serve as catalysts for chemical reactions in living creatures. (A catalyst is a substance that speeds up a chemical reaction.) Though naturally occurring enzymes are complex molecules, Cram hoped to find a way to manufacture relatively simple organic compounds that could imitate the working features of enzymes. Because synthetic enzymes would be cheaper, more stable, and more readily available than natural enzymes, they would make possible large-scale production of a variety of chemicals and pharmaceuticals.

In order to imitate the workings of enzymes, Cram had to solve the problem of molecular recognition—the ability of one molecule to "recognize" another molecule and bind with it. Enzymes, like many other natural compounds, are extremely selective about which molecules they will react with. So far, it had not been possible to duplicate this selectivity with artificial compounds.

In 1967 an industrial chemist named CHARLES J. PEDERSEN published a paper that offered a first step toward solving this problem. Pedersen reported that he had synthesized a new type of molecule whose distinctive shape reminded him of a royal crown. (Because this molecule belonged to the chemical group known as ethers, Pedersen called it a crown ether.) The shape of any molecule is determined by the way its constituent atoms combine with each other. In some molecules, atoms attach in long chains. In others, they form the shape of a cross or a pyramid. In Pedersen's crown ether, atoms of oxygen and carbon combined in an essentially ringlike shape.

The ringlike shape of a crown ether allows it to bind easily with a metal ion. When a crown ether comes in contact with a suitable ion, the ion falls into, and is trapped inside, the ring. By stringing together different atoms in different combinations, Pedersen could vary the shape of the crown ether. He was thus able to design different crown ethers to "select" different ions with a high degree of precision.

Pedersen's crown ethers had practical applications in the laboratory: they were the first synthetic compounds that could form stable complexes with sodium, potassium, and other alkali metal ions that had been previously difficult to bind. More important, however, was their theoretical significance: it was shown that the physical *shape* of a molecule—not just its electrostatic charges—was involved in binding it with other molecules.

Cram used Pedersen's synthetic compounds as a foundation for his own work. Pedersen's crown ethers had a flat shape, and therefore had relatively few contact points at which they could bind to other compounds. A compound that was three-dimensional would have more contact points and therefore would be more selective about what it would bind with. To determine what three-dimensional shapes would best bind with specific molecules, Cram and his colleagues spent hours arranging Corey-Pauling-Koltun (CPK) molecular models, colored interlocking balls that give a close approximation of a molecule's bond lengths and arrangement of atoms. They evaluated these models for desirability as research targets and used them as blueprints for preparing actual samples of the desired compounds.

Cram called his area of research "host-guest chemistry." His aim was to develop a variety of host molecules, each of which would accept one specific guest molecule. (By another analogy, Cram sought to create precise molecular "locks" that could be fitted only by specific "keys.") By the time he received the Nobel Prize for Chemistry in 1987, Cram had succeeded in building more than 500 different host molecules.

Cram shared his Nobel Prize with Pedersen, on whose research he had based his work, and with JEAN-MARIE LEHN, a French organic chemist who independently had developed a number of host molecules. In presenting the award, Salo Gronowitz of the Royal Swedish Academy of Sciences said that the three scientists had "laid the foundation to what today is one of the most expansive chemical research areas, for which Cram has coined the term host-guest chemistry. . . . Their research has been of enormous importance for the development of coordination chemistry, organic synthesis, analytical chemistry, bioinorganic and bioorganic chemistry; it is no longer science fiction to prepare supermolecules which are better and more versatile catalysts than the highly specialized enzymes."

Although no scientist has yet succeeded in creating totally artificial enzymes, the work of Cram, Pedersen, and Lehn has made future success in that area seem more likely. As Gronowitz implied, however, their work points the way toward an even broader range of possible applications. It may someday be possible, for example, to produce superenzymes that are faster and more selective than their natural counterparts. Cram's host-guest chemistry may also make it possible to separate materials with great efficiency. Crown ethers can already be used to remove metallic impurities or to reclaim expensive metals from mixtures. More highly selective molecules, such as those developed by Cram, may someday be able to detect tiny quantities of toxic substances in the environment—and even to remove them.

Since doing the work that won him the Nobel Prize, Cram has continued to develop new forms of synthetic molecules. He has, for example, created structures he calls carcerands—hemispherical molecules that bond together at their rims, thus creating "prison cells" that can trap selected guest molecules inside. Cram expects that these carcerands may someday be used for the slow release of drugs or pesticides. They may also be used as "little laboratories" in which researchers can trap and observe chemical reactions.

Cram married Jean Turner in 1941 and was divorced from her in October 1969. In November 1969, he married Jane Lewis Maxwell, a chemistry professor with whom he has co-written a textbook. His laboratory has served as a training ground for many chemists working in the field of molecular recognition. Outside of the laboratory, he enjoys skiing, surfing, playing tennis, playing guitar, and singing folk songs.

In addition to the Nobel Prize, Cram has won the American Chemical Society Award (1953), a Guggenheim Fellowship (1955), the Herbert Newby McCoy Award (1965 and 1975), the American Chemical Society Award for Creative Work in Synthetic Organic Chemistry (1965), the Society of Chemical Manufacturers Association Award for Creative Research in Organic Chemistry (1965), the California Scientist of the Year Award (1974), the American Chemical Society Arthur C. Cope Award for Distinguished Achievement in Organic Chemistry (1974), and the American Chemical Society Roger Adams Award in Organic Chemistry (1985). He is a member of the National Academy of Sciences and the American Academy of Arts and Sciences. Cram holds honorary degrees from Uppsala University, the University of Southern California, Rollins College, and the University of Nebraska.

SELECTED WORKS: Organic Chemistry, 1964, with others; Foundations of Carbon Ion Chemistry, 1965; Elements of Organic Chemistry, 1967, with D. H. Richards and G. S. Hammond; Essence of Organic Chemistry, 1978, with J. M. Cram.

ABOUT: New Scientist October 22, 1987; New York Times October 15, 1987; Science October 30, 1987; Who's Who in America, 1990.

DALAI LAMA

(July 6, 1935–)
Nobel Prize for Peace, 1989

The fourteenth Dalai Lama (dä lī lä′ mä), Tenzin Gyatso, the political and religious leader of Tibet, was born in the village of Taktser in Amdo

DALAI LAMA

province and named Lhamo Dhondrub by his parents, Chujon and Dekyi Tsering. His birth came two years after the death of the thirteenth Dalai Lama.

The Dalai Lama is revered as the protector of Tibet, the emanation and presence on earth of Chenrezi, the Buddhist personification of divine compassion. According to Buddhist tradition, each Dalai Lama is a reincarnation of the preceding one. Immediately after the death of the thirteenth Dalai Lama in December 1933, a delegation of monks began the customary search for the one chosen as his reincarnation. Using oracles, visions, and signs, a search party was led to eastern Tibet, where, in 1937, in Taktser, the monks found Lhamo Dhondrub, then two years old. From a collection of prayer beads, drums, and walking sticks the boy was able to identify those objects that had belonged to the thirteenth Dalai Lama. The boy was tested and found to possess all of the characteristics necessary to convince the delegation that he was the reincarnated Dalai Lama.

At age four he was taken to the capital city of Lhasa, where, in 1940, he was enthroned and given a new name. Then began nearly two decades of rigorous religious and metaphysical training. By age seven he was leading 20,000 monks in prayer and meeting envoys from foreign countries, including one sent by United States president Franklin D. Roosevelt. He was raised in the company of monks and lived with his immediate older brother as his only companion. In winter he lived in the 1,000-room palace known as the Potala, which was filled with temples, ancient manuscripts, and statues of gold, silver, and precious gems. In summer he lived in the tranquil Jewel

Park enclosure, where he enjoyed the gardens, tamed wildlife, and read old issues of *National Geographic* and *Life* left by his predecessor. He also developed a fascination with mechanical things and taught himself how to repair not only watches but also the movie projector and cars that had belonged to the thirteenth Dalai Lama. Gardening and mechanics remain his favorite hobbies.

Tibet is a small Himalayan country with a spectacular and unique natural environment. Situated on a plateau with an average height of 15,000 feet above sea level and squeezed between the populous countries of China and India, it has often been the pawn in Asian power struggles. In 1950, the year after the Communists gained power in China, they entered Tibet, defeated its small border force, and made it a "national autonomous region" of China. They overthrew the Buddhist theocracy, dynamiting and plundering all but a few of the over 6,000 monasteries, and forcibly annexed the land.

Although the Dalai Lama was only sixteen, he was called upon to assume full leadership of his country. He tried in vain to negotiate a peaceful resolution with Chinese leaders Mao Zedong and Zhou Enlai, but brutalities against monks and others increased. Economic measures introduced by the Chinese resulted in food shortages and famines throughout Tibet.

Repression continued for years. By 1959 Tibetans who were convinced that peaceful means of settlement were impossible staged an uprising against the Chinese, which resulted in the deaths of 87,000 Tibetans. Monks and ordinary citizens were rounded up, tortured, murdered, or sent to labor camps and prisons, many for over two decades.

Heeding warnings that his own capture was imminent, the Dalai Lama, disguised as a soldier, fled over the rugged mountains with his immediate family and a small group of followers to political asylum in India. "I was not afraid of being one of the victims of the Chinese attack," he wrote in his autobiography, but to the Tibetan people, "the person of the Dalai Lama was supremely precious. . . . They were convinced that if my body perished at the hands of the Chinese, the life of Tibet would also come to an end."

Today the Dalai Lama maintains the seat of Tibet's government-in-exile in Dharamsala, in northern India. From there, he travels and works to enlist international sympathy for the plight of his country. However, as Egil Aarvik of the Norwegian Nobel Committee noted when presenting the Dalai Lama with the 1989 Nobel Peace Prize, despite a few "toothless" resolutions passed by the United Nations in the early 1960s, "political support from the outside remained conspicuous by its absence."

Since the Chinese annexation, over 100,000 Tibetans have escaped to asylum in India, Nepal, and other countries. Many more have died as a result of Chinese rule.

In 1987 the Dalai Lama proposed a five-point peace plan for the restoration of peace and human rights in Tibet. It urged "earnest negotiations" on the future of Tibet and the relations between Tibet and China. It called for the restoration of fundamental human rights of Tibetans and a halt to the massive transfer of ethnic Chinese into Tibet which has made the Tibetans a minority in their own country. It called for the protection of the endangered wildlife and environment and the abandonment of China's use of Tibet as a location for the production of nuclear weapons and the storage of nuclear waste. Finally, the plan recommended establishing Tibet as a peace zone.

"It is my dream that the entire Tibetan plateau should become a free refuge where humanity and nature can live in peace and in harmonious balance. . . . The Tibetan plateau would be transformed into the world's largest natural park or biosphere," the Dalai Lama said. "I am convinced that [the peace zone] is of great importance not only for Tibet but for peace and stability in Asia" and it is "in keeping with Tibet's historical role as a peaceful Buddhist nation and buffer region separating the Asian continent's great and often rival powers." The five-point plan failed to initiate any negotiations with China.

In 1988 the Dalai Lama made further conciliatory offers to the Chinese government that would allow the Chinese to handle foreign affairs and defense if the Tibetans were granted full internal autonomy. The Chinese have failed to respond, and the Dalai Lama has stated that these concessions may be withdrawn.

The Dalai Lama speaks of the Chinese not with anger or hatred but with kindness and equanimity. "They too are human beings who struggle to find happiness and deserve our compassion."

The Norwegian Nobel Committee awarded the 1989 Nobel Prize for Peace to the Dalai Lama for his consistent rejection of the use of violence and for advocating "peaceful solutions based upon tolerance and mutual respect in order to liberate Tibet and preserve the historical and cultural heritage of his people." In announcing the award, the committee praised the Dalai Lama for his "great reverence for all living things and upon the concept of universal responsibility embracing all mankind as well as nature." This was the first time that efforts to preserve the environment were mentioned in a Nobel citation.

"It is significant, indeed, that the ecological issue has been put on the agenda of the Nobel Peace Prize committee by a spiritual leader who com-bines rationality, humanism, and religious tradition as a foundation for a moral response to the great challenges of the twentieth century," Aarvik remarked when presenting the award.

Since the Chinese occupation, many of Tibet's herds of wild animals have been extinguished, forests have been stripped for lumber, and soil erosion has contributed to devastating floods in India and Bangladesh. Twelve species of animals are now endangered, including the Tibetan wild yak, the kiang (or wild ass), the black-necked crane, and the snow leopard, in addition to rare plant life. "Both science and the teaching of the Buddha tell us of the fundamental unity of all things. The decision to save the environment must come from the human heart and a genuine sense of universal responsibility based on love, compassion, and clear awareness," the Dalai Lama said in his Nobel lecture.

Some observers saw the awarding of the 1989 Nobel Peace Prize to the Dalai Lama as a condemnation of the Chinese government's crackdown on the country's growing democracy movement. Just three months before the prize was awarded, the Chinese government had violently suppressed student political protests in Beijing's Tiananmen Square. Egil Aarvik said that the award was not politically motivated, but he acknowledged that the award could be interpreted as a sign of support to the demonstrators for their nonviolent prodemocracy demonstrations. China continues to offer to let the Dalai Lama return to Tibet, but only on condition that he abandon his campaign for that land's independence. He will not accept that condition, although he has stated he is open to a compromise or "a middle way."

Throughout the years, the Dalai Lama has traveled extensively to meet with religious and political leaders. In 1991 he met with United States president George Bush, the first ever meeting between an American president and the exiled leader. He has received many international prizes, including the 1973 Palketta Award of Norway, the Peace Medal from the Asian Buddhist Committee for Peace in 1979, the Leopold Lucas Prize in West Germany in 1987, the Albert Schweitzer Humanitarian Award in 1987, and the Raoul Wallenberg Congressional Human Rights Award in New York in 1989. He has also received many honorary degrees and honorary citizenships from the United States and European and Asian nations.

WORKS BY: My Land and My People, 1962, 1987; The Opening of the Wisdom Eye, 1963; Happiness, Karma, and Mind, 1969; The Buddhism of Tibet and the Key to the Middle Way, 1975; A Human Approach to World Peace, 1984; Kindness, Clarity, and Insight, 1984; Freedom in Exile, 1990.

ABOUT: Current Biography, 1982; International Who's Who, 1990; New Republic November 20, 1989; New York Times October 6, 1989; S. Piburn (ed.) The Nobel Peace Prize and the Dalai Lama, 1990; Washington Post October 6, 1989.

DE GENNES, PIERRE-GILLES
(October 24, 1932–   )
Nobel Prize for Physics, 1991

The French physicist Pierre-Gilles de Gennes (də zhen′) was born in Paris to Robert de Gennes and the former Yvonne Morin-Pons. In 1955, after graduating from the École Normale, he took a position as a research engineer with the Atomic Energy Center in Saclay.

At the Atomic Energy Center, de Gennes focused on magnetism, studying how magnets react to changes in temperature. When a magnet is cold, the atoms within it are lined up and rigid, but when the magnet is heated to a certain temperature, that ordered state changes to a disordered one and the atoms move about freely. This "phase transition" from order to disorder occurs at a well-defined temperature called the Curie temperature (named after PIERRE CURIE for his early work on the subject).

De Gennes received a Ph.D. for his work in magnetism in 1957 and spent a large part of the following year continuing his studies at the University of California at Berkeley. After he returned to France, he served two years in the French navy, then became an assistant professor at the University of Paris in Orsay. Moving from the study of magnetism, de Gennes founded the Orsay Superconductivity Group, a group of theorists and experimenters who investigated the properties of superconductors. A superconductor is a substance that expels magnetic fields from its interior and has no resistance to electricity. Like a magnet, a superconductor is affected by temperature changes: if its temperature is raised to a given level, it goes through a phase change and loses its superconductive abilities. De Gennes and his group discovered that the same principles govern the phase transitions of both magnets and superconductors. In 1964 de Gennes published many of the group's findings in the book *Superconductivity in Metals and Alloys,* and in 1965 he was named professor at the university.

In the late 1960s de Gennes changed his focus again, this time to liquid crystals. A common type of liquid crystal has a molecular structure resembling bunches of small rods floating in solution— and it also undergoes dramatic phase transitions. Under some conditions the rodlike molecules move freely like a liquid, the rods being unaligned. However, if they are subjected to certain magnetic,

PIERRE-GILLES DE GENNES

mechanical, or electrical forces, the rods become aligned; that is, they crystallize.

De Gennes showed that a phase change in liquid crystals can transform them from transparent to opaque, permitting the scattering of light. It is this ability to scatter light that makes liquid crystals the material of choice for displays in digital watches and calculators. With the support of a second group—the Orsay Group for Liquid Crystals—de Gennes demonstrated similarities between superconductors and liquid crystals that had never before been observed and developed mathematical expressions to describe the links between the two. De Gennes's 1974 book, *The Physics of Liquid Crystals,* "has become a standard work," noted the Royal Swedish Academy of Sciences when it awarded him the 1991 Nobel Prize for Physics.

In 1971 de Gennes moved from Orsay to the Collège de France in Paris and began to study polymers, an area often explored by chemists but rarely by physicists. Polymers are long chains of repeating units of simpler molecules called monomers. In a dilute solution a polymer resembles a strand of spaghetti, looping and tangling around itself in apparently random patterns. De Gennes found that this apparently disordered arrangement had many similarities to the arrangement of magnetic atoms when they moved from an ordered state to a disordered state. He then sought ways to predict their patterns.

De Gennes took up the challenge of understanding polymer dynamics, that is, the clumping and internal movement of these long molecules. Although the curves and twists appear to be random, de Gennes showed that they are not and went on to develop a mathematical rule to determine the geometrical arrangement of monomer groups within a polymer chain. He also explored the movement of monomers within polymers and showed that within the larger polymer molecule smaller groups of monomers creep along and over each other in predictable patterns. He also discovered mathematical relationships that were shared by polymers and the subjects of his earlier research. His work has had many practical applications in the development and improvement of synthetic polymers such as plastics and adhesives and in the investigation of natural polymers such as proteins and DNA.

As Joshua Deutsch of the University of California at Santa Cruz explained, "De Gennes has had an enormous impact on polymer physics and has contributed to the understanding of virtually every aspect of it." De Gennes helped to create STRASACOL, a polymer physics research group of physicists and chemists from Strasbourg, Saclay, and the Collège de France. In 1979 he presented the group's findings in *Scaling Concepts in Polymer Physics,* a book hailed by Deutsch for successfully "combining physical intuition and mathematical simplicity." Eugene Stanley, a polymer physicist from Boston University, called de Gennes's work "a genuine miracle." Before de Gennes came along, he said, "there was no way to work with polymers as a physicist."

Constantly looking for new areas to explore, de Gennes continues to change his fields of study. He has contributed to the study of gels and the dynamics of the wetting and drying of substances. His most recent work has been on adhesion science, because, as he put it, "We can stick things together very effectively, but we understand little of how this works." He is attempting to develop a "superglue" strong enough to hold airplanes together without rivets, thus making the airplanes lighter and easier to assemble.

De Gennes was awarded the 1991 Nobel Prize for Physics for his work on "order and disorder in nature." In announcing the award, which some scientists have called a lifetime achievement award, the Royal Swedish Academy of Sciences called de Gennes "the Isaac Newton of our time." De Gennes's work is considered remarkable because "he has shown that phase transitions in such apparently widely differing physical systems as magnets, superconductors, liquid crystals, and polymer solutions can be described in mathematical terms of surprisingly broad generality," the Royal Swedish Academy wrote. "Some of the systems de Gennes has treated have been so complicated that few physicists had earlier thought it possible to incorporate them all into a general physical description." The academy congratulated de Gennes for stimulating a great deal of theoretical and experimental work, noting that he had laid a solid foundation for the technical exploitation of materials such as liquid crystals and polymers.

De Gennes remains at the Collège de France. He also serves as the director of the College of Industrial Physics and Chemistry in Paris, a position he began in 1976. He is admired by his colleagues for his daring; his ability to combine physics, mathematics, and chemistry; and his interest in exploring new fields. The chemical engineer William Graessley noted that de Gennes "looks at problems outside the traditional bounds of physics and [has] brought a lot of fresh insights. His work has had dramatic effects in chemistry, material science, and chemical engineering."

De Gennes has received prizes from scientific organizations around the world, including Israel's Wolf Prize in Physics (1990), the Holweck Prize from the joint French and British Physical Society, the Ampère Prize from the French Academy of Sciences, and the Lorentz Medal from the Dutch Academy of Arts and Sciences. He is a member of the French Academy of Sciences, the Dutch Academy of Arts and Sciences, the Royal Society (United Kingdom), the American Academy of Arts and Sciences, and the National Academy of Sciences (U.S.A.). In his spare time he enjoys kayaking, wind surfing, and drawing.

SELECTED WORKS: Introduction to Polymer Dynamics, 1990.

ABOUT: International Who's Who, 1991; Los Angeles Times October 17, 1991; Nature October 24, 1991; New Scientist October 26, 1991; New York Times October 17, 1991; Physics Today June 1990; Science October 25, 1991; Science News October 26, 1991.

DEHMELT, HANS G.

(September 9, 1922–   )
Nobel Prize for Physics, 1989
(shared with Wolfgang Paul and Norman F. Ramsey)

The American physicist Hans Georg Dehmelt (dā′ melt) was born in Goerlitz, Germany. His father, Georg Dehmelt, had studied law and been an artillery officer in World War I. During the depression of the 1930s the family "just managed to make a living in real estate," Dehmelt later recalled. Eventually they were reduced to owning and living in a heavily mortgaged apartment building in "an overwhelmingly communist" part of Berlin. "After a few bloody noses . . . I shifted my interests from roaming the streets more towards playing with rudimentary radio receivers and noisy and smelly experiments in my mother's kitchen."

HANS G. DEHMELT

In 1933 Dehmelt entered the oldest Latin school in Berlin, the Gymnasium zum Grauen Kloster, at the instigation of his mother. Dehmelt recalled that his father "expressed the opinion that I probably would be happier as a plumber. However, he probably didn't quite believe this himself," as he had previously encouraged young Hans's interests in science and general knowledge and later tutored him when he fell behind in his studies.

In addition to learning the classics, Dehmelt studied biology and physics and "supplemented the school curriculum with do-it-yourself radio projects until I had hardly any time left for my class work." Nonetheless, he was able to skip a term and graduate in 1940.

After receiving a draft notice, Dehmelt "found it wise to volunteer" for the army. Despite his radio expertise, he was assigned instead to an antiaircraft gun crew. Sent to relieve the German armies at Stalingrad, he notes, he was lucky to return alive. In 1943 he was "even more lucky" to be ordered back to Germany to study physics at the University of Breslau, but after one year he was sent to the western front and captured in battle. After a year in an American prisoner-of-war camp in France, he returned to Germany in 1946.

Supporting himself by bartering and repairing radios, Dehmelt resumed his studies at the University of Göttingen, West Germany. Here he took an "excellent laboratory class" from WOLFGANG PAUL, with whom he would later share the Nobel Prize for Physics. Dehmelt joined the research institute of Hans Kopfermann, Paul's mentor, and received his master's and doctoral degrees for work in nuclear magnetic resonance (NMR). NMR was first developed to measure the magnetic properties

of atomic nuclei, using microwaves or radio waves. It now has a wide range of uses in physics, chemistry, biology, and medicine.

After receiving his Ph.D. in 1950, Dehmelt stayed at the Kopfermann Institute for two more years, then went to Duke University in North Carolina. Starting as a postdoctoral fellow, he progressed to the rank of associate professor while continuing his NMR work. In 1955 he went to the University of Washington in Seattle. After a one-year stint as a visiting professor, he was offered a tenure-track appointment in the physics department and has remained there ever since.

During the 1950s Dehmelt was experimenting with polarized atoms—atoms with their magnetic axes all aligned—and measuring the light they emitted or absorbed as they changed magnetic orientation. Such changes are called quantum transitions and are described by the theory of quantum mechanics, which says that atoms can only exist in certain magnetic orientations. When an atom changes orientation, it absorbs or emits light of very specific frequencies, called resonance frequencies. High-resolution spectroscopy—the precise measurement of resonance frequencies—can reveal fundamental properties of the atom or provide tests of the theory of quantum mechanics.

Producing polarized atoms required Dehmelt to temporarily trap and hold a beam of polarized electrons, and this led him to consider the advantages of studying trapped particles. One of the fundamental principles of quantum mechanics, the Heisenberg uncertainty principle, developed by WERNER HEISENBERG, predicts that trapping particles for a long time should allow more precise measurements of resonance frequencies. In addition, trapping just a few ions, or even one single charged particle, would remove errors introduced by interactions between particles. Trapped particles could also be slowed down, or "cooled," to eliminate errors caused by their rapid motions.

In 1959 Dehmelt developed his first version of a Penning trap for electrons (so called because of its resemblance to an earlier device called the Penning ion gauge). Though his first experiments with the trap were only partially successful, thirty years of persistence and innovation eventually led him to receive the 1989 Nobel Prize for Physics for his work on trapped electrons and ions.

At about the same time he developed the Penning trap, Dehmelt learned of the ion trap that had just been invented by Wolfgang Paul. Both traps use specially shaped electric fields to confine particles, but the Penning trap takes the plan one step further and also uses a magnetic field. This innovation permitted him to trap, for the first time, a single electron. This he accomplished in 1973.

Dehmelt and his colleagues next turned to measuring the electron's gyromagnetic ratio, the ratio between its magnetic moment (magnetic strength) and its "spin." The quantum-mechanical spin is analogous to the rotation of a top on its axis. Its value has a fixed magnitude, and its axis can take up different orientations. In order to measure this ratio, they needed a way to slow down the electron and a more precise way to measure frequency. By 1978 they had developed "laser side-band cooling" and found a way to measure frequencies with the "continuous Stern-Gerlach technique."

Side-band cooling "tricks" the electron into slowing down by making it absorb light at one frequency and reemit it at a slightly higher frequency. Then the electron is continuously stimulated to emit radio-frequency light so that it can be monitored. The next step is to accurately measure the tiny difference between two of the electrons' resonance frequencies, since this will give the value of the gyromagnetic ratio. However, directly measuring each frequency and then subtracting them won't give a very accurate value. Dehmelt's continuous Stern-Gerlach technique uses a small variation in the strong magnetic field in the trap to create yet another resonance frequency. Stimulating the electron at this second frequency causes a quantum transition that slightly changes the frequency of the continuously emitted light. This frequency shift can be precisely measured, and it turns out to have a simple relationship to the original frequency difference and thus the gyromagnetic ratio.

Dehmelt and his collaborators continued to refine the technique, and in 1987 they succeeded in measuring the gyromagnetic ratio of the electron to an accuracy of 4 parts in a trillion. This ratio is also predicted by quantum electrodynamics, the theory of electromagnetic forces. (In recent years this has been combined with the weak nuclear force, to make a unified program called electroweak theory.) His experiments verified the theory to 11 decimal places, making it the most sensitive test of a physical theory ever made.

In 1974 Dehmelt won an award from the Alexander von Humboldt Foundation, which he used to collaborate with a group in Heidelberg in developing ways to trap single charged atoms of barium. Later, the Heidelberg team was the first to isolate and photograph a single laser-cooled ion in a trap. To take the picture, they stimulated the trapped barium atom to emit visible light.

A number of other scientists, including some of Dehmelt's former students, have used ion traps to make the most accurate measurements to date of the mass of the proton and of the mass ratios of various particles.

Another outgrowth of Dehmelt's work is the "shelved optical electron amplifier," which resembles his continuous Stern-Gerlach technique in using induced transitions to make very accurate frequency measurements. However, it works on ions instead of electrons and uses visible light rather than radio waves. Scientists at the United States National Institute of Standards and Technology (formerly the National Bureau of Standards) are trying to use this method to create an atomic clock more accurate than those currently in use.

Dehmelt, meanwhile, is still striving for better measurements of the electron gyromagnetic ratio. His team has now managed to trap and observe a single electron for nearly a year.

In awarding Dehmelt the 1989 Nobel Prize for Physics, Ingvar Lindgren of the Royal Swedish Academy of Sciences particularly noted Dehmelt's achievements in confining and observing single electrons and ions and his extremely accurate measurement of the electron gyromagnetic ratio. Wolfgang Paul and NORMAN F. RAMSEY also shared the award; Paul for his development of the Paul ion trap, and Ramsey for his key role in the development of atomic clocks.

"The dream of the spectroscopist is to be able to study a single atom or ion under constant conditions for a long period of time. In recent years, this dream has to a large extent been realized," Lindgren said, and he called the trapping of a single ion "a true landmark in the history of spectroscopy." "The continued rapid development of the atomic clock can be foreseen in the near future," Lindgren continued, citing the work based on Dehmelt's techniques. "An accuracy of *1 part in one-billion billions* is considered realistic." Lindgren concluded, "The new technique [will be] even more important for testing very fundamental principles of physics. Further testing of quantum physics . . . may force us to revise our assumptions about . . . the smallest building blocks of matter."

Dehmelt is married to Diana Dundore, a physician. He has a son, Gerd, from a previous marriage to the late Irmgard (Lassow) Dehmelt. He enjoys hatha yoga, waltzing, hiking, reading, listening to classical music, and watching ballet.

In addition to the 1974 Humboldt Prize, Dehmelt has received the Davisson-Germer Prize of the American Physical Society (1970), the International Society of Magnetic Resonance Award (1980), and the Count Rumford Prize of the American Association for the Advancement of Science (1985).

ABOUT: International Who's Who, 1990; New York Times October 13, 1989; Physics Today December 1989; Science October 20, 1989; Scientific American December 1989; U.S. News and World Report October 23, 1989; Washington Post October 13, 1989.

DEISENHOFER, JOHANN
(September 30, 1943–)
Nobel Prize for Chemistry, 1988
(shared with Robert Huber and Hartmut Michel)

The German biophysicist Johann Deisenhofer
(dī′ zen hō fer) was born in Zusamaltheim, a
Bavarian village about 50 miles from Munich. He
and his younger sister, Antonie, grew up on their
parents' farm. Local custom required the oldest
boy to take over the family farm, but Deisenhofer's
parents, Johann and Thekla (Magg) Deisenhofer,
quickly realized that their son lacked interest in
farming. Therefore, when Deisenhofer graduated
from elementary school in 1956, they reluctantly
decided to send him away for further schooling.

Deisenhofer attended several schools over the
next seven years, finally completing his secondary
education at the Holbein Gymnasium in 1963. After eighteen months of military service, Deisenhofer enrolled as a physics student at the Technical
University of Munich.

Deisenhofer had become interested in physics
by reading popular books and articles. He later recalled that "a popular review of the state of astronomy by Fred Hoyle, describing the impact of
modern physics on astronomy" had made him especially eager to become a physicist. At the university, however, he discovered that physics was
"quite different" from what he had expected. As he
became aware that the field encompassed more
than astronomical problems, his attention slowly
shifted to solid-state physics—the study of the
structure of condensed matter.

Deisenhofer pursued his new interest by joining
the laboratory of solid-state physicist Klaus
Dransfeld. Deisenhofer later recalled that "Dransfeld was a person almost as shy as myself, so that
we could not establish a good personal contact at
the time." Dransfeld did, however, succeed in nar-
rowing Deisenhofer's focus from solid-state
physics to biophysics. Under the supervision of
Karl-Friederich Renk, Deisenhofer completed his
experimental work in Dransfeld's lab and earned
his diploma (the equivalent of a master's degree)
in 1971.

By this time, Deisenhofer had developed a
strong interest in the use of X-ray crystallography
to determine the structure and function of biological macromolecules. (Macromolecules are molecules with high molecular weights. Common
macromolecules include proteins, enzymes, nucleic acids, and polysaccharides.) The process of
X-ray crystallography, developed by MAX VON
LAUE in 1912, involves aiming X rays of known
wavelength at crystallized solids (materials that
have regularly repeating molecular structures). By
studying the patterns in which the rays are weak-

JOHANN DEISENHOFER

ened or reinforced as they strike the crystal, the
crystallographer can determine the material's molecular makeup.

Deisenhofer did his doctoral work at the Max
Planck Institute for Biochemistry in Martinsried.
Working under ROBERT HUBER (with whom, along
with HARTMUT MICHEL, he would eventually share
his Nobel Prize), he used X-ray crystallography to
analyze the structure of bovine pancreatic trypsin
inhibitor. After receiving his Ph.D. in 1974, he remained in Huber's lab at the Max Planck Institute,
working first as a postdoctoral fellow and then as
a staff scientist. There he continued his work in X-
ray crystallography, investigating the structure of
such biological macromolecules as the human
myeloma protein Kol and the alpha1-proteinase
inhibitor. He also developed computer software
for use in his investigations.

Deisenhofer's Nobel Prize resulted from his
work relating to photosynthesis—the process by
which plants trap solar energy and convert it to nutrients. Photosynthesis is performed by a protein
that straddles the outer membrane of a cell. The
process begins when a photon (a particle of light)
excites a molecule of chlorophyll that lies near the
inner surface of the membrane. The chlorophyll
releases an electron, which moves through a part
of the membrane referred to as the reaction center
and toward the membrane's outer surface. This reaction creates a charge separation (a difference in
electrical charge) across the membrane, which in
turn provides stored energy to drive the synthesis
of nutritional substances.

In order to learn more about how photosynthesis occurs, Hartmut Michel, a biochemist who also
worked in the Martinsried lab, had begun to study

the photosynthetic reaction center of the purple bacterium *Rhodopseudomonas viridis*. This complex molecule, made up of four different proteins and fourteen other components, is bound to the bacterium's membrane. Earlier research had identified the proteins and other components that made up *Rh. viridis*'s photosynthetic reaction center, but its exact structure—as well as the path electrons followed as they moved through it—remained obscure.

The usual way to determine the structure of a protein is to combine the protein with water. Water causes the protein molecule to take the form of a crystal lattice (a solid, three-dimensional, repeating molecular structure). By analyzing the lattice through X-ray crystallography, a researcher can study the protein atom by atom.

Unlike most proteins, however, membrane proteins—the proteins that make up the photosynthetic reaction center—are not water-soluble; they must interact with water as a part of their function. Therefore, most researchers had considered the crystallization of a membrane protein impossible.

After four years' work, however, Michel developed an additive that could take the place of water in the crystal lattice, thus making it possible to crystallize a membrane protein. In 1981 Michel produced the first high-quality crystals of the *Rh. viridis* photosynthetic reaction center. In 1982, Michel reported his results (which Deisenhofer later characterized as a "spectacular success") in one of Huber's group seminars.

Recognizing that he lacked the background and experience to analyze the crystals he had produced, Michel asked Huber to help him find a collaborator. Huber recommended Deisenhofer as the best person for the job. Over the next four years, Deisenhofer used his crystallographic skills to analyze the structure of the photosynthetic reaction center. With the help of two colleagues, Kunio Miki and Otto Epp, Deisenhofer was able to determine the exact nature and position of each of the molecule's approximately 10,000 atoms. His success marked the first time that anyone had succeeded in giving a complete, three-dimensional analysis of a membrane-bound protein.

The scientific community immediately recognized the tremendous significance of this work, which *New Scientist* magazine called "the most important advance in the understanding of photosynthesis for twenty years." As a result, Deisenhofer, Michel, and Huber were together awarded the 1988 Nobel Prize for Chemistry. In presenting the award, Bo G. Malmström of the Royal Swedish Academy of Sciences acknowledged that their accomplishment had several implications. First, a protein's structure largely determines its biological functions. Therefore, Malmström said,

knowledge of the *Rh. viridis* photosynthetic reaction center's structure "has led to a giant leap in our understanding of fundamental reactions in photosynthesis, the most important chemical reaction in the biosphere of our earth."

Second, the work of Deisenhofer and his colleagues helped verify certain similarities between plant and bacterial photosynthesis. Thus it can help researchers solve the riddles of green plant photosynthesis and, perhaps, eventually lead to the development of artificial photosynthetic reactions, a technology that would have widespread implications.

Third, because it established the exact structure and chemical environment in which electron transfer takes place, the work allowed scientists to calculate the kinetics of this transfer with a precision never before possible. As Malmström stated, the discovery "has given theoretical chemists an indispensable tool in their efforts to understand how biologic electron transfer over very large distances on a molecular scale can occur as rapidly as in one-trillionth of a second."

Finally, membrane proteins play a crucial role in many biological functions other than photosynthesis, including hormone functioning and the activities of viruses. The methods that Deisenhofer and his colleagues developed for crystallizing and analyzing the photosynthetic reaction center will likely provide a means of elucidating the structures of these proteins as well.

In March 1988, Deisenhofer accepted a position as Professor of Biochemistry and Investigator in the Howard Hughes Medical Institute at the University of Texas Southwestern Medical Center at Dallas. There he continues his research into the structure and function of biological macromolecules and the development of crystallographic software.

Deisenhofer has been described by one of his colleagues as "quiet, peaceful, and calm" but "scientifically fearless." In his spare time, he pursues his interests in music, German history, skiing, swimming, reading, and playing chess. He is married to Kirsten Fischer-Lindahl, a fellow scientist.

Deisenhofer belongs to the American Association for the Advancement of Science, the American Crystallographic Association, the Biophysical Society, the German Biophysical Society, and the Protein Society. He is also an honorary member of the International Council for Scientific Development. He and Hartmut Michel have shared the Biological Physics Prize of the American Physical Society (1986) and the Otto-Bayer Prize (1988).

ABOUT: New Scientist October 29, 1988; New York Times October 20, 1988; Science November 4, 1988; Who's Who in America, 1990.

ELION, GERTRUDE B.
(January 23, 1918–)
Nobel Prize for Physiology or Medicine, 1988
(shared with James Black and George H.
   Hitchings Jr.)

GERTRUDE B. ELION

The American chemist Gertrude Belle Elion (el'
i ən) was born in New York City, the first child of
Robert Elion, a Lithuanian immigrant, and Bertha
(Cohen) Elion, a Russian immigrant. Elion later
recalled that, as a child, she had "an insatiable
thirst for knowledge" and therefore found it difficult to settle on one field of interest. "One of the
deciding factors may have been that my grandfather, whom I loved dearly, died of cancer when I
was fifteen. I was highly motivated to do something that might eventually lead to a cure for this
terrible disease." She entered Hunter College, a tu-
ition-free New York women's college, in 1933,
and graduated with a degree in chemistry in 1937.
The Great Depression was now at its height, so
Elion was not able to afford graduate school until
1939. She entered New York University in that
year and earned an M.S. degree in chemistry in
1941.

Though scientific jobs had largely been closed
to women during the depression, such jobs were
now far more available because of World War II.
Nevertheless, Elion was not able to find a satisfac-
tory research position until 1944, when she was
hired by Burroughs Wellcome Research Laboratories in Tuckahoe, New York. She worked as an assistant to GEORGE H. HITCHINGS JR., who was
searching for new pharmaceuticals. "My thirst for
knowledge stood me in good stead in that laboratory," she wrote later, "because Dr. Hitchings permitted me to learn as rapidly as I could and to take
on more and more responsibility when I was ready
for it."

The approach Hitchings and his colleagues
were using was relatively novel. It grew from observations, made in 1940 by the pharmacologists
Donald Woods and Paul Fildes, that the sulfanilamide drugs (which had been discovered by GER-
HARD DOMAGK in the 1930s) worked by interfering
with bacteria's use of certain nutrients. Woods and
Fildes suggested that useful pharmaceuticals
might be found by making "antimetabolites"—
chemicals that are similar enough to a parasite's
necessary nutrients to disrupt its metabolism.

Though the central, directing role of nucleic
acids in the cell would not be established until after 1954 (when FRANCIS CRICK and JAMES D. WAT-
SON determined the structure of DNA), scientists
had realized for many years that nucleic acids were
essential for cellular reproduction and growth.
Hitchings, Elion, and their colleagues observed
later that "parasitic tissues in general depend for

survival on a more rapid growth, hence a more
rapid synthesis of nucleic acid, than that of the host
tissues," so nucleic acid antimetabolites should be
good medicines. They wrote that since "this argument applies equally well to bacterial, viral, rickettsial, and neoplastic diseases . . . one might
say we have been searching for the philosopher's
stone, the universal panacea, of the ancients."

Hitchings's team used a bacterium, *Lactobacil-
lus casei,* to screen for compounds that interfered
with nucleic acid metabolism. ALBRECHT KOSSEL
had discovered, half a century earlier, that nucleic
acids are made up of components called purines
and pyrimidines. Elion concentrated especially on
the purines. "We were exploring new frontiers,"
she later remembered, "since very little was
known about nucleic acid biosynthesis or the enzymes involved with it . . . . Each series of
studies was like a mystery story in that we were
constantly trying to deduce what the microbiolog-
ical results meant, with little biochemical information to help us." Many of their discoveries only
became understandable in the 1950s, when
ARTHUR KORNBERG and other biochemists eluci-
dated the pathways of nucleic acid synthesis.

In 1948 Elion discovered a compound, 2,6-di-
aminopurine, that disrupted *L. casei*'s purine metabolism and inhibited the growth of leukemia
cells. Further testing showed that it had too many
side effects to be useful in human beings, but by
1951 she had found a modified form, 6-mercap-
topurine (6-MP), that was soon recognized as "the
safest and most effective antileukemic agent to
have been discovered." Childhood leukemia had
been a particularly deadly disease, giving victims
a life expectancy of only a few months; 6-MP

Burroughs Wellcome Research Laboratories

raised it to a year, and the combination of 6-MP, other drugs, and radiation treatments eventually made leukemia one of the most curable of cancers.

The unprecedented effectiveness of 6-MP against leukemia persuaded many scientists to study its suitability for other diseases. Robert Schwartz and his colleagues at Tufts University Medical School in Boston, inspired by P. B. MEDAWAR's work on immunological tolerance, had been searching for drugs that might suppress the immune response to foreign tissue and permit organ transplants. Schwartz found that 6-MP was able to suppress the overall activity of the immune system. When Roy Calne (then at Harvard Medical School) tested 6-MP during kidney transplants in dogs, the transplanted kidneys survived five times longer than before. The work of Schwartz and Calne inspired Elion, Hitchings, and their associates to search for more potent immunosuppressants, leading to the discovery of azathioprine (Imuran). This compound was used successfully by JOSEPH E. MURRAY, beginning in 1962, to prevent rejection of transplanted human kidneys.

Elion and her colleagues continued to look for ways to improve 6-MP's effectiveness against leukemia. While searching for drugs that might interfere with the body's breakdown of 6-MP, they discovered allopurinol (Zyloprim). Allopurinol proved to lower the amount of 6-MP a patient needed—but it also reduced the level of 6-MP that was toxic, and it thus offered no therapeutic advantage. In 1966, however, Elion's associate, Dr. Wayne Rundles of Duke University School of Medicine, realized that allopurinol could be used to treat gout, a disorder of purine metabolism. Allopurinol remains the most effective remedy for gout.

When Elion and her associates had first begun to experiment with 2,6-diaminopurine in 1948, they were struck by its strength against certain viruses. At the time, however, the compound had proved too toxic to be useful. But, in 1968, when other scientists discovered that certain natural nucleotide compounds—called arabinosides—inhibited the growth of viruses, "the information started a train of thought." Elion hypothesized that arabinosides based on artificial diaminopurines would persist longer in living animals but would keep the antiviral properties of natural arabinosides. This line of research went through a number of phases before culminating in acyclovir (Zovirax) in 1977. Acyclovir is used to treat infections of herpes viruses and of varicella zoster virus (chicken pox and shingles); it has proved particularly useful for people with inadequate immune systems, such as patients with transplanted organs or AIDS. In 1984, other scientists at Burroughs Wellcome used the antimetabolite principle and the approach to nucleotide analogues pioneered by Elion and Hitchings to produce azidothymidine (AZT), the first drug used to treat AIDS itself.

As Hitchings moved up through the Burroughs Wellcome hierarchy, Elion followed one step behind him, finally becoming head of the Department of Experimental Therapy in 1967. After her retirement in 1983, Elion continued to help with Burroughs Wellcome research and also became a research professor of medicine and pharmacology at Duke University. "In a sense," she reflected, "my career appears to have come full circle from my early days of being a teacher to now sharing my experience in research with the new generations of scientists."

Elion and Hitchings shared the 1988 Nobel Prize for Physiology or Medicine with JAMES BLACK, another industry-based pharmacologist who developed drugs to treat heart disease and gastric ulcers. The Nobel committee honored them not for the practical value of their discoveries alone but because they "succeeded in developing a rational approach to the discovery of new drugs, based upon basic scientific studies of biochemical and physiological processes. As a result, a new era in drug research was born which offers promise for the development of new therapeutic strategies for the treatment of illnesses against which existing drugs are either unsatisfactory or simply do not exist." Elion said that "the Nobel Prize is fine, but the drugs I've developed are rewards in themselves."

When she was first hired by Burroughs Wellcome in 1944, Elion attempted to obtain a Ph.D. by attending night classes at Brooklyn Polytechnic Institute. When she was told she would have to attend full-time, she made what she later called "a critical decision in my life, to stay with my job and give up the pursuit of a doctorate." Elion felt that, for her generation, it was essentially impossible to have both a research career and children, so she never married. She calls her work "both my vocation and avocation"; her other interests include travel, photography, and music, especially opera.

Elion holds eight honorary degrees; her other honors include the Garvan Medal of the American Chemical Society (1968), the Judd Award of the Sloan-Kettering Institute (1983), and the Cain Award of the American Association for Cancer Research (1984). She is a member of numerous scientific societies and has long been an adviser to the National Cancer Institute.

SELECTED WORKS: "The Purine Path to Chemotherapy," Science April 7, 1989.

ABOUT: New Scientist October 22, 1988; New York Times October 18, 1988; New York Times Magazine January 29, 1989; Science October 28, 1988; Who's Who, 1990; Who's Who in America, 1990.

ERNST, RICHARD R.
(August 14, 1933–)
Nobel Prize for Chemistry, 1991

The Swiss physical chemist Richard Robert Ernst was born in Winterthur, Zurich. His father, Johannes Robert Walter Ernst, was a professor of architecture at the Winterthur Technical School. His mother was the former Irma Brunner. Ernst attended the local public school and graduated in 1952.

"That I would become a chemist was already clear when I was fourteen," Ernst later wrote. "I wanted to understand the basic phenomena in nature and technology and started to do experiments at that age." Ernst majored in chemistry at the Swiss Federal Institute of Technology (ETH-Zurich), finished his undergraduate studies in 1956, and received a Ph.D. in physical chemistry in 1962. He won the Silver Medal of the ETH-Zurich for his Ph.D. thesis.

Ernst did his doctoral research on nuclear magnetic resonance (NMR) spectroscopy. NMR spectroscopy was first developed in the 1940s by FELIX BLOCH and EDWARD M. PURCELL. Physicists at that time knew that most atomic nuclei behave like tiny compass needles or magnets: when exposed to a strong magnetic field, they align themselves with that field, similar to the way in which an ordinary compass aligns itself with the magnetic field of the earth. Regardless of their alignment, the atoms also remain in a constant state of spin, rotating on their axes like tops. Each spinning atom wobbles slightly at its own particular rate. This wobble rate is called its resonance frequency.

NMR spectroscopy permits scientists to use these phenomena to determine the atomic composition and structure of molecules. The scientist places the subject material within a strong magnetic field, forcing the atoms to align with the magnet. Then, while the material is still aligned with the magnet, the scientist exposes it to radio waves. If an atom with a particular natural frequency is exposed to a radio wave of the same frequency, it will absorb the energy emitted by that wave and realign itself. When the radio wave is cut off, the atom will return to its earlier magnetic alignment. At the same time, it will release the absorbed energy and resonate, or emit signals that can be detected and recorded. Since resonance frequencies differ for different kinds of atomic nuclei, the frequency and the rate of the emission become a sort of chemical signature that a scientist can read. In addition, the resonance of a particular atom can be affected by its proximity to other types of atoms. This information can be used to determine the placement of atoms within a molecule and thus the molecule's structure.

RICHARD R. ERNST

To do a complete NMR analysis, scientists have to test the material against a wide range of radio frequencies in order to cover all possible nuclear resonances. In the 1950s and 1960s the standard practice was to expose a test material to a long series of signals at slowly increasing frequencies and study the material's reaction to each signal. While this slow, cumbersome method was adequate for small, simple molecules, it was difficult to use for larger ones.

In 1963 Ernst went to work at Varian Associates, a firm specializing in electronic instruments in Palo Alto, California. His supervisor there, the physical chemist Weston A. Anderson, was trying to develop a way to improve the speed of NMR studies. Ernst developed just such a technique.

Ernst showed that they could subject their samples to all the relevant radio frequencies in one quick, broad-band burst rather than one after another. Sir Rex Richards, Oxford biophysicist and president of Britain's Royal Society of Chemistry, later compared Ernst's method to hitting all the keys on a piano simultaneously rather than one at a time.

Since this one burst contained all the frequencies to which the different atoms in the sample might respond, all the atoms would resonate at once, producing a very complicated output. This output represented the sum of all the resonances of all the different atoms present. The individual resonances—the objective of the experiment—still had to be separated out. To do this, Ernst used a complex mathematical technique called a Fourier transform. Fourier's technique had been around for many years (Joseph Fourier, the French physicist who developed the technique, died in 1830).

While the theory behind the technique is simple, it requires massive calculations that are practical only with the aid of computers.

Ernst's new method, called Fourier-transform NMR, took a fraction of the time of the earlier method, and this provided another advantage. One drawback of the earlier method was that "noise" caused by random factors in the instruments or the environment clouded the results. Since this new single-burst method took only a few seconds, each burst could be repeated again and again and the scientist could work with more reliable averaged results.

Ernst introduced Fourier-transform NMR in 1966. Within a few years it had become the method of choice for NMR, and NMR was being ever more widely applied to study chemical structure and the dynamics of chemical reactions. Ernst returned to ETH-Zurich in 1968, continuing his studies of NMR spectroscopy as a lecturer.

As NMR became more widely used, the limitations of even Fourier-transform methods became burdensome. "It soon turned out," Ernst later wrote, "that the information content of an NMR spectrum can become overwhelming." NMR spectroscopy was not sophisticated enough to analyze large, complex molecules such as proteins, which contain thousands of atoms.

In 1971 the Belgian scientist Jean Jeener suggested that NMR could become "two-dimensional," a suggestion Ernst picked up. The two-dimensional NMR methods Ernst and his colleagues proposed in 1976 involve hitting a sample with two separate bursts of radio waves rather than one. Resonances caused by the first burst are modified by the second burst. As the experiment is performed repeatedly with slightly different time intervals between bursts, scientists can gain new insight into the makeup of more complex materials. The difference between one-dimensional NMR and two-dimensional NMR is, as the Royal Swedish Academy of Sciences later wrote, "like looking at the skyline of a mountain range and then looking at the whole range from an aircraft above."

The computations involved in two-dimensional NMR are more complex than those in normal Fourier-transform NMR and rely on improved computer technology. In the 1980s, as computer technology advanced, Ernst worked on extending his methods to produce three- and four-dimensional NMR spectra, which are even more informative.

The methods pioneered by Ernst made NMR useful in the hospital as well as the chemist's laboratory. For example, the hydrogen atoms in water molecules can be detected with NMR. By exposing a person to a strong magnetic field, a physician can judge the water content of various parts of that person's body. Such magnetic resonance imaging (MRI)—as NMR is referred to in hospitals—techniques have become particularly important in studies of the brain and other body tissues. MRI is widely used in hospitals today, as it produces clear images of internal structures through noninvasive means.

Ernst was awarded the 1991 Nobel Prize for Chemistry for his contributions to NMR technology. "NMR spectroscopy has during the last twenty years developed into perhaps the most important instrumental measuring technique within chemistry. This has occurred because of a dramatic increase in both the sensitivity and the resolution of the instruments, two areas in which Ernst has contributed more than anybody else," the Royal Swedish Academy of Sciences wrote in announcing the award.

"I am not aware of any other field of science outside of magnetic resonance that offers so much freedom and so many opportunities for a creative mind to invent and explore new experimental schemes that can be fruitfully applied in a variety of disciplines," Ernst has written. "NMR is intellectually attractive because the observed phenomena can be understood based on a sound theory, and almost all concepts can also be tested by easy experiments. At the same time, the practical importance of NMR is enormous and can justify many of the playful activities of an addicted spectroscopist." NMR studies are used today in biology, biochemistry, materials science, and medicine to analyze drugs and proteins and to study the motions, structures, and interactions of molecules. "With classical techniques it could take years to determine molecular structures," Salo Gronowitz of the academy said. "Now it can take hours or days."

Ernst was named full professor of physical chemistry at ETH-Zurich in 1976 and remains there today. He married Magdalena Kielholz, a teacher, in 1963; they have two daughters and a son. Ernst's hobbies include skiing, hiking, music, and collecting Tibetan art.

Ernst holds fifteen patents related to NMR technology. His honors include Switzerland's Benoist Prize (1986), the Ampère Prize (1990), Columbia University's Horwitz Prize (1991), Israel's Wolf Prize (1991), and honorary doctorates from ETH-Lausanne (1985) and the Technical University of Munich (1989). He is on the editorial board of a number of journals and is a member of Academia Europaea, the National Academy of Sciences of India, and the National Academy of Sciences of the United States, as well as numerous technical societies.

SELECTED WORKS: Principles of Nuclear Magnetic Resonance in One and Two Dimensions, 1987, with G. Bodenhausen and A. Wokann; "Two-Dimensional NMR Spectroscopy: A Powerful Tool for the Investigation of Molecular Structure and Dynamics," Chimia, 41, 323 (1987).

ABOUT: Chemical and Engineering News October 21, 1991; Los Angeles Times October 17, 1991; New Scientist October 26, 1991; New York Times October 17, 1991; Science October 25, 1991; Washington Post October 17, 1991.

JEROME I. FRIEDMAN

FRIEDMAN, JEROME I.
(March 28, 1930–   )
Nobel Prize for Physics, 1990
(shared with Henry W. Kendall and Richard E. Taylor)

The American physicist Jerome Isaac Friedman was born in Chicago, Illinois, the second of two children of Russian immigrants. His father, Selig Friedman, came to the United States in 1913, served in the United States Army during World War I, and later established his own business repairing sewing machines. Friedman's mother, Lillian (Warsaw) Friedman, supported herself until her marriage by working in a garment factory.

Friedman later recalled, "The education of my brother and myself was of paramount importance to my parents, and in addition to their strong encouragement, they were prepared to make any sacrifice to further our intellectual development. When there were financial difficulties, they still managed to provide us with music and art lessons. They greatly respected scholarship in itself, but they also impressed upon us that there were great opportunities available for those who were well educated."

Friedman was originally interested in a career in art and enrolled in a high school art program. While in school, however, he read ALBERT EINSTEIN's *Relativity,* a book that, he noted, "opened a new vista for me and deepened my curiosity about the physical world." Although he was offered a scholarship to the Art Institute of Chicago Museum School, Friedman decided to pursue physics at the University of Chicago. There, working under the physicist ENRICO FERMI, he recalled, "I was indeed fortunate to have seen the practice of physics carried out at its 'very best' at such an early stage in my development." Friedman earned his B.A. (1950), his M.A. (1953), and his Ph.D. (1956) at the university.

While at Chicago, Friedman carried out an important experiment with Valentine Telegdi that demonstrated the lack of mirror symmetry (previously thought valid) in the so-called weak nuclear interaction, the force responsible for the spontaneous breakup (decay) of radioactive particles.

In 1957 Friedman became a research associate under ROBERT HOFSTADTER at Stanford University's High Energy Physics Laboratory, where he studied atomic structure and behavior through electron scattering. Electron scattering involves bombarding atoms with a beam of high-speed electrons and observing the "scattering"—the direction of travel—of the accelerated electrons as they emerge from collisions with the target atoms. If the electrons hit constituent particles in the atom, they emerge at an angle; if they hit nothing, they pass straight through. The higher the speed of the bombarding electrons, the farther into the target atoms they can penetrate and the more information can be obtained from their behavior. Some high-speed collisions, called inelastic scattering, also break apart the target atoms and scatter and reveal their particles.

By the early twentieth century, physicists had settled a few basic facts about the structure of the atom and its subatomic particles. In 1911 ERNEST RUTHERFORD determined that the atom consists of a tiny, positively charged core—a nucleus—that is orbited by negatively charged electrons. In 1919 Rutherford discovered that within the nucleus there is a positively charged particle called the proton. Thirteen years later JAMES CHADWICK discovered another component of the nucleus, a noncharged particle called the neutron. The modern picture of the atom seemed to be complete, and the three basic components—the electron, the proton, and the neutron—were considered to be the fundamental particles of matter.

Further study of the atom showed that this conclusion was incorrect, however. Scattering experiments revealed that these three particles are only a few of the hundreds of different kinds of particles that can be produced by bombarding the atom. As more and more particles were identified, physicists became convinced that there must be something smaller and more fundamental common to all these particles. As Cecilia Jarlskog of the Royal Swedish Academy of Sciences later queried, "Was there a hidden order not yet discovered by man? There could be order but only at the price of postulating an additional, deeper level in nature—perhaps the ultimate level—consisting of only a few building blocks." Scientists struggled to discover those building blocks.

In 1960 Friedman left Stanford to join the faculty of the physics department at the Massachusetts Institute of Technology (MIT). A year later a colleague from Stanford, HENRY W. KENDALL, joined him.

In 1963, under the leadership of Wolfgang K. H. (Pief) Panofsky, Friedman and Kendall began work with RICHARD E. TAYLOR at Stanford and several physicists from the California Institute of Technology (Caltech) on the Stanford Linear Accelerator Center (SLAC), a 2-mile-long linear particle accelerator partially buried under the hills behind the Stanford campus. Particle accelerators are devices that speed the motion of the bombarding particles used in scattering experiments. Linear accelerators such as the SLAC accelerate bombarding particles that travel in a straight line. Their advantage over circular accelerators (cyclotrons) lies in their ability to focus beams on targets more sharply. The SLAC was designed for experiments at energies around 20 billion electron volts, a level far greater than previously possible. With the SLAC, the group began exploring the makeup of subatomic particles.

In 1964 MURRAY GELL-MANN, a physicist from Caltech, devised a way to categorize and group the hundreds of subatomic particles that had been discovered. He theorized a model of these particles, picturing them as clusters of smaller particles, which he called quarks, choosing the name from a passage in James Joyce's *Finnegans Wake*. Six types of quarks, Gell-Mann theorized, make up the fundamental components of many subatomic particles, including protons and neutrons. (A similar model was proposed independently by George Zweig.) Just as atoms are characterized and categorized by the number of electrons and protons they have, subatomic particles can be characterized by the number and types of quarks they have. Gell-Mann's model was widely accepted as a useful way to classify particles, but because no one was able to observe anything as small as quarks in experiments, some physicists thought of them not as real particles but as "mathematical quantities" useful for modeling particle behavior.

Using the new state-of-the-art SLAC accelerator, Friedman, Kendall, and Taylor were able to observe the first traces of quarks and confirm Gell-Mann's theory. In a series of electron-scattering experiments at the SLAC from 1967 to 1973, they sent beams of electrons traveling at nearly the speed of light—faster than ever before possible—toward targets of liquid hydrogen or deuterium, atoms that have the simplest nuclei and thus can be regarded as essentially proton and neutron targets. Their experiments were called deep inelastic scattering experiments: *deep* was a reference to how far into the nucleus of the atom they were able to penetrate, and *inelastic* meant that the bombarding electrons were forceful enough to shatter the proton and neutron targets into their presumed components.

At this new high speed, the electrons penetrated to the center of protons. There, it seemed, the electrons were hitting some hard particles that scattered them at large angles relative to their original direction. These particles could only be Gell-Mann's quarks. Along with the quarks, the three physicists also identified particles called gluons, electrically neutral particles that bind quarks together.

Friedman, Kendall, and Taylor received the 1990 Nobel Prize for Physics for providing evidence that quarks are real particles. In announcing the award, the Royal Swedish Academy of Sciences described the discovery as "a repetition, although at a deeper level, of one of the most dramatic events in the history of physics, the discovery of the nucleus of the atom." Cecilia Jarlskog of the academy said, when presenting the physicists their prizes, that with their discovery, "a new rung on the ladder of creation had revealed itself and a new epoch in the history of physics had begun."

All three scientists credit their achievements to Panofsky and the SLAC. Friedman remembers the chance to work on the SLAC as a rare opportunity: "We were part of a group of physicists who were provided a new accelerator, given the support to design and construct optimal experimental facilities, and had the opportunity to participate in the exploration of a new energy range with electrons. . . . It was a very exciting time for all of us."

In the late 1970s Friedman continued his explorations into subatomic structure at the Fermi National Accelerator Laboratory in Batavia, Illinois. In 1980 he became director of MIT's Laboratory for Nuclear Science, and in 1983 head of the physics department. In 1988 Friedman returned to full-time teaching and research. He and his MIT research group continue to work on the SLAC. He is also involved in design work on the Superconducting Super Collider now under construction near Waxahachie, Texas. The Super Collider, at 54 miles in circumference, will be the largest particle accelerator in the world.

Friedman married Tania Letetsky-Baranovsky in 1956 and has four grown children: Ellena, Joel, Martin, and Sandra. He continues to be interested in art and paints and studies Asian ceramics in his spare time.

Friedman has served on a number of advisory committees at accelerators throughout the world. He was a member of the board of the University Research Association for six years and served as vice president for three years. He is a member of the High Energy Advisory Panel of the United States Department of Energy and chairman of the Scientific Policy Committee of the Superconducting Super Collider. In 1989 Friedman, Kendall, and Taylor shared the W. K. H. Panofsky Prize from the American Physical Society.

ABOUT: American Men and Women of Science, 1989–90; Los Angeles Times October 18, 1990; Newsweek October 29, 1990; New York Times October 18, 1990; Science October 26, 1990; Science News October 27, 1990.

MIKHAIL SERGEYEVICH GORBACHEV

GORBACHEV, MIKHAIL SERGEYEVICH
(March 2, 1931–)
Nobel Prize for Peace, 1990

Soviet political leader Mikhail Sergeyevich Gorbachev (gôr bə chôf′) was born in Privolnoye, a small farming village in the Stavropol territory of southern Russia. His parents, Sergei Andreyevich and Maria Panteleyevna Gorbachev, were peasants, as their parents had been before them. They had witnessed the birth of the Soviet Union and Stalin's takeover of the leadership of the all-powerful Communist party after the death of Lenin in 1924. Gorbachev's father and paternal grandfather were members of the party.

At the time of Gorbachev's birth, Stalin's oppressive campaign to take private land and force Soviet peasants into government-run agricultural collectives was at its bloodiest, resulting in famine and millions of deaths. The Gorbachev family favored collectivization: Gorbachev's maternal and paternal grandfathers worked as procollectivization organizers, and his father operated a combine for a government collective.

The young Gorbachev attended local schools. His education was interrupted by World War II in 1942–1943, when Hitler's army occupied Stavropol for almost six months during the siege of Stalingrad. During the war Gorbachev's father was drafted and served four years as a combat engineer.

In 1950 Gorbachev graduated from secondary school second in his class. By that time he had also joined the Komsomol (Young Communist League) and, in recognition of the several summers he had worked in the local grain fields as a combine operator, had received the Order of the Red Banner of Labor, a rare honor for an eighteen-year-old.

Gorbachev entered the law school of Moscow State University in the fall of 1950. While there, he continued to be active in the Komsomol, and in 1952 he joined the Communist party. At that time he also met Raisa Maximovna Titorenko, a philosophy student at the university. They married several years later, and their daughter, Irina, was born in 1956.

As soon as he finished law school, Gorbachev returned to Stavropol, where he rose quickly through the local ranks of the Communist party. He also studied agriculture, receiving a degree in agronomic economics from the Stavropol Agricultural Institute in 1967. In 1970, at age thirty-nine, Gorbachev was appointed first secretary of the Stavropol territory (a position equivalent to a state governor in the United States), a district of some 2.4 million people. In this position he met many national leaders, including Yuri Andropov, then the director of the KGB (the Soviet state security agency).

Now in the national organization of the Communist party, he continued his rise. In 1978, apparently at Andropov's suggestion, the leader of the Communist party, General Secretary Leonid Brezhnev, named Gorbachev to the Communist party Central Committee as the secretary for agriculture. Thus, at age forty-seven Gorbachev returned to Moscow and became a member of the Soviet equivalent of the United States presidential cabinet. As secretary for agriculture he headed delegations that visited western Europe in 1972, 1975, and 1976. In 1980 he became the youngest full member of the Politburo, the Central Committee's policy-making arm.

Two years later Brezhnev died, and the reformers within the Communist party elected Andropov to the post of general secretary. As Andropov's protégé, Gorbachev helped carry out several reform initiatives and measures intended to provide a degree of economic decentralization. Political observers believed that Andropov was grooming Gorbachev to be his successor.

But when Andropov died in 1984, Brezhnev loyalists picked Konstantin Chernenko to lead the party, although the seventy-two-year-old leader was in poor health. Gorbachev was named chairman of the foreign affairs committee of the Supreme Soviet and served as Chernenko's second in command. When Chernenko died in March 1985, the party quickly named Gorbachev the new general secretary.

Gorbachev inherited many problems. The Soviet Union over the decades had suffered from slow technological development, poor harvests, and strained relations among various Soviet republics as well as with many foreign powers. The communist system, which provided no incentives for workers' efforts, led to slowdowns in production. All these factors had combined to lead to economic decline, shortages, popular unrest, and a thriving black market. In his acceptance speech Gorbachev addressed all these issues, calling for peaceful coexistence with the West, economic modernization, and greater openness within the framework of socialist self-government.

Once in office, Gorbachev attempted to launch an ambitious program of domestic reform. His economic measures were promoted under the banner of *perestroika* (Russian for "restructuring"), the social reforms under the catchword *glasnost* (Russian for "openness").

To increase economic productivity, Gorbachev called for greater discipline on the part of Soviet workers, including a reduction in alcohol consumption; the introduction of cash bonuses, incentive schemes, and new technologies; the elimination of inefficiency, waste, and incompetence; greater attention to the quality and quantity of consumer products; and moves toward "intensification," a euphemism for the introduction of free-market principles within a planned economy.

By all accounts, perestroika was a failure. The Soviet economy and standard of living continued to decline, and inflation and consumer dissatisfaction continued to rise. Glasnost, in contrast, succeeded in revolutionizing everyday Soviet life. Gorbachev's policies allowed for the easing of media censorship, the release of political dissidents (including ANDREI SAKHAROV), the relaxation of restrictions on the practice of religion, a more

truthful rewriting of Soviet history, and the open airing of domestic problems. Nonetheless, relapses occurred: In April 1986 Gorbachev's government tried to cover up the scope of the disaster at the nuclear reactor at Chernobyl; in January 1990 Gorbachev imposed martial law to quell ethnic unrest in Baku, Azerbaijan, which led to the killing of a hundred civilian protestors; several months later Gorbachev called for a blockade on Lithuania when that republic declared independence from the Soviet Union.

Gorbachev also resumed a campaign begun by Andropov to purge the party of incompetent and corrupt officials. In 1988 he announced a plan to dismantle the Supreme Soviet and turn the government over to smaller bodies composed of elected officials. The party members approved these plans and other constitutional reforms, one of which created the office of president of the Soviet Union. In the following year the newly elected legislature named Gorbachev to that post.

Despite Gorbachev's commitment to political pluralism and economic restructuring and his personal charisma and oratorical skill, his domestic programs had little success during the late 1980s. Far more impressive were his achievements in foreign affairs, especially his dealings with the United States and eastern Europe.

In November 1985 Gorbachev and United States president Ronald Reagan met in Geneva for the first of their four summit meetings. The principal topics were arms reduction and the renewal of cultural exchanges, which had been limited over the years because of Soviet expansionism and the cold war between the two nations. At a December 1987 summit in Washington, D.C., the two leaders signed a treaty to eliminate medium-range nuclear missiles.

In 1989 Gorbachev ended what had been called "the Soviet Union's Vietnam war" when he ordered the withdrawal of Soviet troops from Afghanistan after a bloody ten-year standoff. Later that year, citing the inalienable right to self-determination, Gorbachev took no military action when members of the eastern European defense alliance known as the Warsaw Pact—Poland, Hungary, East Germany, Czechoslovakia, Bulgaria, and Romania—overthrew their communist governments and declared their independence from the Soviet sphere of influence. Gorbachev also actively promoted the reunification of East and West Germany.

In recognition of his leading role in international affairs, Gorbachev was awarded the 1990 Nobel Prize for Peace. In announcing the award, the Norwegian Nobel Committee praised Gorbachev for his "many and decisive contributions" to the "dramatic changes" that had recently taken place in East-West relations: "Confrontation has been replaced by negotiations. Old European nation-states have regained their freedom. The arms race is slowing down, and we see a definite and active process in the direction of arms control and disarmament. Several regional conflicts have been solved or at least come closer to a solution. The UN is beginning to play the role which was originally planned for it in an international community governed by law."

In his Nobel lecture Gorbachev described his vision of world peace that would transcend "mere coexistence" and move toward the "universality of civilization" and "cooperation and common creative endeavor among countries." He also linked the fate of the "new world order" to the health of the Soviet economy: "If Soviet perestroika succeeds, there will be a real chance of rebuilding a new world order. And if perestroika fails, the prospect of entering a new peaceful period in history will vanish, at least for the foreseeable future."

In 1990, when Gorbachev's requests for massive foreign aid and credit could not be met, the Soviet economy continued to deteriorate. Rising prices and shortages of food and basic consumer goods stirred up widespread anger in Moscow. Despairing over the fate of the national economy, inspired by the secession of the USSR's Baltic republics, and buoyed by new tides of nationalism, various Soviet republics declared their independence in 1991. In August 1991 Gorbachev survived a coup launched by hard-line insiders.

After the coup Gorbachev tried unsuccessfully to stem the tide of independence and keep the republics united. He proposed a more democratic, decentralized Soviet Union, but the republics wanted nothing less than the total eradication of the central government. In December three republics—Russia, Ukraine, and Byelorussia (now called Belarus)—drew up a treaty that would unite them loosely as the Commonwealth of Independent States, a union with no central government and no role for Mikhail Gorbachev. In a very short time most of the other former Soviet republics voted to join the new commonwealth.

When the USSR dissolved on December 25, 1991, Gorbachev resigned and became the head of the International Foundation for Social, Economic, and Political Research, a Moscow think tank he created after the August coup. While the role of the Commonwealth of Independent States and the viability of the newly independent nations are still unclear, the Soviet Union's place in international affairs has largely been taken over by Russia, the former union's largest republic.

WORKS IN ENGLISH TRANSLATION: A Time for Peace, 1985; The Coming Century of Peace, 1986; Moratorium, 1986; Peace Has No Alternative, 1986; Speeches and Writings, 1986; Perestroika, 1987; The August Coup, 1992.

ABOUT: Butson, T. Gorbachev: A Biography, 1986; Current Biography Yearbook, 1985; International Who's Who, 1991–92; Medvedev, Z. Gorbachev, 1986; Schmidt-Hauer, C. Gorbachev: The Path to Power, 1986; Smith, H. The New Russians, 1990; Time January 4, 1988; White, S. Gorbachev and After, 1991; Zemtsov, I., and Farrar, J. Gorbachev: The Man and the System.

GORDIMER, NADINE
(November 20, 1923–)
Nobel Prize for Literature, 1991

The South African novelist Nadine Gordimer (gôr′ di mər) was born in Springs, which was then a small mining town thirty miles west of Johannesburg, in the province of the Transvaal. Both her parents were Jewish immigrants; her father, Isidore Gordimer, a jeweler, came from Lithuania, and her mother, the former Nan Myers, came from England.

In the Union of South Africa of her childhood, although over 70 percent of the population was black—as it is today—black people had virtually no influence in government. Racism was legally sanctioned in a system called *apartheid,* or separateness, under which black, white, and Asian racial groups were rigidly defined and required to live under separate laws and institutions and often in separate places.

Gordimer, who was born, as she said, "on the soft side of the color bar," attended elementary school at the all-white Convent of Our Lady of Mercy. At an early age she realized that she had little in common with her peers. She spent long hours alone in the whites-only library, reading. Recalling her formal schooling as "sketchy, at best," she later noted, "My school was the local library. Proust, Chekhov, and Dostoyevski . . . were my professors."

Although her parents did not express strong political convictions, Gordimer's reading led her to question the attitudes of white South Africans. She found that she did not share their prejudices against black South Africans. She discovered, she later wrote in an autobiographical essay, that she "lived with and among a variety of colors and kinds of people. This discovery was a joyous personal one, not a political one, at first, but, of course, as time has gone by it has hardened into a sense of political opposition to abusive white power."

Gordimer began to express herself through fiction. She published her first short story, "Come Again Tomorrow," when she was fifteen. After graduating from secondary school, she drifted for a few years, then moved to Johannesburg to attend

NADINE GORDIMER

the University of Witwatersrand. She quit after a year and chose to pursue writing, although she later recalled, "I did not, at the beginning, expect to earn a living by being read. I wrote as a child out of the joy of apprehending life through my senses . . . and soon out of the emotions that puzzled me or raged within me and which took form, found some enlightenment, solace, and delight, shaped in the written word."

She wrote short stories, quite a few of which were published in *The New Yorker* and *Harper's,* and the first collection, *Face to Face,* appeared in 1949, when she was twenty-five; another volume of her short stories, *The Soft Voice of the Serpent,* appeared in 1952. Gordimer's first novel, *The Lying Days,* was published in 1953. It depicts a young South African woman who, like Gordimer, gradually gains a widened social perspective. The critic Leon de Kock wrote of the heroine that she "triumphs against the provincial narrowness and racial bigotry of her parents' mining village existence, yet she discovers that she, too, is sealed within her social limitations."

Throughout her career Gordimer has kept her focus on the same theme: the destructive influence of apartheid on human relationships among both blacks and whites. In the 1958 novel *A World of Strangers* she writes of an Englishman who comes to South Africa to work and finds himself to be "a stranger among people who were strangers to each other." In *A Guest of Honor* (1970) she describes the conflicts of a man who returns to a newly independent nation whose previous government had ousted him for his ties to nationalistic black groups. A short story in the 1991 book *Jump and Other Stories* depicts a suburban family whose

members build increasingly strong barriers around their home to keep outsiders from encroaching. Despite the political overtones and interpretations of her work, Gordimer emphasizes that it is the country and its people, not apartheid, that are the subjects of her work. Nevertheless, several of her books have been banned in her home country.

Outside her fiction Gordimer takes a vocal political stand against apartheid. "I think when you're born white in South Africa, you're peeling like an onion. You're sloughing off all the conditions that you've had since you were a child," she has explained. "I'm not by nature a political person . . . and I think if I had lived in another country, I would have remained like that," but to do so, she contends, is impossible in South Africa. In 1987 Gordimer helped found the mostly black Congress of South African Writers, and she is a member of the recently legalized African National Congress.

Gordimer received the 1991 Nobel Prize for Literature. In announcing the award the Swedish Academy noted that she "writes with intense immediacy about the extremely complicated personal and social relationships in her environment. At the same time as she feels a political involvement—and takes action on that basis—she does not permit this to encroach on her writings. Nevertheless, her literary works, in giving profound insight into the historical process, help to shape this process." She is the first South African to win the award and only the seventh woman in the ninety-year history of the prize.

The Swedish Academy identified the 1981 novel *July's People* as one of her best works. The story is set in what Gordimer saw then as the near future of South Africa, in the aftermath of a revolution in which the white government has been toppled and rioting blacks have taken over the country. The story describes a white, middle-class liberal family who must rely on their former black manservant to provide refuge for them in his village. Critic Betty Thompson said of the book, "*July's People* is a slim book, but it conveys all that is necessary to understand the situation of whites and blacks in Africa, of masters and servants everywhere, and how quickly it can all be reversed."

Another of her masterpieces, *Burger's Daughter* (1979), reveals white ambivalence about apartheid through the fictional character Rosa Burger, the daughter of a martyred leader of the South African Communist party. When her father dies, Rosa is expected to take on his cause. Instead she leaves the country to remove herself from politics and establish a new life. Only when she is away from her homeland does she begin to resolve her feelings about the system under which she was raised. She concludes that "the real definition of loneliness

. . . is to live without social responsibility," and she returns to South Africa to continue her father's struggle against social injustice.

When Gordimer was told that she had won the Nobel Prize, she called it the second greatest thrill of the past two years. The first, she said, was the release of Nelson Mandela, the leader of the African National Congress, who was freed in 1990 after nearly thirty years of political imprisonment. While she is pleased with the recent loosening of apartheid, including the legalization of the African National Congress and the release of Mandela, she feels that not enough is being done to help the blacks in her country. "We've gone halfway there," Gordimer has said. "It's not enough for whites to say that they would be prepared to live under black majority rule. . . . You have to help bring that about."

Gordimer tries to keep some distance between her fiction and her politics; she says that although her work is clearly biased, "I don't think that a writer like myself . . . should put whatever talent he or she has at the service of a revolution, no matter how much you believe in it yourself. . . . In practical terms this means that because I am a member of the African National Congress, I must not then in my fiction suggest that everything members of that organization do is right."

Gordimer was married to Gerald Gavronsky from 1949 to 1952, then married Reinhold Cassirer, an art dealer and gallery owner, in 1954. She has a daughter from her first marriage and a son from her second. Despite her successful career and her abhorrence of apartheid, Gordimer continues to live in a suburb of Johannesburg. "I was born there," she has said of her homeland. "And it's my situation—by that I mean it's something I feel I have to deal with. Jean-Paul Sartre once said that to go into exile is to lose your place in the world."

Gordimer has taught at universities around the world and has received honorary doctorates from the University of Leuven (Belgium, 1980), Smith College (1985), the City College of New York (1985), Mount Holyoke College (1985), Harvard University (1987), and Yale University (1987). Her awards include the United Kingdom's W. H. Smith Literary Award (1961) for *Friday's Footprint,* the South African English Academy's Thomas Pringle Award (1969), the University of Edinburgh's James Tait Black Memorial Prize (1972) for *A Guest of Honor,* the United Kingdom's Booker Prize (1974) for *The Conservationist,* and France's Golden Eagle Award (1975). She has won South Africa's CNA (Central News Agency) award three times, and in 1981 she won the Scottish Arts Council Neil Gunn Fellowship, the Common Wealth Award, and the Modern Language Association of America Award. In 1990 she won the Royal Society of Literature's Benson Medal.

Gordimer is vice president of the writer's group International PEN. She is a member of the Royal Society of Literature, a foreign honorary member of the American Academy and Institute of Arts and Letters and the American Academy of Arts and Sciences, and an honorary fellow of the Modern Language Association of America.

ADDITIONAL WORKS: Six Feet of the Country, 1956; Occasion for Loving, 1963; Not for Publication, 1965; The Late Bourgeois World, 1966; Livingstone's Companions, 1971; Selected Stories, 1975; A Soldier's Embrace, 1980; Something Out There, 1984; Lifetimes Under Apartheid, 1986; A Sport of Nature, 1987; The Essential Gesture, 1988, with S. Clingman; My Son's Story, 1990; Crimes of Conscience, 1991.

ABOUT: Bazin, N., and Seymour, M. Conversations with Nadine Gordimer, 1990; Clingman, S. The Novels of Nadine Gordimer, 1986; Contemporary Authors, 1990; Contemporary Literary Criticism, 1989; Contemporary Novelists, 1986; Current Biography, 1980; Haugh, R. Nadine Gordimer: The Meticulous Vision, 1974; Newman, J. Nadine Gordimer, 1988; World Authors, 1950–1970, 1975.

HAAVELMO, TRYGVE

(December 13, 1911–)
Nobel Memorial Prize in Economic Sciences, 1989

The Norwegian economist Trygve Haavelmo (haw vel' mo) was born in Skedsmo, Norway. He received his undergraduate degree in political economy from the University of Oslo in 1933. From 1933 to 1938 he served as a research assistant at the university's Institute of Economics, which had been established by RAGNAR FRISCH.

Haavelmo later described general economics in those days as having "lots of deep thoughts, but a lack of quantitative results." At Frisch's new institute, "The work of quantifying economic interrelations was taken up with great enthusiasm, and the volume of quantitative results grew very rapidly."

Researchers at the institute were trying to deduce cause-and-effect relationships from observations of economic activity. The most dangerous pitfall they faced was the problem of spurious correlation (the danger of mistaking a coincidence for an instance of cause and effect). Haavelmo later recalled that "Frisch used to imprint his warnings on this point upon his students by giving the following horrifying illustration. It can be observed that there is a high positive intercorrelation between the number of flies on the western coast of Norway and the number of tourists visiting that region. From this observation it is probably not a very good idea to try to promote tourism by breeding more flies."

TRYGVE HAAVELMO

At the institute, Haavelmo and the other researchers also worked on problems concerning the verification of economic theories. Unlike chemists or physicists, economists cannot conduct laboratory experiments. So how could economists prove or disprove statements about causal relationships? How could they decide which factors influenced a particular economic activity, and how could they most accurately measure each factor? The goal of econometrics—an approach pioneered by Frisch and JAN TINBERGEN, among others—was to resolve such questions of validity and verifiability by developing methods for expressing economic theories in mathematical and statistical formulas that could be empirically tested.

After five years of working under Frisch and a yearlong lectureship in statistics at the University of Aarhus in Denmark, Haavelmo received a scholarship to visit the United States in 1939. "For reasons beyond my control," he later explained, referring to the Nazi invasion of Norway in April 1940, "the visit lasted for seven years." During those years he continued his studies, first as a Rockefeller Fellow at Harvard University (1940–1942) and later as a research associate at the Cowles Commission for Research in Economics at the University of Chicago (1946–1947). He also worked for two years as a statistician in New York City and for a year as a commercial attaché at the Norwegian Embassy in Washington, D.C.

In 1946 the University of Oslo awarded Haavelmo his doctoral degree. He had earlier presented his dissertation, "The Probability Approach in Econometrics," at Harvard University (1941), and it had been published as a supplement to the journal *Econometrica* in 1944. Haavelmo's innov-

ative argument was that economists could overcome some of the inherent inexactness involved in measuring economic activities and in deducing theoretical hypotheses from their data by using probability theory and statistical methods.

Haavelmo's probability approach directly challenged the orthodox position held by most economists up until the 1930s. The traditionalists held that probabilities could not be usefully applied to economic data because probability distributions were not an accurate characterization of economic behavior in the real world. In his dissertation Haavelmo took the contrary view: "The question is not whether probabilities *exist* or not, but whether—if we proceed *as if* they existed—we are able to make statements about real phenomena that are 'correct for practical purposes.'" Probability distribution, he argued, could be a powerful analytic tool for economists, a useful abstraction that could help economists understand, explain, and forecast economic activity in the real world.

The particular statistical model Haavelmo proposed in his dissertation concerned the relationships between supply, demand, and prices. In classical economic theory, the influence of supply and demand on price is stated simply: When the supply of an item exceeds purchasers' demand for that item, the price of the item falls; when demand exceeds supply, the price rises. Similarly, changes in prices affect supply and demand: When price of an item rises, producers are motivated to produce more and the supply increases; when price falls, purchasers are motivated to buy more and demand increases.

But these observations do not help you very much if you are trying to discover if the quantity is high or the price has moved because of shifts in the supply or the demand. If both supply and demand curves remained stable, so would prices and quantities. If supply and demand changed at different times so that only one of them moved in any single time period, then the problem of learning which function had shifted to cause prices and quantities to move would be straightforward. Typically, however, both supply and demand are shifting simultaneously, creating a difficult problem of identifying the cause of any price or quantity change. Haavelmo argued that the methods of statistical probability could be used to solve this identification problem.

Though Haavelmo published several other papers in *Econometrica* during the 1940s, none of his later articles or books was to prove as influential as his dissertation.

Upon returning to Norway in 1947, Haavelmo served as a division head at the Ministry of Trade and Ministry of Finance. In 1948 he was appointed professor of economics at the University of Oslo.

At this point, he turned his attention away from econometrics and toward economic theory. In 1954 he published *A Study in the Theory of Economic Evolution,* a broad-ranging survey of the causes of economic inequality among highly industrialized and less-developed nations. At the time, the book was welcomed as a pioneering study of the relatively ignored area of economic underdevelopment. Though the mathematical models and theorems Haavelmo presented have been superseded by subsequent researchers, the text has been cited as a testimonial to his professional creativity and imagination.

In *A Study in the Theory of Investment* (1960), Haavelmo examined the relationships between the activities of individual households or companies and a national economy's rate of capital accumulation (the amount by which production exceeds consumption) and investment. Classical economists viewed the reduction of consumption as the key to capital accumulation, but John Maynard Keynes countered by arguing that frugality in itself would not necessarily lead to economic growth. Following his lead, modern economists have focused on the ways in which capital accumulation is affected by increased production and increased productivity. Haavelmo's study of the microeconomic (small-scale) basis of macroeconomic (national) investment activity contributed another piece to this neoclassical theory of capital accumulation.

An active and well-respected teacher, Haavelmo retired from the University of Oslo in 1979. Haavelmo was awarded the 1989 Nobel Prize in Economic Sciences "for his pioneering contributions to the development of econometrics." In presenting the award, Bengt-Christer Ysander of the Royal Swedish Academy of Sciences praised Haavelmo for having laid the foundations of modern econometric methods: "You have shown that—despite difficulties in performing controlled experiments—empirical estimates and tests of economic theories can be derived by statistical methods. Quantitative studies of economic relations, used today as bases for private and public decision making, are to large extent structured according to the methodological development you initiated."

Assar Lindbeck of the Royal Swedish Academy of Sciences cited the enormous influence Haavelmo's work has had on the practice of economic forecasting: "Every time you open a newspaper and see an analysis made of economic trends, how consumption changes if income is reduced by [budget or tax] policies, it is based on Haavelmo's econometric theories." Earlier Nobel laureates in economics enthusiastically concurred in Lindbeck's assessment. PAUL SAMUELSON

noted, "The whole modern stage in economics has tried to use statistics to test out different theories. It was Haavelmo who made the great breakthrough." LAWRENCE KLEIN commented that Haavelmo "set the whole tone for modern econometrics." "When you dig down to the foundations," ROBERT M. SOLOW noted, "you find Haavelmo."

Haavelmo is a member of the Norwegian Academy of Science and Letters, the Council of the Econometric Society, the American Economic Association, the Royal Danish Academy of Sciences and Letters, and the American Academy of Arts and Sciences. In 1979 he received the Fridtjof Nansen Award for Outstanding Research.

ABOUT: Business Week October 23, 1989; Encyclopedia of Economics; New Palgrave Dictionary; New York Times October 12, 1989; Washington Post October 12, 1989.

HITCHINGS, GEORGE H., JR.

(April 18, 1905–   )
Nobel Prize for Physiology or Medicine, 1988
(shared with Gertrude B. Elion and James Black)

The American pharmacologist George Herbert Hitchings Jr. was born in Hoquiam, Washington. He grew up in a variety of towns on the west coast of the United States, including Berkeley, San Diego, and Seattle. His father was a shipbuilder and marine architect, descended from a family of English loyalists who left the United States for Canada during the American Revolution. His mother, Lillian (Matthews) Hitchings, was descended from another shipbuilding family of English and Scottish ancestry. George Jr. was the youngest of their three children and the only boy. Later in life, he recalled that "when I was baptized, my father held me up and dedicated my life to the service of mankind."

His father died a lingering death when Hitchings was twelve years old, and Hitchings later wrote that "the deep impression made by this event turned my thoughts toward medicine." In high school, Louis Pasteur became his scientific role model: "The blending of Pasteur's basic research and practical results remained a goal throughout my career."

Hitchings entered the University of Washington as a premedical student but soon became a chemistry major. After graduating cum laude in 1927 and earning a master's degree in 1928, he enrolled at Harvard—first in the chemistry department and later in the biological chemistry department at the medical school.

Hitchings began working with the analytic chemist Cyrus Fiske and quickly became caught

GEORGE H. HITCHINGS JR.

up in Fiske's research. Fiske was one of a number of scientists who, in the late 1920s and early 1930s, were trying to trace the role of adenosine triphosphate (ATP) in muscles and metabolism. ATP is a member of the chemical class called purines. In his work for Fiske, Hitchings developed methods for analyzing very small quantities of purines.

Hitchings earned his Ph.D. in 1933 at the height of the Great Depression and had to wait until 1942 to be hired by Burroughs Wellcome Research Laboratories in Tuckahoe, New York. There, he founded the company's biochemistry department. For his staff, he hired the chemists Elvira Falco in 1942 and GERTRUDE B. ELION in 1944.

Hitchings now had the opportunity to revive his research. In 1940, the pharmacologists Donald Woods and Paul Fildes had suggested "a rational approach to research in chemotherapy" that they called the "antimetabolite principle." They argued that the best way to fight infectious diseases was to find compounds that are similar—but not identical—to a parasite's natural nutrients. Once these compounds were accepted by the parasite, they would disrupt its metabolism (preferably without affecting the metabolism of the host). At the time, Hitchings later noted, "the world of chemotherapy was sharply divided between the screeners and the fundamentalists. The screeners were dutifully poisoning mice with whatever came in hand . . . hop[ing] that if they tested enough compounds, sooner or later they would run across one that did more damage to the infecting organism than the host. The fundamentalists disdained all this as being devoid of intellectual interest. . . . Our group thought that some kind of middle course might be

possible, a course that would generate basic information which chemotherapy could then exploit."

Hitchings used his knowledge of purine chemistry as the basis for a study of the nucleic acids, which, as ALBRECHT KOSSEL had discovered at the turn of the century, are composed of purines and pyrimidines. Though the central, directing role of nucleic acids in the cell would not be established until after 1954 (when FRANCIS CRICK and JAMES D. WATSON determined the structure of DNA), scientists had realized for many years that nucleic acids were essential for cellular reproduction and growth. Hitchings and his colleagues observed that "parasitic tissues in general depend for survival on a more rapid growth, hence a more rapid synthesis of nucleic acid, than that of the host tissues," so nucleic acid antimetabolites should be good medicines. They wrote that "this argument applies equally well to bacterial, viral, rickettsial, and neoplastic diseases, so that, in a sense, one might say we have been searching for the philosopher's stone, the universal panacea, of the ancients."

Hitchings and his team made chemical variations on natural purines and pyrimidines, looking for artificial compounds that would enter and disable a parasite's nucleic acid-synthesizing machinery. By 1948 they had developed two promising leads: the purine analogue 2,6-diaminopurine, which showed some activity against leukemia, and pyrimidine variants called the diaminopyrimidines. Though Hitchings supervised the group, Elion was largely responsible for the purine work, while Falco and the chemist Peter Russell were responsible for the pyrimidines.

Hitchings's team soon discovered that their pyrimidine analogues were interfering with a particular enzyme in the nucleic-acid production pathway, called dihydrofolate reductase (DHFR). This was an important result, because though every organism has a DHFR, the enzyme varies considerably between species. It was therefore possible, in principle at least, to create an antimetabolite that would block the DHFR of a parasite but not that of a human being.

Their first success came in 1949 with the compound pyrimethamine (Daraprim), which is used to treat malaria. They soon produced another DHFR-blocking chemical, trimethoprim, which was called co-trimoxazolre (Septrin or Bactrim) when sold in combination with a sulfanilamide drug. (The sulfanilamides, discovered by GERHARD DOMAGK in the 1930s, worked by blocking a bacterium's synthesis of folic acid. As the subsequent research of ARTHUR KORNBERG showed, DHFR acts later along the same pathway, so the combination of trimethoprim and sulfanilamide was particularly effective.)

Meanwhile, Hitchings's and Elion's research on purine derivatives also started to bear fruit. Their original purine analogue, 2,6-diaminopurine, had too many side effects to be useful in human beings. In 1951, however, Hitchings, Elion, and their colleagues found a modified compound called 6-mercaptopurine (6-MP). Sold under the name Puri-Nethol as a treatment for leukemia, 6-MP was soon recognized as one of the safest and most effective antileukemic agents to have been discovered. Efforts to improve 6-MP further led to azathioprine (Imuran), used since 1962 to prevent the immunological rejection of transplanted organs (especially kidneys), and allopurinol (Zyloprim), which has been used since 1966 to treat gout.

In 1967 Hitchings became vice president of Burroughs Wellcome, and the next year the company moved from New York to the Research Triangle area of North Carolina. Though he now held an administrative position, Hitchings continued his interest in research, and he remained active even after his retirement in 1976. He and his team developed several other drugs during this period, the most important of which was acyclovir (Zovirax), the first effective antiviral agent, which was introduced in 1977 to treat infections of herpes and other viruses.

Hitchings and Elion shared the 1988 Nobel Prize for Physiology or Medicine with JAMES BLACK, whose work led to important drugs for the treatment of heart disease and gastric ulcers. According to Folke Sjöqvist of the Karolinska Institute, who presented the award, the three laureates had "succeeded in developing a rational approach to the discovery of new drugs, based upon basic scientific studies of biochemical and physiological processes." Hitchings, however, felt that his work had value beyond its establishment of new scientific principles. "I've had many awards," he said, "but my real awards have come from patients whose lives have been saved by the drugs I've invented."

Hitchings married M. Beverly Reimer, the daughter of a Boston minister, in 1933. They had two children, Laramie Ruth and Thomas Eldridge. Beverly Hitchings died in 1985 after a long illness, and Hitchings married the physician Joyce Carolyn Shaver four years later. Hitchings's main interests outside of scientific research are philanthropy and travel. By his own estimate, Hitchings has traveled "about one million miles all over [the] globe."

Hitchings's numerous awards include the Gairdner Award (1968), the Royal Society of London's Mullard Award (1976), and the Albert Schweitzer International Prize for Medicine (1989). He holds eleven honorary doctorates and is a member of the United States National Academy of Sciences, the Royal Society of London, the Royal Society of Medicine, the Royal Society of Chemistry, and many other scientific organizations. His philanthropic positions include that of founder and director of the Greater Triangle Community Foundation, and directorships of the United Way, the American Red Cross, and the Royal Society of Medicine Foundation. In addition, he has served since 1968 as director of the Burroughs Wellcome Fund, a nonprofit biomedical research foundation.

SELECTED WORKS: Inhibition of Folate Metabolism in Chemotherapy, 1983.

ABOUT: New Scientist October 22, 1988; New York Times October 18, 1988; New York Times Magazine January 29, 1989; Science October 28, 1988; Who's Who in America, 1990.

HUBER, ROBERT
(February 20, 1937–   )
Nobel Prize for Chemistry, 1988
(shared with Johann Deisenhofer and Hartmut Michel)

The German chemist Robert Huber (hōō' ber) was born in Munich, the son of Sebastian and Helene (Kebinger) Huber. His father worked as a bank clerk; his mother was a homemaker who raised Huber and his sister through the trying war years—a task he later described as "a continuous struggle for some milk and bread and search for air-raid shelters." Huber's education was interrupted for two of these years, 1945 and 1946, when the grammar school closed. He entered secondary school in 1947 at Munich's Humanistisches Karls-Gymnasium, where he had "intense" studies in Latin and Greek, some natural science, and the option of studying chemistry for a few hours every month. Huber became fascinated by chemistry, which he learned on his own by reading all the textbooks he could find.

In 1956 Huber entered the Technical Academy of Munich (later called the Technical University of Munich), supported by stipends from the Bavarian Ministry for Education and Culture and the Foundation for the Study of the German People. He joined the laboratory of the crystallographer W. Hoppe, where he investigated ecdysone, an insect metamorphosis hormone.

His work in Hoppe's lab familiarized Huber with the process of X-ray crystallography, a technique in which X rays of known wavelength are beamed at crystallized solids (materials that have regularly repeating molecular structures). By studying the patterns in which the rays are weakened or reinforced as they strike the crystal, the

ROBERT HUBER

crystallographer can determine the material's molecular makeup. The process of X-ray crystallography, developed in 1912 by MAX VON LAUE, has led to such major discoveries as the structure of DNA.

By means of a "simple crystallographic experiment," Huber determined the molecular weight and probable steroid nature of ecdysone. This work earned him a diploma in chemistry (the equivalent of a master's degree) in 1960. Huber continued to work with Hoppe, earning his Ph.D. three years later. He and Hoppe then returned to studying ecdysone and eventually developed an atom-by-atom account of its structure. "This discovery," he wrote later, "convinced me of the power of crystallography and led me to continue in this field."

Huber was thus launched on what has been his life's work, exploring the structure of biological macromolecules. In 1967 he and his colleague H. Formanek began crystallographic studies of the insect protein erythrocruorin. The studies showed the insect protein to be remarkably similar to globin proteins in mammals.

In 1968 Huber was appointed a lecturer at the Technical University of Munich. In 1971 he had two job offers: the chair of structural biology at the Biozentrum at the University of Basel and a directorship at the Max Planck Institute for Biochemistry at Martinsried, just outside Munich. Huber accepted the latter position and continued his affiliation with the Technical University of Munich, where he became a full professor in 1976.

At the Martinsried laboratory, Huber headed a team of researchers who explored the structure of a variety of macromolecules. The team also re-

fined and developed crystallographic techniques, including computer programs that aided in their work, which are now used in laboratories around the world. With time, Huber's crystallographic laboratory became internationally renowned for, in the words of the *New York Times,* "solv[ing] problems that other scientists thought were too difficult to tackle."

The formidable reputation of Huber's laboratory led HARTMUT MICHEL, a biochemist who also worked at Martinsried, to ask Huber for assistance in completing a project relating to photosynthesis. Photosynthesis—the process by which plants convert energy from the sun into nutrients—is performed by a protein that straddles the outer membrane of a cell. The process begins when a photon (a particle of light) excites a molecule of chlorophyll that lies near the inner surface of the membrane. The chlorophyll releases an electron, which moves through a part of the membrane referred to as the reaction center and toward the membrane's outer surface. This reaction creates a charge separation (a difference in electrical charge) across the membrane, which in turn provides stored energy to drive the synthesis of nutritional substances.

In order to learn more about how photosynthesis occurs, Michel had begun to study the photosynthetic reaction center of the purple bacterium *Rhodopseudomonas viridis.* This complex molecule, made up of four different proteins and fourteen other components, is bound to the bacterium's membrane. Earlier research had identified the proteins and other components that made up *Rh. viridis*'s photosynthetic reaction center, but its exact structure—as well as the path electrons followed as they moved through it—remained obscure.

The usual way to determine the structure of a protein is to combine the protein with water. Water causes the protein molecule to take the form of a crystal lattice (a solid, three-dimensional, repeating molecular structure). By analyzing the lattice by means of X-ray crystallography, a researcher can study the protein atom by atom. Unlike most proteins, however, membrane proteins—the proteins that make up the photosynthetic reaction center—are not water-soluble; they must interact with water as a part of their function. Therefore, most researchers had considered the crystallization of a membrane protein impossible.

After four years, however, Michel developed an additive that could take the place of water in the crystal lattice, thus making it possible to crystallize a membrane protein. In 1981 Michel produced the first high-quality crystals of the *Rh. viridis* photosynthetic reaction center. In 1982 he reported his results at a seminar organized by Huber.

After announcing his achievement, Michel was unsure how to proceed. He did not feel that he had the knowledge and experience necessary to identify and describe the more than 10,000 atoms that made up the photosynthetic reaction center. It was at this point that he asked Huber for help. Huber responded by assigning JOHANN DEISENHOFER, a talented crystallographer in his department, to work with Michel in analyzing the crystals. Deisenhofer, Michel, and others spent three years analyzing vast amounts of data; finally, in 1985, they completed the task. For the first time in history, they had provided a complete, three-dimensional analysis of a membrane protein.

For his contribution to the analysis of the photosynthetic reaction center, Huber shared the 1988 Nobel Prize for Chemistry with Deisenhofer and Michel. In part, the prize recognized Michel's discovery of a technique for crystallizing membrane-bound proteins—a technique that suddenly made it possible to analyze a whole range of biologically important materials.

More important, however, according to Bo G. Malmström of the Swedish Academy of Sciences, the work of Huber, Deisenhofer, and Michel in analyzing the photosynthetic reaction center "has given theoretical chemists an indispensable tool in their efforts to understand . . . biologic electron transfer," such as that which takes place in photosynthesis. It has, in fact, given scientists a deeper understanding of photosynthesis itself, which Malmström has called "the most important chemical reaction in the biosphere of our earth."

The work of Huber and his colleagues "really has revitalized investigation in photosynthesis," according to Dr. Wayne Hendriksson of Columbia University. It has helped verify similarities between green plant and bacterial photosynthesis, opened up a range of new questions for exploration, and led some scientists, including Malmström, to predict the eventual development of artificial photosynthetic reactions.

An untiring worker, Huber typically spends ten hours in his laboratory on Monday through Saturday, then returns for a half-day on Sunday. He married Christa Essig in 1960, and the couple has four children—Ulrike, Martin, Robert, and Julia. The three oldest are grown and have studied economics; Huber retains some hope that the youngest may pursue a career in science.

Huber's achievements have led to his receiving such awards as the E. K. Frey Medal of the Society for Surgery in Germany (1972), the Otto Warburg Medal of the Society for Biological Chemistry in Germany (1977), the Emil von Behring Medal from Marburg University (1982), the Keilin Medal of the London Biochemical Society (1987), and the Richard Kuhn Medal of the

German Chemists' Society (1987). In 1988 he was named a member of the Bavarian Academy of Sciences. Huber has received two honorary doctorates, one from the Catholic University of Louvain, Belgium (1987), and the other from the University of Ljubljana, Yugoslavia (1989). He belongs to the German Chemical Society, the Society for Biological Chemistry in Germany, the European Molecular Biology Organization (EMBO), and the EMBO council. He is also an honorary member of the American Society of Biological Chemists and the Swedish Society for Biophysics.

ABOUT: New Scientist October 29, 1988; New York Times October 20, 1988; Science November 4, 1988; Who's Who, 1990.

KENDALL, HENRY W.
(December 9, 1926–)
Nobel Prize for Physics, 1990
(shared with Jerome I. Friedman and Richard E. Taylor)

The American physicist Henry Way Kendall was born in Boston, Massachusetts, the eldest child of businessman Henry P. Kendall and the former Evelyn Way. In the early 1930s his parents moved the family, which by then included a younger brother and sister, to Deerfield, Massachusetts. Kendall graduated from the Deerfield Academy, a college preparatory school, in 1945. "My academic work was poor," he later explained, "for I was more interested . . . in things mechanical, chemical, and electrical." Kendall's father encouraged his young son's many explorations "except when they involved hazards, such as the point, at about age eleven, when I embarked on the culture of pathogenic bacteria."

The summer after his high school graduation, Kendall entered the United States Merchant Marine Academy. "I was there, in basic training, when the first atom bombs were exploded over Japan. I was unaware of the human side of these events and only recall a feeling that some of the last secrets of nature had been penetrated and that little would be left to explore."

Kendall resigned from the academy in 1946 and entered Amherst College. Although he majored in mathematics, he was also interested in history, English, biology, and especially physics. He and a college companion took advantage of summer breaks to run a diving and salvage operation. Kendall later recalled, "We wrote our first books after that; one on shallow water diving, another on underwater photography, with a considerable success for both. These activities, mostly self-taught, were a good introduction to two skills very helpful in later experimental work: seeing projects

HENRY W. KENDALL

through to successful completion and doing them safely."

In 1950, after receiving his bachelor's degree in mathematics, Kendall entered the Massachusetts Institute of Technology (MIT) in Cambridge. In 1954 he earned a Ph.D. in nuclear and atomic physics. He spent the next two years as a National Science Foundation postdoctoral fellow at MIT and at Brookhaven National Laboratory in New York. In 1956 he joined the faculty of Stanford University's physics department and became a member of the Stanford research group headed by ROBERT HOFSTADTER. Hofstadter's group was studying the structure of the subatomic particles called protons and neutrons.

Until the 1930s physicists believed that there were only three components of the atom—the negatively charged electron, the positively charged proton, and the uncharged neutron—and that these three particles were the fundamental particles of nature. Further study of the atom showed that these beliefs were incorrect; in fact, there are hundreds of different subatomic particles, such as muons, pions, baryons, kaons, and neutrinos. As more particles were identified, physicists became convinced that there must be something still smaller and more fundamental common to all these particles. As Cecilia Jarlskog of the Royal Swedish Academy of Sciences later asked, "Was there a hidden order not yet discovered by man? There could be order but only at the price of postulating an additional, deeper level in nature—perhaps the ultimate level—consisting of only a few building blocks." Although at the time, as Kendall later explained, "the very notion of 'internal structure' [of subatomic particles] was foreign," Hof-

stadter's group and other scientists struggled to find out whether there are any such building blocks inside subatomic particles.

One common way to study particle structure was through electron-scattering experiments. Electron scattering involves bombarding atoms with beams of high-speed electrons and observing the motion, or "scattering," of the bombarding electrons as they emerge from collisions with the target atoms. The higher the speed of the incoming electrons, the farther into the target atoms they can penetrate and the more information scientists can obtain from their behavior. At the highest speeds, these collisions also break apart the target atoms, scattering and revealing their particles. This is called inelastic scattering.

To speed the motion of the bombarding particles used in scattering experiments, physicists use particle accelerators, devices that propel the particle along a straight line (linear accelerator) or in a circle (cyclotron) toward the target atoms. When Kendall joined the Stanford physics department, it had a 300-foot-long linear accelerator.

It was during his years at Stanford that Kendall first met and began working with JEROME I. FRIEDMAN. In 1960 Friedman took the position of assistant professor of physics at MIT, and a year later Kendall did the same. At around the same time, Kendall became troubled by the buildup of nuclear arsenals by the United States and the Soviet Union. From 1960 to 1971 he served as a member of the Jason Group, a group of academic scientists advising the United States Department of Defense. That experience gave him, he later recalled, "the opportunity to observe the operation of the defense establishment from the 'inside,' both in the nuclear weapons area and in the counterinsurgency activities that later expanded to be the United States military involvement in Southeast Asia."

In 1963 Kendall and Friedman began a collaboration with Stanford physicist RICHARD E. TAYLOR on a new linear accelerator. The Stanford Linear Accelerator Center (SLAC), built under the direction of Wolfgang K. H. (Pief) Panofsky, is a 2-mile-long linear particle accelerator located near the Stanford campus. This was a vast improvement over its 300-foot precursor. With this new accelerator, the three physicists could conduct scattering experiments at energy levels never before possible and delve even deeper into the makeup of subatomic particles.

In 1964 MURRAY GELL-MANN, a physicist from the California Institute of Technology (Caltech), devised a way to categorize and classify the hundreds of subatomic particles that had been discovered. He theorized a model of these particles, picturing them as clusters of smaller particles, which he named quarks. (He chose the name from a passage in James Joyce's *Finnegans Wake*.) Six types of quarks, Gell-Mann theorized, make up the fundamental components of such subatomic particles as protons and neutrons. (Essentially the same model was proposed independently by physicist George Zweig.) Just as atoms are categorized and classified by the number of electrons and protons they have, subatomic particles can be classified by the number and types of quarks they have. Gell-Mann's model was widely accepted as a useful way to classify particles, but because no one was able to observe anything as small as quarks in experiments, some physicists (including Gell-Mann) thought of them not as real particles but as "mathematical quantities" useful for modeling particle behavior.

Using the new state-of-the-art SLAC, Kendall and his colleagues were able to observe the first traces of quarks and confirm Gell-Mann's theory. In a series of electron-scattering experiments conducted at the SLAC from 1967 to 1973, they sent beams of electrons traveling at nearly the speed of light—faster than ever before possible—toward targets of liquid hydrogen or deuterium. (Hydrogen and deuterium were chosen for these experiments because they have the simplest nuclei: hydrogen, a single proton; deuterium, a proton plus a neutron.)

At this new speed, the electrons were able to penetrate to the center of the protons or neutrons. There, the electrons hit some hard particles that scattered them at large angles relative to their original direction. These particles could only be Gell-Mann's quarks. Along with the quarks, the three physicists also identified particles called gluons, electrically neutral particles that bind quarks together. "The picture of [subatomic particles] . . . as diffuse, structureless objects was gone for good, replaced by a successful, nearly complete theory," Kendall concluded.

Kendall, Friedman, and Taylor received the 1990 Nobel Prize for Physics for providing evidence that quarks are indeed actual particles. "A new rung on the ladder of creation had revealed itself, and a new epoch in the history of physics had begun," noted Cecilia Jarlskog of the Royal Swedish Academy of Sciences when presenting the award. All three physicists noted that their accomplishments would have been impossible without the work of Panofsky and the SLAC. "The linear accelerator that provided the electron beam employed in the inelastic scattering experiments was, and remains . . . a device unique among high-energy particle accelerators," Kendall acknowledged when discussing their work.

In 1967 Kendall was made a full professor at MIT. In 1969 he became a founding member of the Union for Concerned Scientists (UCS), a public interest group that, Kendall explained, "presses for control of technologies that may be harmful or dangerous. . . . The activities of the organization are part of a slowly growing interest among scientists to take more responsibility for helping society control the exceedingly powerful technologies that scientific research has spawned." Kendall has been chairman of the UCS since 1974.

Kendall is currently collaborating with Friedman on the design of monitoring equipment that will be used with the Superconducting Super Collider. The Super Collider, to be built near Waxahachie, Texas, by the year 2000, will be the largest particle accelerator in the world.

Kendall was married to Ann C. G. Pine in 1972. That marriage ended in divorce in 1988. He retains the love for the outdoors he exhibited in college and enjoys mountaineering and mountain photography. He has gone on climbing expeditions in Yosemite Valley, the Andes, the Himalayas, and the Arctic.

Kendall has served on numerous scientific committees and panels, including the planning committees of the National Academy of Sciences and the American Physics Society. He was a member of the board of directors of the Bulletin of the Atomic Scientists from 1975 to 1984 and has been a member of the board of the Arms Control Association since 1979. Among Kendall's many awards are an honorary doctorate from Amherst College in 1975, a 1976 public service award from the Federation of American Scientists, the Leo Szilard Award (shared with HANS A. BETHE) from the American Physical Society in 1981, and the Bertrand Russell Society Award in 1982. In 1989 he received the W. K. H. Panofsky Prize (shared with Friedman and Taylor) from the American Physical Society. He has been a fellow of the American Academy of Arts and Sciences since 1982, a fellow of the American Physical Society since 1985, and a fellow of the American Association for the Advancement of Science since 1988.

ABOUT: American Men and Women of Science, 1990; Los Angeles Times October 18, 1990; Newsweek October 29, 1990; New York Times October 18, 1990; Science October 26, 1990; Science News October 27, 1990.

LEDERMAN, LEON M.

(July 15, 1922–)
Nobel Prize for Physics, 1988
(shared with Melvin Schwartz and Jack
   Steinberger)

The American physicist Leon Max Lederman was born in New York City, the elder son of Russian immigrants. His father, Morris Lederman, ran a hand laundry; his mother, Minna (Rosenberg)

LEON M. LEDERMAN

Lederman, was a homemaker. Lederman was educated entirely in New York City: he attended elementary school at P.S. 92 in 1927, graduated from James Monroe High School in the Bronx in 1939, and completed a B.S. at City College of New York in 1943. Although his degree was in chemistry, his scientific interests had already begun to shift toward physics.

After spending three years in the United States Army during World War II, Lederman returned to New York and entered Columbia University's physics department, where what has been called a "unique postwar flowering of physics talent" had just begun to blossom. (The work of Columbia physicists over the next fifteen years would eventually earn six independent Nobel Prizes.) Lederman specialized in particle physics (the study of the constituents of the atom and its nucleus) and completed his doctoral thesis in 1951. Then, as he recalls, "I was invited to stay on, which I did, for the next twenty-eight years." He became a full professor in 1958.

Lederman completed the experiment that brought him the Nobel Prize relatively early in his career. By the late 1950s, scientists were aware of the existence of four fundamental forces that govern the physical interactions of matter: gravitation, electromagnetism, the strong nuclear force, and the weak nuclear force. The latter two forces operate only at the subatomic level: the strong force affects the interactions of protons and neutrons, and the weak force affects the nuclear interactions of less massive particles, such as electrons.

Gravitation, the weakest of the four forces, does not play any significant role on the subatomic scale. The effects at short distances of electromag-

netic and strong nuclear interactions can be experimentally investigated by the use of beams of particles, such as protons and electrons, accelerated in machines such as cyclotrons and synchrotrons. Although the weak nuclear force was known to be responsible for one form of radioactivity, called beta decay, no one had gathered any information about the weak nuclear force by using the technique of colliding particle beams. One difficulty was that the weak force was masked by the much stronger electromagnetism and the strong nuclear force.

During a coffee-hour discussion in 1959, TSUNG-DAO LEE, a colleague of Lederman's in the Columbia physics department, challenged his colleagues to come up with a way to observe and measure the weak force in collision. Thinking about the challenge later that night, MELVIN SCHWARTZ, another Columbia physicist, realized that the best promise for a solution lay in the neutrino.

Neutrinos are particles with no electrical charge and virtually no mass. They are therefore not affected by either the electromagnetic force or the strong force. They rarely interact with other particles—billions pass unnoticed through every square centimeter of the earth every day—but the rare neutrino interactions that do occur involve only the weak force. Schwartz realized that if enough neutrinos could be gathered in one place, the probability of interaction would rise. Therefore, if he could create a concentrated beam of neutrinos, he might be able to study uncontaminated weak force interactions.

Schwartz discussed his ideas with Lederman and another colleague, JACK STEINBERGER. "We yelled and screamed at each other for a while," said Lederman, "and then we decided, 'Hey! This is a doable experiment.'" The first step of the experiment—conducted at Brookhaven National Laboratory's newly completed alternating gradient synchrotron—involved firing a beam of protons at a beryllium target. The energy of the protons was large enough to tear the nuclei of the beryllium atoms apart, creating a flood of subatomic particles. Among those particles were pions, which decay (break down) in one hundred-millionth of a second into neutrinos and muons. (A muon is a particle similar to, but much heavier than, an electron.)

The next task was to eliminate all the particles except the neutrinos. Steinberger and his colleagues blocked the particles' path with a 10-ton wall of steel salvaged from a scrapped battleship. All the particles except the neutrinos were blocked by the steel; the neutrinos passed straight through. The result was a neutrino beam.

This new tool could be used for investigating the weak force. It also proved useful for investigating the neutrino itself, about which relatively little was known. Physicists, for example, had suggested that there might be two kinds of neutrinos. That is, the neutrino formed from the decay of a pion might be different from the neutrino produced by beta decay. (In beta decay, a neutron decays into a proton, an electron, and a neutrino.) The two kinds of neutrinos were referred to as the muon type and the electron type, because the first—which resulted from pion decay—was always accompanied by a muon, and the second—which resulted from beta decay—was always accompanied by an electron. Steinberger and his colleagues realized that their neutrino beam was ideally suited to test this two-neutrino hypothesis because the neutrinos in the beam were all necessarily of the muon type—that is, they were all produced by the decay of pions.

To conduct the experiment, Lederman, Schwartz, and Steinberger built a 10-ton spark chamber containing ninety aluminum plates and focused the neutrino beam on it. (A spark chamber is a detection device in which particles are shot through neon gas, creating electric currents that cause the gas to glow. Different types of particles create different types of visible "trails" in the chamber.) Every time a neutrino collided with the nucleus of an aluminum atom, it would give off particles that could be identified by their distinctive trails. If the collisions yielded equal numbers of muons and electrons, the experimenters could conclude that the neutrinos associated with these particles did not differ. If the collisions yielded no electrons, however, the experimenters would have confirmed the two-neutrino hypothesis (according to which collisions from muon-type neutrinos should generate only muons).

During the eight months in which they conducted the experiment, approximately 100,000 billion neutrinos passed through the spark chamber. Fewer than 60 of those neutrinos collided with other particles. Significantly, however, every one of these collisions produced a muon rather than an electron. The scientists had confirmed the existence of two distinct kinds of neutrinos.

Both the method and the results of their experiment had enormous repercussions, as Gösta Ekspong of the Royal Swedish Academy of Sciences recognized in awarding the three scientists the 1988 Nobel Prize for Physics. Crediting them with discovering "a new law of nature," he noted that confirmation of the two-neutrino hypothesis made an "indispensable" contribution to the development of the standard model. The standard model is a continually evolving theory describing the functions and behavior of all subatomic particles. Lederman has described it as "the grand theory which will ultimately lead us to a unification of all the forces in nature."

In addition, the neutrino-beam technique itself has become a mainstay at accelerators throughout the world. As Ekspong put it, the experiment "started a bold new line of research, which gave rich fruit from the beginning."

Lederman accepted the award for the three scientists, expressing their "feelings of pleasure and gratitude for the decision to award us the 1988 Nobel Prize in physics, thus making us experts on the Brazilian debt, women's fashions, and social security." On a more serious note, he conveyed his longstanding concern with what he has termed the "crisis in public understanding of science." As he put it in his Nobel lecture, "How does one make this research comprehensible to ordinary people? . . . This is a dilemma and an anguish for all scientists because the public understanding of science is *no longer* a luxury of cultural engagement, but it is an *essential* requirement for survival in our increasingly technological age." Since he received the Nobel Prize, Lederman's interest in this problem has led him to focus his attention on teaching. Currently a professor at the University of Chicago, he works with both graduates and undergraduates, science and nonscience majors. He also helped found and is on the board of the Illinois Mathematics and Science Academy, a three-year residential public school for gifted children.

Lederman has had a distinguished career in the years since he completed the two-neutrino experiment. He maintained an active involvement in particle experiments at CERN (European Center for Nuclear Research) from the late 1950s through the mid-1970s, directed Columbia's Nevis Laboratory from 1961 to 1978, and became director of the Fermi National Accelerator Laboratory (Fermilab) in 1979. He has described his attitude toward his work by saying, "Part of being a scientist is compulsive dedication—the insistence on working without rest until you get what you're after." His intense determination has created remarkable results; colleagues believe that he could have won a Nobel Prize for any of a number of his groundbreaking discoveries.

Lederman has three children from his marriage to Florence Gordon, from whom he was divorced in 1981. His daughter Rena is an anthropologist; his son, Jesse, an investment banker; and his daughter Rachel, a lawyer. Lederman married Ellen Carr in 1981. They live in Batavia, Illinois, near Fermilab, from which Lederman retired in 1989.

Lederman has received fellowships from the Ford and Guggenheim foundations (1958), the Ernest Kempton Adams Foundation (1961), and the National Science Foundation (1965). He has earned the National Medal of Science (1965) and the Wolf Prize for Physics (1982). Institutions that have awarded him honorary doctorates include City College of New York (1981), the University of Chicago (1983), the Illinois Institute of Technology (1987), Carnegie Mellon University (1988), and the University of Pisa (1989).

SELECTED WORKS: From Quarks to the Cosmos, 1989.

ABOUT: New Scientist October 29, 1988; New York Times October 20, 1988; Who's Who in America, 1990.

LEHN, JEAN-MARIE
(September 30, 1939–)
Nobel Prize for Chemistry, 1987
(shared with Donald J. Cram and Charles J.
    Pedersen)

The French chemist Jean-Marie Pierre Lehn (lān) was born in the Alsatian city of Rosheim to Pierre Lehn, a baker and organist, and Marie (Salomon) Lehn. He attended high school at the Collège Freppel, where he studied classics, languages, philosophy, and chemistry and received his diploma in both philosophy and experimental sciences in 1957. He continued his studies at the University of Strasbourg, where a young professor named Guy Ourisson stimulated his interest in organic chemistry. He became especially interested in the experimental side of organic chemistry, which seemed to have the power, he wrote later, "to convert . . . complicated substances into one another following well-defined rules and routes."

After obtaining his bachelor's degree in 1960, Lehn joined Ourisson's laboratory at the National Center for Scientific Research. In Ourisson's lab, he explored the physical and chemical properties of triterpenes, enzymes used in the synthesis of vitamin A. He published his first paper in 1961 and earned his Ph.D. in 1963. He spent the next year as a visiting researcher at Harvard University, working with R. B. WOODWARD on the synthesis of vitamin B_{12} and studying quantum mechanics with ROALD HOFFMANN.

After his year in the United States, Lehn returned to Strasbourg and decided to specialize in physical organic chemistry, hoping to combine his interests in organic chemistry and physics. Recalling his early training in biology and philosophy, he began to wonder how a chemist might contribute to studies of biological processes.

The foundation of biological processes, of course, is chemical: the ability of molecules to recognize each other allows them to interact in the ways that make life possible. The work of proteins, enzymes, and antigens—even the transcription of the genetic code—takes place through highly specific and selective molecular interactions. In order

JEAN-MARIE LEHN

to explore these interactions, Lehn began studying the human nervous system. He understood that the nervous system worked through a chemical process that distributed sodium and potassium ions across membranes. Ions that cannot normally penetrate membranes bind selectively with "carrier" molecules, creating a compound that can then pass through. Lehn reasoned that if such a compound can occur through natural processes, he could develop an artificial compound that would do the same thing. Such an artificial compound would have great value to the pharmaceutical industry because it would be cheaper, more stable, and more readily available than its naturally occurring counterpart.

In 1966 Lehn was promoted to assistant professor in the chemistry department at the University of Strasbourg. By 1967 his work on the human nervous system had advanced considerably, developing into what he would later call supramolecular chemistry. Supramolecular chemistry is the chemistry of the intermolecular bond, the process by which molecules recognize and react to each other. Lehn's work in this field led to a promotion in 1970 to associate professor and, later that same year, to full professor.

Lehn continued to explore different aspects of supramolecular chemistry. He became involved in the field of artificial photosynthesis, investigating how plants store and chemically convert solar energy. He also worked on developing supramolecular catalysts that act similarly to natural enzymes.

A breakthrough in the area of supramolecular chemistry occurred in 1967, when CHARLES J. PEDERSEN, an American industrial chemist, published the results of work he had begun in 1960.

Pedersen reported that he had synthesized a new type of molecule whose distinctive shape reminded him of a royal crown. (Because this molecule belonged to the chemical group known as ethers, Pedersen called it a crown ether.) The shape of any molecule is determined by the way its constituent atoms combine with each other. In some molecules, atoms attach in long chains. In others, they form the shape of a cross or a pyramid. In Pedersen's crown ether, atoms of oxygen and carbon combined in an essentially ringlike shape.

Pedersen had discovered that the ringlike shape of a crown ether allows it to bind easily with a metal ion. When a crown ether comes in contact with a suitable ion, the ion falls into, and is trapped inside, the ring. By stringing together different atoms in different combinations, Pedersen could vary the shape of the crown ether. He thus was able to design different crown ethers to "select" different ions with a high degree of precision.

Pedersen's crown ethers had practical applications in the laboratory: they were the first synthetic compounds that could form stable complexes with sodium, potassium, and other alkali metal ions that had been previously difficult to bind. More important, however, was their theoretical significance: it was shown that the physical *shape* of a molecule— not just its electrostatic charges—was involved in binding it to other molecules.

Lehn read about Pedersen's work in 1967 and immediately began to elaborate on it by expanding the crown into three dimensions. Lehn realized that crown ethers react with other molecules at only a few contact points, and that a molecule with more contact points would be more selective. For example, a molecule that is three-dimensional and has a cavity would be more selective than a flat or convex molecule.

In 1969 Lehn succeeded in producing such elaborate three-dimensional molecules in the laboratory. Because these structures, which he called cryptands, were more rigid and complex than crown ethers, they resembled biological "locks" that could be fitted only by very specific molecular "keys." During the same period, DONALD J. CRAM, an American chemist who had no connection with Lehn, made similar strides in increasing molecular selectivity. Both scientists were able to develop synthetic molecules that, to some extent, mimic the actions of naturally occurring enzymes.

In 1979 Lehn was elected to the chair of Chemistry of Molecular Interactions at the Collège de France in Paris; in 1980 he took charge of the chemistry laboratory. He still directs that lab and the one at Strasbourg. He also has held visiting professorships at the Swiss Federal Institute of Technology (ETH) in Zurich and at the universities of Cambridge, Barcelona, and Frankfurt.

Pedersen, Cram, and Lehn shared the 1987 Nobel Prize for Chemistry "for achievements in the development and use of molecules that can recognize each other and choose with which other molecules they will form complexes." As Salo Gronowitz of the Royal Swedish Academy of Sciences said in his presentation speech, "Through their work the laureates laid the foundation to what today is one of the most expansive chemical research areas. . . . Lehn calls it supramolecular chemistry. Their research has been of enormous importance for the development of coordination chemistry, organic synthesis, analytical chemistry, bioinorganic and bioorganic chemistry; it is no longer science fiction to prepare supermolecules which are better and more versatile catalysts than the highly specialized enzymes."

The work of Lehn, Cram, and Pedersen promises to have significant practical applications in the future. Lehn, for example, produced a synthetic molecule that acts as a "host" for acetylcholine, one of the most important substances in the chemical process that sends messages through the nervous system to the human brain. This research raises the possibility of creating totally artificial enzymes with clear advantages over the natural substances that control the destinies of cells. Artificial enzymes would be more stable, and might also be more selective, than naturally occurring enzymes. They could be used to treat health problems, synthesize pharmaceuticals, and catalyze chemical reactions that up to now have been difficult to reproduce in the laboratory.

The laureates' work also makes possible the chemical separation of substances with greater precision than was possible before. Crown ethers can already be used to remove metallic impurities or to reclaim expensive metals from mixtures. More highly selective molecules, such as those developed by Lehn, someday may be able to extract radioactive or toxic substances from soil, water, air, or living tissue.

In 1965 Lehn married Sylvie Lederer, with whom he had two sons. Lehn has played the piano since childhood, and music remains his main interest outside of science.

In addition to the Nobel Prize, Lehn has received the Bronze, Silver, and Gold medals of the National Center for Scientific Research (1963, 1972, 1981), the Gold Medal of the Pontifical Academy of Sciences (1981), the Pierre Bruylants Medal (1981), the Paracelsus Prize of the Swiss Chemical Society (1982), the badge of a chevalier of the Legion of Honor (1983), the Prize of the CEA, awarded by the French Academy of Sciences (1984), the Prize of the Alsace Foundation (1986), the George Kenner Prize, University of Liverpool (1987), the Sigillum Magnum, University of Bologna (1988), the badge of an officer of the Legion of Honor (1988), and the Vermeil Medal of the City of Paris (1989), among others. He is a member of the United States National Academy of Sciences; the American Academy of Arts and Sciences; the Royal Netherlands Academy of Arts and Sciences; the German Academy of Leopoldina Naturalists; the Accademia Nazionale dei Lincei; the Union des Physiciens; the Institut de France, Académie des Sciences; the American Philosophical Society; the Royal Society of Chemistry of Belgium and Great Britain; and the Académie d'Alsace. Lehn holds honorary degrees from the Hebrew University of Jerusalem (1964), the University of Madrid (1985), the Georg-August University of Göttingen (1987), the University of Brussels (1987), and Iraklion University in Greece (1989).

ABOUT: International Who's Who, 1990; New Scientist October 22, 1987; New York Times October 15, 1987; Science October 15, 1987.

MAHFOUZ, NAGUIB
(December 11, 1911–)
Nobel Prize for Literature, 1988

The Egyptian writer Naguib Mahfouz (mä fōōz'), sometimes spelled Najib Mahfuz, is generally credited with bringing the Arabic novel to maturity. He has lived in Cairo since his birth in 1911. Indeed, he has almost never left his native land, having traveled abroad only once, when he went on official business to Yugoslavia. Even when Mahfouz won the Nobel Prize for Literature in 1988, he did not go to Sweden to receive the award. Instead, his daughters, Om Kalsoum Naguib Mahfouz and Fatma Naguib Mahfouz, accepted the prize for him, while a friend delivered his address to the Swedish Academy.

Mahfouz grew up in a suburban Cairo neighborhood, the son of Abdel Aziz Ibrahim, a merchant, and Fatma Mostapha Mahfouz. Little else is known about his early years, in part because he rarely gives interviews. Yet the city of Cairo, as well as the culture of Egypt, clearly captured the love and imagination of this prolific writer. He has set virtually all of his more than forty novels, short story collections, and short plays in his native city, and he has acknowledged the importance of the Islamic and Pharaonic civilizations in which he grew up. In his Nobel lecture, he wrote, "It was my fate . . . to be born in the lap of these two civilizations, and to absorb their milk, to feed on their literature and art. From the inspiration of all this— as well as my own anxieties—words bedewed from me."

NAGUIB MAHFOUZ

Mahfouz began writing fiction in the early 1930s, while he was completing a degree in philosophy at the University of Cairo. He published *Whisper of Madness,* his first novel, in 1939, five years after entering the Egyptian civil service, where he continued to work full-time until 1972. Between 1944 and 1952, he produced a series of works that made his reputation in Egypt and the rest of the Arab world. In his fiction of that period, including the novels *Midaq Alley* and *The Beginning and the End,* Mahfouz captured the struggles of the middle and lower classes of Cairo during a time of social upheaval. His social-realist style served as a model for a generation of Arab writers to follow.

The work of this period culminated in a series of three long novels, *Palace Walk, Palace of Desire,* and *Sugar Street,* that tell the story of a Cairo family between the two world wars. Completed in 1952 but not published until 1956 and 1957, these novels, sometimes called the Cairo Trilogy, earned Mahfouz the Egyptian State Prize for Literature in 1957 and made him the most important figure in Arabic fiction. The novels also offered Egyptians perhaps the first vivid fictional portrayal of the political and social trends, confusions, and contradictions that they had experienced in the first half of the century. Professor Sasson Somekh of Tel Aviv University noted, "No future student of Egyptian politics, society, or folklore will be able to overlook the material embodied in Mahfouz's trilogy."

The middle of the twentieth century was a tumultuous time in Egyptian history. Before the turn of the century, Egypt had borrowed large sums from Great Britain and other European countries. When a nationalist revolt occurred in Egypt in

1881, Great Britain took control. The country remained under British rule until 1922, when it became an independent monarchy under King Fuad. In 1937 Fuad was succeeded by his son Farouk, a much less popular leader. Then, in 1952, the Egyptian army, demoralized by its defeat in the 1948 war with Israel, seized power from King Farouk. The following year, Egypt became a republic and elected General Muhammad Naguib, the leader of the revolt, to be its first president. In 1954 Colonel Gamal Abdel Nasser removed Naguib from office and assumed the presidency. The years that followed were marked by international conflicts (especially with Israel) and domestic unrest.

The revolution of 1952 marked the beginning of a seven-year hiatus in Mahfouz's fiction writing. Some have attributed this break in an otherwise prolific career to his uncertainties about the new social and political situation. (The change of government had left many Egyptians unclear about their country's future direction.) Others attribute Mahfouz's fallow period to the sheer amount of work he had to do in his post at the Ministry of Culture, where he took an active role in the development of Egyptian cinema. When he did write again, however, his work contrasted markedly with his earlier novels. *The Children of Gebelawi,* published in serial form by the Cairo newspaper *Al-Ahram* in 1959, presented a complex view of the roles of religion and science in the modern world and included disguised but easily recognizable characters based on Adam, Satan, Jesus, Mohammed, and other major figures of Judaism, Islam, and Christianity. The novel's treatment of religious subjects was condemned as blasphemy, and the novel has still not been published as a book in Egypt.

With *The Children of Gebelawi,* Mahfouz broadened his range of novelistic techniques, moving from the objective realism prominent in his early works to a closer focus on characters' internal worlds, which he portrayed vividly through the use of interior monologue and stream of consciousness. His style also became allegorical and symbolic, with much of the symbolism conveying his social concerns and frequently concealing political judgments that showed his disillusionment with the outcome of the revolution. Some critics have in fact suggested that his reliance on symbolism during this time reflected not just an artistic choice but a well-founded fear that the Nasser government would censor his work.

In 1958 Egypt and Syria had joined together into a single country called the United Arab Republic (UAR). The union ended in 1961, when Syrians became concerned that the union was lowering their standard of living. Syrian officers in the union's army revolted, and Syria seceded. The collapse of the UAR was a great blow to the pride of the Nasser government, which responded by passing stringent laws regulating the personal freedoms of Egyptians.

In that year, Mahfouz published *The Thief and the Dogs,* a criminal adventure story set against a background of religious commentary. Its scathing portrayal of exploitation and political hypocrisy captured the uneasiness of Egypt in the early 1960s. Mahfouz's subsequent novels—*Autumn Quail, The Search,* and *The Beggar*—continued these trends, and his 1966 work, *Chatter on the Nile,* presented an almost unequivocally disillusioned view of the Egyptian cultural and intellectual elite. In *Miramar,* published in 1967, Mahfouz continued his indirect criticism of the course that the Egyptian government had taken. John Fowles has called the novel "a courageous anticipation of a subsequent 'loosening of tongues' or release of steam after the thirteen years of tight control of the press and the arts practiced by the Nasser regime." Here he also expanded his range of technique, using multiple narrative perspectives for the first time in a single work.

In 1967 the Six-Day War with Israel left Egypt's armed forces and economy in ruins and a part of its territory lost. Mahfouz responded to these events with a series of questioning and highly symbolic short stories. When he returned to writing longer works, in the early 1970s, he expressed his doubts about and criticisms of Egyptian politics, and especially the widening gap between rich and poor, more directly than he had in his earlier novels. *Karnak Cafe,* for instance, dealt with the brutality of the secret police in suppressing political dissent during the 1960s, while *Respected Sir* described a self-serving bureaucrat as he manipulated his rise to power. The force of Mahfouz's challenge led the government briefly to prevent him from publishing.

Mahfouz's later work has continued in much the same vein, emphasizing social concerns and humanistic values while continuing to examine Egyptian and Arab realities and struggles, including the plight of the Palestinians in the occupied territories. Nevertheless, his support for the Camp David accords with Israel has led some Arabs to advocate that his works be banned. Even where such bans have been initiated, however, they have been largely unsuccessful, for Mahfouz's reputation as the greatest of Arab novelists, along with the difficulties of controlling book distribution in many Arab states, has ensured him a large readership throughout the Arab world.

Mahfouz's works gained a broader public when, in 1988, the writer became the first Arab to receive the Nobel Prize for Literature. In awarding the prize, Sture Allén of the Swedish Academy described Mahfouz's novels as providing "a committed, perceptive, almost prophetic commentary on the world around him." Allén stated that Mahfouz has "an unrivaled position as spokesman for Arabic prose. Through him, in the cultural sphere to which he belongs, the art of the novel and the short story has attained international standards of excellence, the result of a synthesis of classical Arabic tradition, European inspiration, and personal artistry." Mahfouz himself used the platform of the Nobel lecture as an opportunity to broaden his role as a spokesperson for the dispossessed of the Third World. Addressing the members of the Swedish Academy, he asked, "Where can the moans of mankind find a place to resound if not in your oasis of civilization planted by its great founder for the service of science, literature, and sublime human values?"

Thus Mahfouz is both the trailblazer and the master of the Arabic novel. He transformed conventions developed in other lands into a form suited to Arab culture, and he explored how the Arabic language could be used most expressively in this new form. At the same time, he has confronted social and political evils even when others remained silent, risking censure and worse from both religious and political interests. His novels record, reflect, and help us understand one of the most turbulent periods in Middle Eastern history, even as they contribute to a long and rich tradition in the art of storytelling.

Since retiring from the Egyptian civil service, Mahfouz is often to be found meeting with friends in Cairo cafés. According to critic R. Z. Sheppard, "He is also known as one of the best joke tellers in Cairo, no small compliment in a land noted for its wit."

English translations of most of Mahfouz's works were hard to find until recently. Since the awarding of the Nobel Prize, however, major publishers in the United States and Great Britain have begun to bring out his novels and stories. As a result, the list of his works available in English is steadily growing.

ADDITIONAL WORKS IN ENGLISH TRANSLATION: God's World, 1974; Mirrors, 1977; Fountain and Tomb, 1988; Wedding Song, 1989.

ABOUT: Allen, R. "Some Recent Works of Najib Mahfuz: A Critical Analysis," Journal of the American Research Center in Egypt, 1977; Allen, R. The Arabic Novel: An Historical and Critical Introduction, 1982; Jad, A. Form and Technique in the Egyptian Novel 1912–1971, 1983; Mahmoud, M. "The Unchanging Hero in a Changing World: Najib Mahfuz's Al-Liss wa 'l-Kilab," Journal of Arabic Literature, 1984; Sakkut, H. The Egyptian Novel and its Main Trends from 1913–1952, 1971.

MARKOWITZ, HARRY M.

(August 24, 1927–)
Nobel Memorial Prize in Economic Sciences, 1990
(shared with Merton H. Miller and William F. Sharpe)

The American financial economist Harry M. Markowitz was born in Chicago, Illinois. He was the only child of Morris and Mildred (Gruber) Markowitz, who owned a small grocery store. As Markowitz later recalled, "We lived in a nice apartment, always had enough to eat, and I had my own room. I was never aware of the Great Depression."

As a child, Markowitz played baseball, read comic books, and played violin, but he also was fascinated with physics and astronomy. By high school he was reading "original works of serious philosophers" and studying Charles Darwin.

Markowitz received his bachelor's degree in liberal arts from the University of Chicago in 1947 and chose to remain at the university to study economics. He took courses offered by MILTON FRIEDMAN and TJALLING C. KOOPMANS and was invited to serve as a student member of the Cowles Commission for Research in Economics, an organization that has greatly influenced the field of economics and produced a number of Nobel laureates, including FRANCO MODIGLIANI, GERARD DEBREU, JAMES TOBIN, and LAWRENCE KLEIN. In 1950, after earning his master's degree in economics, Markowitz began work toward his doctorate.

By that time Markowitz had become interested in finding a way to apply mathematics and statistical methods to analysis of the stock market. His doctoral dissertation, which explained how an investor in stocks, bonds, or other securities can realize the greatest return, was the first step in his ground-breaking portfolio theory.

A portfolio is a collection of assets (such as stocks and bonds) held by a single investor. Economists and investors alike had always known intuitively that it is dangerous to "put all your eggs in one basket"—that is, to invest exclusively in one company's stock—although there was no mathematical rationale for that understanding. In spite of their intuition, investors generally continued to focus primarily on picking a "winner" in the stock market by trying to estimate the expected profitability of a single company. Markowitz's research showed that to realize the greatest gain from investment, picking winners was far less productive than diversifying one's portfolio among different companies and, better yet, different industries.

The earnings of all companies of a single type, such as automobile manufacturers, depend on the same economic conditions and thus are apt to rise or fall together. If an investor were to put only

HARRY M. MARKOWITZ

some money in that industry and put other money in different industries, such as real estate or oil— investments that depend on different economic conditions—thereby spreading the risk, there would be a much greater probability that the investor would realize at least some gains even during times when automobile companies were not doing well. This theory would later lead to the development of mutual fund investments.

In 1952, while completing his dissertation, Markowitz joined the Rand Corporation, a research company. He earned his Ph.D. from the University of Chicago two years later. In 1955 he accepted an invitation from James Tobin to take a year's leave from Rand to work at the Cowles Foundation at Yale. He used that opportunity to write his first and most widely acclaimed book, *Portfolio Selection: Efficient Diversification of Investments,* which detailed his portfolio theory and laid out formulas for determining the best mix of investments. "It is not clear that [my book] would ever have been written if it were not for Tobin's invitation," Markowitz recalls.

Markowitz's book, published in 1959, showed how investors can use mathematical analysis to select a portfolio with the best chance of a high return. His technique—putting factors such as risk and potential return into existing statistical formulas—was a new way to view the stock market. Even after the book was published, Markowitz continued to devise still more refined ways to measure the relationship of risk to return among the various securities that make up a portfolio. As it developed, Markowitz's portfolio theory began to require calculations so complicated that large, sophisticated computer systems and data resources

were needed to predict how a set of stocks or other securities would behave over time.

In 1956 WILLIAM F. SHARPE joined the staff at Rand. For several years he and Markowitz worked closely analyzing investors' choices. Sharpe, using Markowitz's calculations about stocks' risks and returns, went on to develop methods of measuring risks and pricing financial assets.

After spending time at Rand and a year at General Electric, Markowitz moved back and forth between academic and private research. In 1963 he became chairman of the board and technical director of Consolidated Analysis Centers, a position he left in 1968 to become professor of finance at the University of California at Los Angeles (UCLA). From 1969 to 1972 he was president of Arbitrage Management Company. He joined the finance faculty at the University of Pennsylvania's Wharton Business School from 1972 to 1974. He then became a member of the research staff of the T. J. Watson Research Center of the IBM Corporation, where he remained until 1983. During the early 1980s Markowitz also taught finance at Rutgers University. In 1982 he joined the faculty of the finance department at Baruch College of the City University of New York, where he is the Marvin Speiser Distinguished Professor of Finance and Economics.

Markowitz shared the 1990 Nobel Memorial Prize in Economic Sciences with Sharpe and MERTON H. MILLER. Miller, considered the originator of modern theories of corporate financing strategies, had shown that a company's value does not depend on its method of financing or on its dividend policy. His work led to a revolution in the way corporations finance acquisitions and other projects. When the prizewinners were announced, many scholars applauded the Royal Swedish Academy of Sciences' decision to recognize, for the first time, pioneers in financial theory. For too long, some said, the field of finance had been considered a stepchild of economics, not a fullfledged discipline. As Gregg Jarrell of the University of Rochester explained, "Financial economists in academia were treated as secondclass citizens at the universities. . . . [Now] every academic in the field of financial economics will work a little harder and teach with a little more conviction, for the Nobel committee has just said to the world that [financial economics] is legitimate and important."

Markowitz had felt the prejudice against his field in 1954, when he defended his dissertation. In his speech to the academy, he recalled that Milton Friedman, a member of his dissertation committee, had "argued that portfolio theory was not economics and that they could not award me a Ph.D. degree in economics for a dissertation that was not in economics. I assume he was only half serious, since they did award me the degree without long debate." Thanking the academy, he said, "We take this award to be a recognition and acceptance of financial economics as a branch of economics, equal to any, as much as a reward for the efforts of three individuals."

The work of these three individuals has had a major influence on the decisions of stockbrokers, bankers, mutual fund managers, and individual investors. "Widows live safer lives because their portfolios are invested according to the diversification principles developed by Markowitz and elaborated by Sharpe," Harvard economist Lawrence Summers said after the announcement of the 1990 Nobel award.

Markowitz and his wife, the former Barbara Gay, have two children.

In 1990 Markowitz spent a semester as a visiting professor at the University of Tokyo, and in 1991 he worked at the London School of Economics. He has been president of the American Finance Association and director of the Institute of Management Sciences. He is a fellow at the Econometric Society and the American Academy of Arts and Sciences. In 1989 Markowitz won the Von Neumann Theory Prize in operations research theory.

ADDITIONAL WORKS: Simscript: A Simulation Programming Language, 1963, with B. Hausner and H. Kerr; Studies in Process Analysis, 1963, with A. S. Manne; The Simscript II Programming Language, 1969, with P. Kiviat and R. Villanueva; Adverse Deviation, 1981, with others; The EAS-E Programming Language, 1981, with A. H. Malhotra and D. P. Pazel; Mean-Variance Analysis in Portfolio Choice and Capital Markets, 1989.

ABOUT: Los Angeles Times October 17, 1990; Newsweek October 29, 1990; New York Times October 17, 1990; Wall Street Journal October 17, 1990; Washington Post October 17, 1990; Who's Who in America, 1990.

MICHEL, HARTMUT

(July 18, 1948–   )
Nobel Prize for Chemistry, 1988
(shared with Johann Deisenhofer and Robert
   Huber)

The German biochemist Hartmut Michel (mi shel) was born in Ludwigsburg, the elder son of Karl and Frieda (Kachler) Michel. His ancestors had farmed in the Württemberg region of southwestern Germany for generations. Yet because of the local tradition of dividing property equally among all of a family's children, the Michels' landholdings had dwindled in size over the years. Hartmut's father had to work as a joiner, and his mother as a dressmaker, in order to support the

HARTMUT MICHEL

family. The Michels took care of the "huge gardens" that remained of their farm on Saturdays and in the evenings.

In an autobiographical essay, Michel describes himself as having been a lively child, "an active member of the local children's gang, frequently being chased by field guards and building supervisors." An excellent student, he joined his hometown library at age eleven and began to read "subjects ranging from archaeology to ethnology and geography to zoology. Needless to say," he adds, "I did not do much homework." Nevertheless, Michel continued to do well in school, enjoying history, biology, chemistry, and physics. By the time he graduated from the Friedrich Schiller Gymnasium in 1967, he had become particularly interested in biochemistry and molecular biology.

In 1969, having completed his military service, Michel enrolled at the University of Tübingen— the only German university that permitted students to study biochemistry from their first year. Michel spent the 1972 school year doing lab work at the University of Munich and the Max Planck Institute for Biochemistry. At the end of that year, he said, "I was convinced that academic research was what I wanted to do."

As a result, after passing his examinations in 1974, Michel joined the Friedrich Miescher Laboratory of the Max Planck Society in Tübingen, where he worked under the biochemist Dieter Oesterhelt. In 1975 he followed Oesterhelt to a new position at the University of Würzburg, completed his thesis, and received his diploma (the equivalent of a master's degree). Continuing to work under Oesterhelt, he attained his Ph.D. in 1977.

For much of this time, Michel had been studying photosynthesis. Photosynthesis is the process by which plants trap energy from the sun and convert it to nutrients. The process of photosynthesis is performed by a protein that straddles the outer membrane of a cell. Researchers had for years tried to determine the structure of membrane proteins, in order to determine how they converted solar energy to chemical energy.

The usual way to determine the structure of a protein is to combine the protein with water. Water causes the protein molecule to take the form of a crystal lattice (a solid, three-dimensional, repeating molecular structure). By analyzing the lattice through a process called X-ray crystallography, a researcher can study the protein atom by atom. This process, developed by MAX VON LAUE in 1912, involves aiming X rays of known wavelength at crystallized materials and studying the patterns in which the rays are weakened or reinforced as they strike the crystal.

Unlike most proteins, however, membrane proteins—the proteins involved in photosynthesis—are not water-soluble; they must interact with water as a part of their function. Therefore, most researchers had considered the crystallization of a membrane protein impossible. Decades of attempts at developing new techniques had been unsuccessful.

Michel was working with a membrane protein called bacteriorhodopsin. As part of an experiment, he removed the fat from this protein and stored it in the freezer. To his surprise, when he removed the protein from the freezer, it had been converted into "solid, glasslike aggregates." This "accidental observation," as he called it, convinced him that it should be possible to crystallize membrane proteins, even though they were not water-soluble. Once crystallized, the proteins could be analyzed by X-ray crystallography just like any water-soluble protein.

Working with Oesterhelt, he used a detergent to free the bacteriorhodopsin from the cell membrane. Within four weeks, he had developed two-dimensional crystals of bacteriorhodopsin. These two-dimensional crystals could be examined with an electron microscope but not with the more exacting technology of X-ray crystallography, which requires three-dimensional crystals. Michel continued his efforts, and in April 1979 he produced the first three-dimensional crystals of a membrane protein. These crystals did diffract X rays, but they were still too small and disordered for structural analysis. Nevertheless, Michel's excitement over his achievement led him to cancel his original postdoctoral plans and to move again with Oesterhelt, this time to the Max Planck Institute for Biochemistry at Martinsried.

At Martinsried, Michel realized that he might achieve better results by working with a membrane protein other than bacteriorhodopsin. He turned his attention to the photosynthetic reaction center of the purple bacterium *Rhodopseudomonas viridis*. This complex molecule, made up of four different proteins and fourteen other components, is bound to the bacterium's membrane. Working with the photosynthetic reaction center, Michel tried a number of detergents and additives in search of a molecule that could take the place of water in the crystal lattice. Success finally came in 1981, after four years' effort. As Michel wrote later, "During September 1981 the first reaction center crystal was X-rayed . . . and turned out to be of excellent quality."

In the spring of 1982, Michel started collecting data for the X-ray analysis of the molecule he had successfully crystallized. Recognizing that he lacked the background and experience to complete this analysis on his own, he asked ROBERT HUBER, a department head at Martinsried who specialized in the structure of biological macromolecules, to help him find a collaborator. Huber and Michel soon came to the conclusion that JOHANN DEISENHOFER, a crystallographic researcher in Huber's department, was the ideal choice. Deisenhofer, Michel, and others spent three years analyzing vast amounts of data; finally, in 1985, they completed the task. For the first time in history, they had provided a complete, three-dimensional analysis of a membrane protein, in which they identified and described each of more than 10,000 atoms.

Scientists around the world instantly recognized the implications of this achievement. First, simply by crystallizing a membrane protein, Michel had blazed a trail for investigating a type of molecule with tremendous biological and medical significance. In awarding the 1988 Nobel Prize for Chemistry to Michel, Deisenhofer, and Huber, Bo G. Malmström of the Royal Swedish Academy of Sciences noted that membrane proteins are associated not only with photosynthesis and respiration, but with "many other central biological functions, e.g., the transport of nutrients into cells, hormone action, or nerve impulses." He predicted that crystallizing these proteins and analyzing their structures would lead to great advances in scientific understanding of fundamental life processes.

Furthermore, by determining the exact structure of the photosynthetic reaction center, the team had provided theoretical chemists with what Malmström called an "indispensable tool" for understanding the process of photosynthesis. The photosynthetic reaction center plays an essential role in photosynthesis, not only in bacteria, but in algae and green plants as well. Some researchers predict that detailed understanding of photosynthetic reaction centers eventually will lead to the development of artificial photosynthetic reactions, a process that would have broad applications in nearly every area of technology.

In October 1987 Michel became a department head and director at the Max Planck Institute for Biophysics in Frankfurt/Main. He enjoys time off with his wife, Ilona Leger, and his children, Andrea and Robert. He also loves orchids, which he grows in such profusion that they fill his apartment and spill into his laboratory.

Michel's achievement has brought him many honors in addition to the Nobel Prize, including the Lecturer Stipend of the German Chemical Industry (1986), the Otto Klung Prize for Chemistry (1986), and the Leibniz Prize of the German Research Association (1986). With Johann Deisenhofer, he was also awarded the Biophysics Prize of the American Physical Society (1986) and the Otto-Bayer Prize (1986). He belongs to the European Molecular Biology Organization. In Germany he belongs to the Max Planck Society, the Society for Biological Chemistry, the German Chemists' Society, and the Society for Physical Biology.

ABOUT: New Scientist October 29, 1988; New York Times October 20, 1988; Science November 4, 1988; Who's Who, 1990.

MILLER, MERTON H.

(May 16, 1923–)

Nobel Memorial Prize in Economic Sciences, 1990

(shared with Harry M. Markowitz and William F. Sharpe)

The American financial economist Merton H. Miller, the only child of Joel and Sylvia Miller, was born and raised in Boston, Massachusetts. His father, an attorney, was a Harvard graduate, and Miller continued that tradition by entering Harvard in 1940. He graduated magna cum laude with a degree in economics.

During World War II Miller held several government jobs, first in the Division of Tax Research of the United States Treasury Department and then in the Division of Research and Statistics of the Board of Governors of the Federal Reserve System. Having decided to attend graduate school in 1949, he selected Johns Hopkins University because he was impressed with its "small but very distinguished faculty." Miller earned his doctorate in economics in 1952, then spent a year as a visiting assistant lecturer at the London School of Economics. He then moved to the Carnegie Institute of Technology (now Carnegie-Mellon University) in Pittsburgh, Pennsylvania.

Miller later recalled that Carnegie's then-new Graduate School of Industrial Administration was "the first and most influential of the new wave of research-oriented United States business schools." During his years there he had the opportunity to work with HERBERT SIMON, one of the founders of the school, and FRANCO MODIGLIANI. At Carnegie, Miller and Modigliani began a collaboration that was to continue for many years. The first of their joint papers, which came to be known as "the M&M papers," was published in American Economic Review in 1958. Entitled "The Cost of Capital, Corporation Finance, and the Theory of Investment," the paper laid out theories that are regarded today as definitive in the field of corporate finance.

When a corporation needs to raise money, it can do so in either of two ways: It can sell additional shares of its stock, or it can borrow. Traditional assumptions suggested that it was innately risky to borrow too much and that investors would not be attracted to companies with large debts. Therefore, corporations should limit their risk—and thus remain attractive to investors—by doing most of their financing through the issuing of stocks.

However, another financial economist, HARRY M. MARKOWITZ, had already shown that some of these traditional assumptions were incorrect. Investors would be foolish, Markowitz determined, if they selected only companies that employed less risky financing methods, because stocks in risk-taking companies provide higher rates of return than do stocks in conservatively managed companies. Wise investors should diversify and choose a mixture of both. Their portfolios (collections of assets) should include many types of companies, and those companies should reflect a variety of financing methods. Since investors need to balance safe companies and risky companies with the prospect of a higher return, Markowitz's portfolio theory concluded, there is always a market for companies that finance largely through debt.

Based on this theory of investment diversification, Miller and Modigliani asserted that a company's financing method per se has no effect on the value of that company. Since stockholders control the risks they take by diversifying their investments among different companies with different financing methods, the best way a company can maximize its capital value is to employ the method of financing that is the least expensive.

In subsequent papers, Miller and Modigliani expanded their conclusions about capital financing. Their model of dividend policy choice holds that a company's dividend policy, like its decision about debt financing, does not affect the appeal of the firm to investors. In all cases, what really matter to investors, the M&M theories state, are the skills of the company's managers and the value actually produced by the company's machinery or internal work force.

When first introduced, their ideas were controversial and were rejected by many, but after further substantiation over the years, they became widely adopted. Although the theories developed by Modigliani and Miller were limited because they were based on "perfect" markets and did not take into account such real-world considerations as taxes and the costs of bankruptcy, their techniques are still in use today and their theories are considered a foundation of corporate finance. Modigliani received the 1985 Nobel Memorial Prize in Economic Sciences for this and other innovative work.

In 1961 Miller joined the faculty of the Graduate School of Business at the University of Chicago. There he continued his explorations of corporate finance and the relationships among a firm's method of financing, its dividend policy, and its value. He worked to move his theorems from the "perfect" world of theory to more practical applications by incorporating the effects of taxes and bankruptcy on corporate finance.

Much of Miller's work at the University of Chicago focused on leverage. Leverage is the use of borrowed funds to increase the purchasing power of a business and, ideally, to increase that firm's profitability. While Miller generally espoused the use of leverage, the economist Robert Kuttner noted that "unfortunately, his disciples have tended to take [his words] as a literal description of the world, a sprinkling of scholarly holy water on the extreme claims of the 1980s: Let market forces rip—whatever they do is by definition optimal." Many see this as the cause of wild swings in the stock market and the crash of 1987.

In the 1980s American business news was full of stories of leveraged buyouts, or takeovers of companies using borrowed money. In general, the acquiring firm used the assets of the company being taken over to secure loans. Those loans then could be repaid out of cash generated by the company that was taken over. Although this scheme stems directly from Miller's theories, Miller explained, when accepting the Nobel Prize, that "contrary to what you may have read in some press accounts . . . I am not the co-inventor of the leveraged buyout. That Franco Modigliani and I should be credited with inventing these takeovers is doubly ironic since the central message of our M&M propositions was that the value of the firm was independent of its capital structure." However, firms in the 1980s were routinely buying out others in attempts to increase their values.

Miller has remained at the University of Chicago except for the academic year 1966–1967, during which he visited the University of Louvain

MERTON H. MILLER

in Belgium. In 1987 the stock market crash in the United States led to a renewed emphasis on diversification, and immediately after the crash Miller was chosen by the Chicago Mercantile Exchange to chair a special postmortem panel to analyze the effects of the crash.

Miller shared the 1990 Nobel Memorial Prize in Economic Sciences with Harry Markowitz and WILLIAM F. SHARPE. Sharpe, starting with Markowitz's portfolio theory, developed mathematical formulas that investors could use to assess the risk of particular investments and formulas that financial analysts could use to determine the value of a company. His methods have become standard among investors and analysts.

The announcement of the award was a surprise to many, as the Nobel Prize had up to then been given for work in traditional economics rather than finance. Miller, Markowitz, and Sharpe are widely recognized as the founders of modern financial economics—pioneers who developed methods for valuing corporate stocks and other securities and for weighing the risks and returns of different types of investments. They are credited with having changed Wall Street, business schools, and the investment habits of millions. "The fact that they gave it to the three of us shows that they were honoring the whole field [of finance]," Miller said when he heard about the award.

Miller is a past president of the American Finance Association. He continues to serve as public director of the Chicago Mercantile Exchange and of the Chicago Board of Trade. He is the Robert R. McCormick Distinguished Service Professor at the University of Chicago. His current research interests include economic and regulatory problems of the financial services industry, particularly securities and options exchanges.

Miller's first wife, Eleanor, died in 1969, leaving him with three daughters. A few years later he married his current wife, Katherine, the treasurer of the Sanwa Leasing Corporation. Miller and his wife divide their time between Hyde Park, Illinois, and "a country retreat on a working farm (though not worked by us) in Woodstock, Illinois. . . . Like some other weekend retreaters, my hobby has become brush cutting and maintenance," he said. "Unlike some of my more athletic fellow laureates, however, the closest I get to recreational exercise these days is watching the Chicago Bears from my season ticket seats . . . in the south end zone of frigid Soldier Field."

WORKS BY: The Theory of Finance, 1972, with E. Fama; Macroeconomics: A Neoclassical Introduction, 1974, with C. Upton and R. Irwin.

ABOUT: Los Angeles Times October 17, 1990; Newsweek October 29, 1990; New York Times October 17, 1990; Wall Street Journal October 17, 1990; Washington Post October 17, 1990.

MÜLLER, K. ALEX

(April 20, 1927–)
Nobel Prize for Physics, 1987
(shared with J. Georg Bednorz)

The Swiss physicist Karl Alexander Müller was born in Basel, Switzerland. He spent his early childhood in Salzburg, Austria, where his father, Paul Rudolf Müller, was studying music. Later, he and his mother, Irma (Feigenbaum) Müller, went to live with his grandparents in the Swiss town of Dornach. They moved next to Lugano, Switzerland, where Müller attended an Italian-speaking school and became fluent in that language.

Müller's mother died when he was eleven, and he moved again, this time to a mountain valley in eastern Switzerland. There, he attended Evangelical College, a school that he described as "liberal in the spirit of the nineteenth century, and intellectually quite demanding." As World War II raged throughout the rest of Europe, Müller and his friends followed its events from the safety of a neutral country. Müller became active in sports, especially in alpine skiing. In his spare time, he developed a fascination with building radios and dreamed of becoming an electrical engineer. A chemistry tutor, however, convinced him that his abilities were better suited to physics.

Müller graduated just as the war ended. After completing basic military training, he enrolled in the department of physics and mathematics at the Swiss Federal Institute of Technology (ETH) in

Zurich. He joined a huge freshman class in what became known as the " 'atom-bomb semester,' as just prior to our enrollment nuclear weapons had been used for the first time, and many students had become interested in nuclear physics." Müller found many of his courses disappointing and considered switching to electrical engineering. Again, however, an adviser dissuaded him. Studying with WOLFGANG PAULI also revived his interest in physics. By the time he completed his diploma (equivalent to a master's degree), he retained his interest in applied science but had also developed a taste for solid-state physics.

In 1956 Müller's fondness for applied science led him to the Department of Industrial Research at the ETH, where he developed an interest in oxides (compounds of metallic elements and oxygen). For his doctoral thesis, he investigated a newly synthesized oxide—a compound with strontium and titanium. Also in 1956, Müller married Ingeborg Winkler, with whom he later had two children, Eric and Sylvia. He completed his Ph.D. in 1958.

Müller then spent five years at the Battelle Memorial Institute in Geneva, where he became the manager of a magnetic resonance group. In 1962 Müller also became a lecturer at the University of Zurich and joined a magnetic resonance group that was forming there. The following year, his position at the university led to a job offer with the IBM Zurich Research Laboratory, where he has remained ever since.

During the years that followed, Müller continued his studies in solid-state physics. Frequently working in collaboration with Walter Berlinger, he did extensive research on oxides, particularly the strontium-titanium compound that had been the subject of his doctoral work. He developed a reputation as a strong personality with an abiding faith in his own ideas. In addition, as head of the laboratory's physics group from 1972 on, Müller closely followed the work of HEINRICH ROHRER and GERD BINNIG, whose development of the scanning tunneling microscope earned them the Nobel Prize for Physics in 1986.

Müller's own Nobel Prize was awarded for his work with J. GEORG BEDNORZ. In 1972 Bednorz was a young university student who worked in Müller's department as a summer researcher. Bednorz returned to the laboratory in 1973 and again in 1974, this time to do the experimental work for his diploma. His experiments centered on the same strontium-titanium oxide that had occupied so much of Müller's attention. With Müller's encouragement, Bednorz came to Zurich permanently in 1977, and Müller advised him on his doctoral thesis. Bednorz completed his Ph.D. in 1982 and immediately joined the IBM laboratory, where he and

K. ALEX MÜLLER

Müller began a close collaboration. In 1985 Müller decided to give up management entirely in order to dedicate himself to his work with Bednorz.

The object of Müller's and Bednorz's attention was superconductivity—a technology with extraordinary potential ramifications. Superconductivity had first been observed in 1911, when the Dutch physicist HEIKE KAMERLINGH ONNES cooled mercury to 4°K and found that electricity would flow through it with no loss of energy to resistance. (This temperature is very close to "absolute zero"—0°K—the point at which atomic motion effectively ceases.) This discovery captured the imagination of the scientific community. If electricity could be conducted with 100 percent efficiency, the costs of generating and transmitting electric power would drop precipitously. To add to the excitement, later investigations revealed that superconductors are able to float above a magnetic field. Therefore, engineers predicted that further research in superconductivity would bring about the invention of low-cost, frictionless, high-speed trains.

These dreams, however, were tempered by an unfortunate reality: the effort and expense of cooling mercury to 4°K made superconductivity impractical for most applications. Nevertheless, because superconductors seemed to offer such extraordinary promise, researchers began a long and painstaking search for substances that would superconduct at higher temperatures. By 1973 the maximum temperature for superconductivity had reached 23°K.

At this point, however, all progress stopped. A temperature of 23°K remained far too cold for most practical applications, yet many scientists believed that this temperature represented a natural barrier that could not be passed.

Müller and Bednorz set out to test this belief. Rather than work with metals, however, they decided to work with oxides. Although oxides (which resemble ceramics) normally do not conduct electricity at all, some oxides were known to become conductors at very low temperatures. Inspired by this knowledge, the researchers began a painstaking process of synthesizing various compounds, cooling them, and measuring their conductivity. They occasionally discovered that a minor change in a molecule's structure created a conductor where none had existed before, but their efforts to achieve superconductivity went unrewarded.

Then Bednorz read a French paper that described a newly synthesized oxide—a compound of copper, barium, and lanthanum. The team decided to test the substance for superconductivity. On January 27, 1986, they measured a sharp drop in resistance at a temperature far higher than ever before observed. By April, Müller and Bednorz were able to achieve superconductivity at 35°K. Although this temperature still fell below the limits of practical applicability, it surpassed by 12° the barrier that had stymied researchers for thirteen years.

Hoping to pursue their discovery quietly for at least a year or two, the scientists published a modest account of their work in the German journal, *Zeitschrift für Physik,* which they expected few physicists to read. Despite these efforts, however, word of the team's results spread rapidly around the world. Within a year, the American researcher Paul Chu had raised the maximum temperature for superconductivity to 90°K. This temperature is a full 13° warmer than the temperature of liquid nitrogen, a common laboratory coolant. For the first time, superconductivity had become a practical reality.

In honoring Müller and Bednorz with the 1987 Nobel Prize for Physics, the Nobel committee offered what may be the fastest recognition it had ever given to a scientific achievement. Gösta Ekspong of the Royal Swedish Academy of Sciences explained the quickness of the award by saying, "This discovery is quite recent—less than two years old—but it has already stimulated research and development throughout the world to an unprecedented extent." Crediting the researchers with having "reopened and revitalized" scientific debate over superconductivity, he noted that their work had provoked an explosion in research that succeeded in producing a practical superconductor. Furthermore, their discovery had provoked a new interest in the theory of superconductivity. No one yet understands how oxides can function as superconductors. Therefore, no one can say what factors might limit the temperatures at which they do so. Indeed, some scientists have even entertained the possibility of eventual room-temperature superconductivity.

Müller is the author of over 200 technical publications. He is a member of the Executive Committee of the Groupement Ampère, the Ferroelectricity Group of the European Physical Society, and the Swiss Physical Society. He served as president of the Zurich Physical Society in 1968. He has also become a Fellow of the American Physical Society and a Foreign Associate Member of the United States Academy of Sciences. His work in superconductivity has earned him honorary doctorates from universities around the world, along with a special award from the Second International Superconductivity Symposium in Tsukuba, Japan. With Bednorz, he has also received such awards as the German Physical Society's Robert Wichard Pohl Prize (1987), the Hewlett-Packard Europhysics Prize (1988), and the American Physical Society's International Prize for New Materials Research (1988).

ABOUT: International Who's Who, 1990; New York Times October 15, 1987; New York Times Magazine August 16, 1987; Physics Today December 1987; Science October 25, 1987.

MURRAY, JOSEPH E.

(April 1, 1919–   )
Nobel Prize for Physiology or Medicine, 1990
(shared with E. Donnall Thomas)

The American surgeon Joseph Edward Murray was born in Milford, Massachusetts, to William Andrew Murray, a district court judge, and the former Mary DePasquale, a schoolteacher. "Both parents had benefited from and stressed the value of the educational opportunities this country offered. By example and precept they emphasized the need for service to others," Murray recalled. "From earliest memory I wanted to be a surgeon, possibly influenced by the qualities of our family doctor."

Murray majored in humanities at the College of the Holy Cross in Worcester, Massachusetts, receiving his B.A. in 1940. He then attended Harvard Medical School, graduating in 1943. After a surgical internship at Peter Bent Brigham Hospital in Boston (now Brigham and Women's Hospital), he joined the military and in 1944 was assigned to Valley Forge General Hospital in Pennsylvania, where he worked under the plastic surgeon James Barrett Brown.

The casualties flowing into Valley Forge from the battlefields of World War II included a large number of burn victims. Murray and his colleagues followed the standard practice of auto-grafting—grafting, or transplanting, skin from unburned parts of the patient's body to cover areas where the skin had been burned away. In some cases, though, the victim no longer had enough unburned skin to do the job, and surgeons would take skin from other people to use as a surface cover. This practice was called allografting.

Allografting was only a temporary solution, because the foreign grafts were always slowly rejected and cast off. Brown, who had studied the process in the 1930s, found that the only allografts that were not rejected were those from identical twins. Murray credited Brown's work as the impetus for his own study of organ transplantation: "The slow rejection of the foreign skin grafts fascinated me. How could the host distinguish another person's skin from his own?"

The problems of transplant rejection had been studied in the first part of the twentieth century, when ALEXIS CARREL was developing techniques for transplant surgery. Carrel's results indicated that rejection is similar to an allergic reaction: It is somehow related to the body's resistance to infectious diseases, or immunity. There was no explanation at the time for the connection between disease resistance and transplant rejection.

In addition to the immunological problem of rejection, a transplant operation involving different individuals presented great difficulties with surgical technique and with caring for the patient after the operation. Transplantation, for example, required two operations: the careful removal of the intact organ from one body and the proper insertion of that organ into the recipient. These problems, though, struck surgeons as more interesting than intractable, if only they could get around the obstacle of rejection.

Murray left the army in 1947 and returned to the Brigham Hospital, where he joined a team of physicians studying kidney failure. Murray's task was to develop a repeatable, effective surgical procedure for transplanting kidneys. He first experimented with dogs, trying different placements and surgical techniques. The method he developed, in which a kidney is transplanted into the lower abdomen, is still the standard transplant operation.

In 1954 a man with kidney failure who had an identical twin brother was referred to the Brigham Hospital. "Needless to say, the transplant team was interested in the possibility of transplanting a genetically compatible kidney," Murray recalled. The urologist J. Hartwell Harrison removed a kidney from the healthy donor twin, and Murray transplanted the organ into the sick twin. The operation was successful, and the recipient lived eight years. To Murray this was "a clear demonstration that organ transplantation could be lifesaving. In a way it was spying into the future

JOSEPH E. MURRAY

because we had achieved our long-term goal by bypassing, but not solving, the issue of biological incompatibility. . . . The impact was worldwide and stimulated widespread laboratory attempts to breach the immunological barrier."

Meanwhile, the immunologist P. B. MEDAWAR and his colleagues in Great Britain were also studying graft rejection. In 1953 they experimentally injected pairs of unrelated newborn mice with each other's cells and showed that these animals, once fully grown, were able to exchange skin grafts. They thus proved (as had been predicted by MACFARLANE BURNET) that an organism's ability to differentiate between self and nonself is not innate but is acquired early in life. "Although not applicable to the clinical situation," Murray said, "their experimental breaching of the immunological barrier was another impetus for optimism in the problem so many considered hopeless."

Murray's research in the late 1950s focused on ways to suppress or inactivate the recipient's immunities (which later came to be known as the immune system) so the recipient would tolerate a transplanted organ. His first approach was to use doses of X rays strong enough to knock out the immune system. He had little success in this area, although one transplant recipient lived twenty-five years after accepting an allograft from his fraternal twin.

By this time scientists knew that immune functions are largely based in the bone marrow. Murray experimented with transplanting bone marrow along with a kidney, hoping to reconstitute the patient's immune system so that the patient would be able to tolerate the foreign tissue. These experiments were failures; it was many years before E.

DONNALL THOMAS performed the first successful bone marrow allograft.

In 1951 GERTRUDE B. ELION and GEORGE H. HITCHINGS JR. of the Burroughs Wellcome Research Laboratories had discovered the drug 6-mercaptopurine (6-MP), which is used to treat leukemia, a cancer of the immune system. In 1959 Robert Schwartz and his colleagues at Tufts University Medical School in Boston, studying the effects of 6-MP on immune functions, found that 6-MP prevents the body from developing an immune response to a foreign compound, or antigen, introduced along with the drug. The British surgeon Roy Calne then tested 6-MP during kidney transplants in dogs. Calne's results were so encouraging that Peter Medawar advised him to move to the United States to work with Murray, which he did in 1960. Calne introduced Murray to Elion and Hitchings, and they all began to collaborate.

Almost immediately, Murray recalled, "we knew we had hit on something big! Suppression of the immune response by drugs was a whole new game. Drug-induced immune suppression was more specific than X-ray treatment, less toxic, easier to give, and could be started at the time of the transplant." Hitchings and Elion developed new drugs, which Calne, Murray, and their colleagues tested in dogs undergoing kidney transplants. The most promising such drug was azathioprine (Imuran), a drug related to 6-MP.

Murray and his colleagues performed the first human kidney transplant using azathioprine in 1961. The patient died a month later because of problems with the drug's toxicity, but the transplant itself had worked. After adjusting the drug dosage, they performed the first successful transplant of a kidney from an unrelated donor in 1962. The impact was immediate and worldwide. "By 1965," Murray noted, "one-year survival rates of . . . kidneys from living related donors were approaching 80 percent, and from cadavers 65 percent. . . . Optimism and enthusiasm were high as new drugs and other methods of immune suppression were tested." Surgeons were also learning to transplant other organs, such as the liver, heart, pancreas, lungs, and bone marrow.

Murray and Thomas shared the 1990 Nobel Prize for Physiology or Medicine "for their discoveries concerning organ and cell transplantation in the treatment of human disease." Even though by 1990 over 200,000 kidney transplants had been performed, their work was an unusual choice for a Nobel Prize, which is most often given for work in basic science. "I was totally surprised by this," said Thomas. "I really felt the prize would never go to patient-oriented research."

Even without the prize, though, Murray feels that "my life as a surgeon-scientist, combining hu-

111

manity and science, has been fantastically rewarding. In our daily patients we witness human nature in the raw. . . . If alert, we can detect new problems to solve, new paths to investigate."

Murray married the former Virginia (Bobby) Link, a pianist and singer, in 1945; they have six children. Murray has described himself as "a physical enthusiast" and a lover of the outdoors. "We have been blessed in our lives beyond my wildest dreams," he notes. "My only wish would be to have ten more lives to live on this planet."

Murray is a member of numerous medical societies and has been president or vice president of the American Association of Plastic Surgeons, the American College of Surgeons, the American Surgical Association, the Boston Surgical Society, and the Harvard Medical Alumni Association. He is an honorary fellow of the royal colleges of surgeons in London, Ireland, and Australasia. His awards include the Francis Amory Prize of the American Academy of Arts and Sciences (1962), the Gold Medal of the International Society of Surgeons (1963), and the Olof Af Acrel Medal of the Swedish Society of Medicine (1990).

ABOUT: The Chimera August 1990; Los Angeles Times October 9, 1990; New York Times October 9, 1990; Science October 19, 1990; Science News October 3, 1990; Time October 22, 1990; U.S. News and World Report October 22, 1990; Washington Post October 9, 1990; Who's Who in America, 1991.

NEHER, ERWIN

(March 20, 1944–)

Nobel Prize for Physiology or Medicine, 1991
(shared with Bert Sakmann)

The German biophysicist Erwin Neher (nā′ her) was born in Landsberg am Lech, in Bavaria, to Franz Xavier and Elisabeth Neher. He earned his bachelor's degree in physics at the Institute of Technology in Munich in 1965 and his master's degree two years later from the University of Wisconsin. He then returned to Germany and the institute and received a Ph.D. in 1970. He spent the next two years in Munich at the Max Planck Institute for Psychiatry, then moved to Göttingen to take the position of research associate at the Max Planck Institute for Biophysical Chemistry.

At Göttingen, Neher chose to apply his training in physics to the study of biology, specifically to the role of electrically charged particles—ions—in nerve cells.

Scientists had recognized a connection between nerve cells and electricity since the late eighteenth century. By the early part of the twentieth century the basis for this connection had become clear: an unequal distribution of ions—most commonly positively charged sodium, potassium, and calcium atoms and negatively charged chlorine atoms—between the inside and the outside of nerve cells.

In the 1940s and early 1950s the English physiologists ALAN HODGKIN and ANDREW HUXLEY established that sodium and potassium ions move across the nerve cell membrane (the cell's outer wall) in response to electrical, physical, or chemical stimulation from other cells. This movement in turn spreads an electric current along the membrane, resulting in a nerve impulse. Their work indicated that the ions do not simply move through passive holes in the membrane. They hypothesized that embedded in the membrane are gates or channels that can control the flow of specific ions and that the channels are controlled by electrical stimulation or another form of stimulation.

Despite knowing nothing about the physical and chemical structure of ion channels, Hodgkin, Huxley, and their associate BERNARD KATZ were able to derive exact formulas to describe ionic movements during a nerve impulse. Other scientists followed up this work and investigated the channels, trying to determine their properties. By the mid-1970s a picture was starting to emerge. The ion channels appeared to be large protein molecules, or collections of molecules, with a closable hole in the middle. When this hole is open, ions can slip through the cell membrane. When it is closed, the channel is impenetrable.

In 1974 the physiologist BERT SAKMANN became an assistant professor at the institute and moved into Neher's laboratory. In conversation one day, Sakmann recalled, the two men agreed that ion channels represented "one of the most urgent problems in membrane biophysics." While a great deal had been deduced about their structure and function, all the research to date had involved indirect methods: no one had ever been able to isolate a single ion channel and study its individual properties.

At that time one of the most common tools for studying ion channels was the voltage clamp, which had been invented by K. C. Cole of Columbia University in the mid-1930s and refined by Hodgkin and Huxley. A voltage clamp is a device that "freezes" the electric field of a portion of the cell membrane at the level the experimenter chooses, so that the flow of selected ions at a given point can be measured at any time.

Voltage clamps were the basis of most experiments in neurophysics for several decades, but they have several drawbacks. First, the clamp controls a comparatively large area of cell membrane in which thousands of ion channels are opening and closing. Second, some ions are able to bypass the ion channels and leak through the cell membrane by way of pores. This flow creates addi-

ERWIN NEHER

tional electrical activity, or background noise, against which the activities of the channels must be studied.

Neher and Sakmann first solved these problems in 1976, using hollow glass tubes (pipettes) with ultrafine tips only a few microns (millionths of a meter) in diameter. When such a pipette is pressed against a nerve cell membrane, the glass forms a seal with very high electrical resistance. Instruments within the pipette respond only to the patch of membrane surrounded by the pipette's wall—a patch perhaps only a micron in diameter. Such a small piece of membrane can contain only a very few ion channels and sometimes just one. When the pipette is connected to a voltage clamp, scientists can study the behavior of a single ion channel under various conditions.

Neher and Sakmann called their technique "patch clamping." The original method had a few problems, principally leakage between the pipette and the membrane, which led to bothersome levels of background noise. Initial attempts to eliminate the noise proved unsuccessful. "By about 1980 we had almost given up on attempts to improve the seal," Neher later recalled, but then he stumbled upon the solution. He found that they could achieve the results they needed by applying suction to the pipette, using freshly made and polished pipettes for each experiment, and being scrupulously careful to avoid contaminating the pipette or the cell surface. The resulting seal would be tremendously strong both physically and electrically.

The refined patch-clamp technique opened a scientific cornucopia. The seal is so strong that experimenters can tear the patch of membrane, ion channel and all, right out of the cell. They can then study the isolated channel or leave the pipette in place and study the inside of the cell. Since background noise has been almost entirely eliminated, they can measure the tiniest electric currents and observe the behavior of an individual ion channel with great clarity.

Frances Ashcroft of the University of Oxford has recalled that after they discovered patch clamping, Neher and Sakmann "opened their lab to the whole world, and the whole world went to Mecca." As other scientists learned the technique, they began to apply it more widely. Nerve and muscle cells were the first targets, but patch clamping revealed ion channels in many other cell types as well. For example, patch clamping let scientists study pancreatic cells, which malfunction in patients with diabetes, and chloride channels in lung cells, which are defective in patients with cystic fibrosis. Neher's own research involved applying patch clamps to a great variety of cells, including those from the immune system and the adrenal glands.

Neher and Sakmann were awarded the 1991 Nobel Prize for Physiology or Medicine for their invention of the patch-clamp technique. They "conclusively established with their technique that ion channels do exist," the Nobel Assembly at the Karolinska Institute noted. "This new knowledge and this new analytical tool have during the past ten years revolutionized modern biology, facilitated research, and contributed to the understanding of the cellular mechanisms underlying several diseases."

The assembly emphasized the practical effects of the pair's prizewinning work. "Many . . . diseases [including cystic fibrosis, epilepsy, several cardiovascular diseases, and neuromuscular disorders] depend entirely or partially on a defect [in the] regulation of ion channels, and a number of drugs act directly on ion channels. Many pathological mechanisms have been clarified during the eighties through ion channel studies. . . . With the help of the technique of Neher and Sakmann, it is now possible to tailor-make drugs to achieve an optimal effect on particular ion channels," the assembly wrote. "Neher and Sakmann's contributions have meant a revolution for the field of cell biology."

Except for a year at Yale University in 1975–1976 and one at the California Institute of Technology in 1988–1989, Neher has remained at Göttingen. In 1983 he was appointed head of the Department of Membrane Biophysics. Since 1987 he has also been a professor at the University of Göttingen. Neher is described by his colleagues as a "soft-spoken, friendly, precise" man devoted to his wife, microbiologist Eva-Marie (Ruhr) Neher, whom he married in 1978, and their five children.

Neher has received many awards, including the German Society for Physical Chemistry's Nernst Prize (1977), Great Britain's Feldberg Foundation Award (1979), the American Biophysical Society's K. C. Cole Award (1982), Columbia University's Spencer Award (1983) and Louisa Gross-Horwitz Award (1986), and the Gairdner Foundation's International Research Award (1989). He is a member of the Bavarian Academy of Scientists, the Academia Europaea, and the National Academy of Sciences (U.S.A.).

SELECTED WORKS: Elektronische Masstechnik in der Physiologie, 1974; Single Channel Recording, 1983; "The Patch Clamp Technique," with B. Sakmann, Scientific American March 1992.

ABOUT: Chemical and Engineering News October 14, 1991; New Scientist October 12, 1991; New York Times October 8, 1991; Science October 25, 1991; Washington Post October 8, 1991.

WOLFGANG PAUL

PAUL, WOLFGANG
(August 10, 1913–   )
Nobel Prize for Physics, 1989
(shared with Hans G. Dehmelt and Norman F. Ramsey)

The German physicist Wolfgang Paul was born in Lorenzkirch, a small village in Saxony. He was the fourth of six children of Theodor and Elisabeth (Ruppel) Paul. Paul recalls spending time in the laboratory of his father, who was a professor of pharmaceutical chemistry at the University of Munich. By the time his father died, when Paul was just fifteen, the boy had developed a strong interest in science, even though his parents, as he put it, "were very much in favor of a humanistic education." When he graduated from high school, with "nine years of Latin and six years of ancient Greek, history, and philosophy," he immediately decided to become a physicist.

Under the advice of his father's former colleague, the physicist Arnold Sommerfeld, Paul began his career with an apprenticeship in precision mechanics (the study of forces and motion). He then entered the Technical University of Munich in 1932. In 1934 he transferred to the Technical University of Berlin and began work with physicist Hans Kopfermann, a collaboration that was to last for the next sixteen years.

Paul received his diploma (the equivalent of a master's degree) in 1937 and followed Kopfermann to the University of Kiel. Just before completing his doctoral thesis on the properties of the nucleus of the element beryllium, he was inducted into the air force, only a few days before the beginning of World War II. "Fortunately," he re-

called, "a few months later I got a leave of absence to finish my thesis," which he completed in 1939. In 1940 he was exempted from military service.

Paul promptly rejoined Kopfermann's group, which moved to the University of Göttingen two years later. There, in 1944 he became an assistant professor.

At the university, Paul used mass spectrometry to study the separation of isotopes. Isotopes are atoms of an element that have the same number of protons (and the same charge) but a different number of neutrons, and therefore a different atomic mass. A mass spectrometer uses a strong magnetic field to deflect a molecular beam, or stream, of ions (charged particles) from a particular element. This deflection separates ions from different isotopes—those with heavier atomic masses are deflected less.

After World War II, Göttingen became a part of West Germany, which was placed under a military government. "Due to the restriction in physics research imposed by the military government, I turned for a few years my interest to radiobiology [the study of the effect of radiation on living organisms] and cancer therapy by electrons," Paul recalled. Eventually, he returned to his earlier studies.

The sad state of German physics research may have stimulated Paul's inventiveness. "It was a scanty period," he later wrote. "In order to become in a few years competitive with the well-advanced physics abroad we tried to develop new methods and instruments in all our research." One method Paul developed to improve measurements of atomic properties was to devise electric and magnetic "lenses" that could help to focus beams of molecules more precisely. Some of his inventions have become standard equipment in molecular beam labs.

In 1952 Paul was appointed professor at the University of Bonn and director of its Physics Institute. He has remained at Bonn ever since, working in the fields of mass spectrometry, molecular beam physics, and high-energy electron physics (the use of particle accelerators to study atomic properties).

Several factors determine how precisely one can make measurements of an atom: how little it moves while under observation, how little interference there is from nearby atoms, and how long it can be observed. In the late 1950s, Paul and his students developed the first ion traps, which improved all these factors: they permitted scientists to slow down, isolate, and study atoms for a very long time. "Such traps permit the observation of isolated particles, even of a single one, over a long period of time and therefore . . . enable us to measure their properties with extremely high accuracy," Paul wrote.

Now called Paul traps, these electrical "bottles" for charged particles were a natural extension of his work with lenses. "If one extends the rules of two-dimensional focusing to three dimensions, one possesses all ingredients for particle traps," Paul explained. Paul's development of ion traps has greatly advanced high-precision measurements of atoms, such as electrical charge, magnetic strength, and mass. Also, these traps can be used to test the theory of quantum mechanics, which predicts how atoms emit and absorb light.

Paul was awarded the 1989 Nobel Prize for Physics for his invention of the ion trap. While many scientists have used and refined ion traps, HANS G. DEHMELT's contributions have been so outstanding that he too was awarded the 1989 Nobel Prize for Physics. Dehmelt developed the Penning trap, and with it he confined a single electron for nearly a year. He has also developed better methods for slowing down particles and measuring the frequencies of their emissions. Dehmelt's work measuring the properties of electrons has earned him the distinction of making the most sensitive test ever of a physical theory. Researchers have also used ion traps to study other single-charged particles, measure frequencies very exactly, and make the most accurate measurements of the mass of a proton.

As Ingvar Lindgren of the Royal Swedish Academy of Sciences said when awarding Paul the Nobel Prize, "The dream of the spectroscopist is to be able to study a single atom or ion under constant conditions for a long period of time. In recent years, this dream has been to a large extent realized," thanks to the ion trap.

"The technique is now being used in development of improved atomic clocks," Lindgren continued. (NORMAN F. RAMSEY shared in the 1989 Nobel Prize for Physics for his key contributions to the development of atomic clocks—ultraprecise timekeepers.) "The continued rapid development of the atomic clock can be foreseen in the near future. An accuracy of *1 part in one-billion billions* is considered realistic."

Lindgren concluded, "The new technique [will be] even more important for testing very fundamental principles of physics. Further testing of quantum physics . . . may force us to revise our assumptions about . . . the smallest building blocks of matter."

Paul has four children by his late wife, the former Liselotte Hirsche, whom he married in 1940. "She shared with me the depressing period after the war, and due to her optimistic view of life she gave me strength and independence for my profession," he recalls. She died in 1977; Paul is now married to Dr. Doris Walch-Paul, a professor of medieval literature at the University of Bonn.

Paul became a professor emeritus in 1981 but remains active in research. He is currently developing "magnetic bottles" for confining non-charged particles, such as neutrons. His two sons, Lorenz and Stephan, have joined him in his work.

Paul has served in various executive positions with CERN (the pan-European accelerator organization) and DESY (the West German national accelerator laboratory). He has been a member of many advisory bodies, including German government committees on higher education and research planning. Paul is also president of the Alexander von Humboldt Foundation, a group which fosters international collaboration and exchange between scientists. His awards include the Grosses Verdienstkreuz mit Stern (literally, Great Cross of Merit with Star) of the Federal Republic of Germany, the Robert W. Pohl Prize of the German Physical Society, and the Gold Medal of the Academy of Sciences in Prague.

ABOUT: International Who's Who, 1990; New York Times October 13, 1989; Physics Today December, 1989; Science October 20, 1989; Scientific American December 1989; U.S. News and World Report October 23, 1989; Washington Post October 13, 1989.

PAZ, OCTAVIO

(March 31, 1914–   )
Nobel Prize for Literature, 1990

Octavio Paz (päs), poet and essayist, grew up in a town on the outskirts of Mexico City in what he described as "an old dilapidated house that had a junglelike garden and a great room full of books."

OCTAVIO PAZ

The son of Josefina Lozano Paz, whose family had come from Andalusia, in Spain, and Octavio Paz Sr., a lawyer and social reformer, the young Paz was deeply influenced by his paternal grandfather, a public official and novelist who was among the first to write sympathetically about Mexico's Indian population.

In his childhood home, Paz remembered, "The garden soon became the center of my world; the library, an enchanted cave. . . . Books with pictures, especially history books, eagerly leafed through, supplied images of deserts and jungles, palaces and hovels, warriors and princesses, beggars and kings. We were shipwrecked with Sinbad and with Robinson, we fought with D'Artagnan, we took Valencia with the Cid. . . . The world was limitless, yet it was always within reach; time was a pliable substance that weaved an unbroken present."

By his teens Paz had become familiar with modern works in Spanish as well as with foreign authors such as Nietzsche, Marx, Hugo, and Rousseau. T. S. ELIOT's *The Waste Land* particularly impressed him. In 1931, at age seventeen, Paz founded his first literary review, *Barandal* (Banister); at age nineteen, he published his first book of poetry, *Luna silvestre* (Forest Moon). Paz attended the National University of Mexico but did not get a degree. Instead, he went to the Yucatán to found a secondary school and explore the Mexican past.

In 1937 Paz left Mexico for Madrid. There, along with many other North American artists and intellectuals, he supported the Loyalists in their unsuccessful struggle to protect their republic against General Francisco Franco's fascist forces

in the Spanish Civil War. Paz's experiences in Spain confirmed in him the leftist perspective that was to dominate his early and middle years.

On his return to Mexico, Paz founded another literary journal, *Taller* (Workshop). In this journal and its successor, *El Hijo Pródigo* (The Prodigal Son), Paz's work reflected a surrealist inspiration and his deep interest in Mexican culture, tradition, and history. In addition to original works, Paz contributed translations from French, German, and English.

In 1943 Paz received a Guggenheim fellowship and went to study and travel in the United States. Two years later he joined Mexico's diplomatic service. He was posted to Paris, where he spent five years and met writers such as André Breton, AL-BERT CAMUS, and JEAN-PAUL SARTRE and became immersed in surrealist poetry and existentialist philosophy.

In 1950 he published a major prose work, *El labertino de la soledad (The Labyrinth of Solitude),* a probing and original study of the Mexican national character. This book explores the effect of the Indian and Spanish heritages and of influences from the United States on modern Mexicans. The book continues to have such a tremendous impact that Alice Reckley, a University of Missouri professor of Latin American literature, recently noted, "No one can talk about the Mexican character without referring to Paz." The concerns that inspired this book remain central to Paz's work today; as he wrote, "In Mexico the Spaniards encountered history as well as geography. That history is still alive: it is a present rather than a past. The temples and gods of pre-Columbian Mexico are a pile of ruins, but the spirit that breathed life into that world has not disappeared; it speaks to us in the hermetic language of myth, legend, forms of social coexistence, popular art, customs. Being a Mexican writer means listening to the voice of that present, that presence."

From Paris, Paz was sent as Mexico's ambassador to Switzerland, then to Japan, and finally to India. His years in Asia inspired a deep and abiding interest in Oriental poetry, painting, and architecture as well as the classic writings of Buddhism and Taoism, all of which left their mark on his poetry. He published an influential collection of essays on poetics, *El arco y la lira (The Bow and the Lyre),* in 1956.

Paz resigned from the diplomatic corps in 1968 in protest against the Mexican government's violent suppression of student demonstrations at the Olympic Games in the Plaza de Tlatelolco. His essays from this period, which focused on themes of religion, sexuality, and culture, were published in his 1970 collection *Posdata* (published in English in 1972 and 1985, with additional essays, as *The*

Other Mexico). During the 1970s Paz taught at both Harvard University (where in 1971–1972 he delivered the Charles Eliot Norton lectures) and Cambridge University and continued to write poetry, critical essays, and political commentary. His poetry became increasingly experimental. His most complex poem, *Blanco* (1967), can be folded in a variety of ways to permit alternative readings. Paz also experimented with multilingual poetry and cooperative works done with several poets.

In all its forms, Paz's work has been dominated by his deep interest in Mexico and his social consciousness. His bent toward mysticism distinguishes his writing from that of many other politically oriented writers. Those who comment on his writing almost invariably note its breadth and sheer change over time: in approaching fields as diverse as modern and ancient art, philosophy, religion, anthropology, psychology, and politics, Paz has successfully incorporated surrealist and classical styles and contemporary Western, ancient Mexican, and traditional Asian influences.

Paz characterizes his development as a writer as a quest for modernity, a quest that he has come to see as an effort to rediscover the unbroken present that he lived so vividly in the garden of his childhood: "Only now have I understood that there was a secret relationship between what I have called my expulsion from the present and the writing of poetry. Poetry is in love with the instant and seeks to relive it in the poem, thus separating it from sequential time and turning it into a fixed present." As he commented when he accepted the Nobel Prize, "I returned to the source and discovered that modernity is not outside but within us. It is today and the most ancient antiquity; it is tomorrow and the beginning of the world; it is a thousand years old and yet newborn. It speaks in Nahuatl, draws Chinese ideograms from the ninth century, and appears on the television screen."

In announcing that Paz had won the 1990 Nobel Prize for Literature, Sture Allén of the Swedish Academy recognized the surprising extent to which he has succeeded in his ambitious efforts. The academy described him as "a writer of Spanish with a wide international perspective" whose "poetry and essays evolve from an intractable but fruitful union of cultures: pre-Columbian Indian, the Spanish Conquistadors, and Western modernism." When presenting the prize, Kjell Espmark of the academy drew attention to Paz's "welding together of thought and sensuousness" and to his ability to capture the eternal moment. As an example, he pointed to Paz's 1957 work *Piedra de sol (Sunstone),* an epic inspired by the so-called calendar stone, an ancient Aztec sculpture in the National Museum in Mexico City. Espmark praised the way in which the poem "precisely

forced different times, regions, and identities to merge in one single here, now, and I, dictated by the logic of the dream."

To Paz, Espmark said, "It has been my task to give a picture of your writing in a few minutes. It is like trying to press a continent into a walnut shell—a feat for which the language of criticism is poorly equipped. This is, however, what you have managed to do, again and again."

Scholars generally applauded the Swedish Academy's choice. According to Roberto González Echevarría, a professor of Spanish at Yale University, Paz's Nobel Prize was long overdue. "He's clearly one of the major poets of the twentieth century. He was able to cull from the language of the avant-garde the very best to create a Latin American poetic language, to domesticate it."

Besides his poetry and literary essays, Paz continues to write extensively about politics, although his views have changed from the fervently secular socialism of his youth to current positions such as supporting the present right-of-center Mexican government, encouraging closer ties with the United States, and arguing for the integration of Catholic tradition into Mexican political culture. These changes have made Paz a controversial figure among Mexican leftists: Though his poetry remains almost universally admired, his more conservative political beliefs have rendered him suspect to many of his country's intellectuals.

Paz became an honorary member of the American Academy of Arts and Letters in 1972 and received an honorary doctorate from Harvard in 1980. His many awards include the 1981 Cervantes Prize (the most prestigious award in the Spanish-speaking world), the 1982 American Neustadt Prize, and literature prizes from Belgium, Israel, Spain, Mexico, and West Germany. He continues to publish *Vuelta* (Return), a magazine dedicated to the arts and politics. He and his wife, the former Marie José Tramini, whom he married in 1964, have one daughter.

ADDITIONAL WORKS IN ENGLISH TRANSLATION: Configurations, 1971; Renga: A Chain of Poems, 1972; Early Poems: 1935–1955, 1973; Eagle or Sun? 1976; Selected Poems, 1976; A Draft of Shadows and Other Poems, 1979; Airborn, 1981; The Monkey Grammarian, 1981; Obsidian Butterfly, 1983; Selected Poems, 1984; The Four Poplars, 1985; One Earth, Four or Five Worlds, 1985; On Poets and Others, 1986; Convergences, 1987; Homage and Desecrations, 1987; Sor Juana: Or, the Traps of Faith, 1988; A Tree Within, 1988; Alternating Current, 1991; The Collected Poems: 1957–1987, 1991; In Search of the Present, 1991.

ABOUT: Chantikian, K. Octavio Paz: Homage to the Poet, 1980; Contemporary Authors, 1990; Contemporary Literary Criticism, 1989; Current Biography, 1974; Fein, J. Toward Octavio Paz, 1986; Guibert, R. Seven Voices, 1973; International Who's Who, 1991–92; Ivask, I. The Perpetual Present, 1973; Phillips, R. The Poetic Modes of Octavio Paz, 1973; Wilson, J. Octavio Paz, 1986; World Authors, 1970.

PEDERSEN, CHARLES J.
(October 3, 1904–October 26, 1989)
Nobel Prize for Chemistry, 1987
(shared with Donald J. Cram and Jean-Marie
   Lehn)

The American chemist Charles J. Pedersen was
born in Fusan, Korea. His father, Brede Pedersen,
was a Norwegian mechanical engineer employed
by the Unsan Mines, an American-owned gold
mining operation in Korea. His mother, Takino
(Yasui) Pedersen, belonged to a Japanese merchant family that had moved to Korea to deal in
soybeans and silkworms. Pedersen and his older
sister, Astrid, grew up speaking English in the
Americanized environment of the Unsan Mines.

Pedersen later speculated that his unusual upbringing may have influenced his decision to become a chemist. Living in an isolated enclave that
resembled the frontier mining towns of the American West, he learned what he later described as "a
certain independent approach to problem solving."
He also was inspired by the sight and odor of the
pouring of molten gold.

Because English-language schools did not exist
in Korea, Pedersen was sent to convent school in
Nagasaki, Japan, at the age of eight. At age ten, he
moved on to Saint Joseph College, a preparatory
school in Yokohama, where he took his first course
in chemistry. In 1922, at his father's suggestion, he
went to the United States to study chemical engineering at the University of Dayton (Ohio). After
his graduation in 1926, he enrolled at the Massachusetts Institute of Technology and earned a master's degree in organic chemistry a year later.

Though Pedersen's professors encouraged him
to continue his studies, he wanted to relieve his father of the burden of supporting him financially. He
therefore decided not to pursue a Ph.D. but instead
to take a job as a research chemist at E. I. du Pont
de Nemours and Company in Wilmington, Dela-
ware. Pedersen later described Du Pont as "a productive center of research where many interesting
and important problems were being solved. . . .
The atmosphere was vibrant and exciting, and success was expected." Pedersen remained at Du Pont
for his entire forty-two-year career as a chemist. He
produced twenty-five technical papers and sixty-
five patents, mainly in petrochemicals.

At the time, Du Pont manufactured a variety of
products made from petroleum and rubber. Like
many other materials, petroleum and rubber can be
broken down by oxidation—the chemical reaction
that occurs when their molecules come in contact
with oxygen. (A more familiar form of oxidation is
the rust that forms on iron and steel.) Pedersen
found that trace metals found in petroleum and
rubber, such as copper and vanadium, serve as cat-

CHARLES J. PEDERSEN

alysts—that is, they speed up the oxidation process. Therefore, he began searching for "metal deactivators"—chemical compounds that would
suppress the catalytic activity of metals.

Pedersen's search for metal deactivators led
him into the field of coordination chemistry—the
study of how metallic ions bond with nonmetallic
ions. (In such a union, the nonmetallic ion is
called a ligand.) Pedersen began to investigate
whether various ligands could halt the catalytic
properties of copper, and thus the oxidative degra-
dation of petroleum and rubber. His work led to
the first good metal deactivator for petroleum
products.

By the mid-1940s, Pedersen had become an acknowledged expert in the field of oxidative degra-
dation and stabilization. He was given the title of
research associate, which at that time was the
highest position a Du Pont scientist could achieve.

His most important work, however, was not to
come until 1960. During that year, he had begun to
investigate the effects of various ligands on the
metallic element vanadium. One of his experiments yielded an unexpected byproduct—a small
quantity of silky white crystals that Pedersen had
never seen before.

Instead of discarding the byproduct, he experimented with it. He suspected that it was a member
of the family of organic compounds called phenols, which typically appear as white crystals at
room temperature. To test this hypothesis, he
mixed the unknown crystals with methane. They
dissolved in the methane to the same degree that a
phenol would. He then added a small amount of
sodium hydroxide (commonly known as caustic
soda). If the unknown substance were a phenol, the

sodium hydroxide would not dissolve, because phenols do not bind to sodium ions. To Pedersen's surprise, however, the sodium hydroxide dissolved completely.

Pedersen computed the molecular weight of the unknown substance and discovered that it was exactly twice the molecular weight of a phenol. From these and other observations, he determined the crystals' unusual molecular structure.

A molecule's structure is determined by the way the atoms that make up the molecule attach to each other. In some molecules, atoms attach in long chains. In others, they form the shape of a cross or a pyramid. In Pedersen's new molecule, the atoms formed a large ring. Ring-shaped molecules are not in themselves unusual—benzene, for example, is also ring-shaped—but Pedersen's molecule was an unusually large ring, consisting of 18 atoms. (In contrast, the central ring of a benzene molecule consists of only 6 atoms.)

Pedersen's molecule was a ring of 12 carbon atoms and 6 oxygen atoms, with 2 carbons between each oxygen. With the oxygen atoms protruding from the ring at regular intervals, the structure reminded Pedersen of a royal crown. Therefore, Pedersen called this new molecule a *crown ether.* (An ether is a molecule in which an oxygen atom is attached to 2 carbon atoms in hydrocarbon radicals.)

Pedersen named his first crown ether 18-crown-6, or 18C6, because it had 18 atoms in its ring, 6 of which were oxygen. He later explained, "I created the system of crown nomenclature chiefly because the official [chemical] names of the crown ethers were so complex and hard for me to remember." Pedersen's delight in his discovery was motivated by aesthetics as much as by science. The crown-like appearance of the molecule intrigued him, and he was taken with the elegant simplicity of its structure.

Having determined the structure of the crown ether, Pedersen was now able to explain the results of his experiment. He realized that the sodium ion from each molecule of caustic soda had fallen into the hole at the center of a crown ether. Once it entered the hole, the ion was trapped there—not just because of electrostatic attraction but also because of the physical shape of the molecule. In the absence of the sodium ion, the crown ether ring was "floppy," but with the ion bound at its center, it assumed a stiffer, more platelike shape.

Pedersen went on to create other crown ethers, each designed to bond to a different type of metallic ion. In the meantime, Du Pont held back Pedersen's findings until it was able to take out patents on his discovery. When his results were finally published in 1967, they created a stir among organic chemists around the world.

Up until this point, no one had ever made a synthetic compound that could form stable bonds with sodium ions. Pedersen's crown ethers could also bond with other alkali metal ions—such as potassium, lithium, rubidium, and cesium—that had been previously difficult to bind. The way in which metal ions bind to crown ethers has helped biochemists understand how cells transport sodium and potassium ions across membranes. It has been suggested that natural molecules similar in structure to crown ethers may open up channels in a cell membrane, through which metal ions can pass.

Crown ethers have practical applications as well. Because crown ethers can be designed to bond to specific metal ions, they can be used to separate metal mixtures—thereby making it easy to reclaim expensive metals. If a crown ether is attached to an electrical circuit, it can serve as a sensor for detecting specific metal ions.

Pedersen's pioneering work in organic synthesis made it possible for DONALD J. CRAM and JEAN-MARIE LEHN, working independently, to design more complex molecules that can bind a greater variety of ions with a greater degree of selectivity. Their work laid the foundation for the field of supramolecular chemistry. Both Cram and Lehn eventually produced synthetic molecules that, to some extent, mimic the actions of enzymes (naturally occurring proteins that are essential to many biochemical reactions).

Pedersen, Cram, and Lehn shared the 1987 Nobel Prize for Chemistry "for achievements in the development and use of molecules that can recognize each other and choose with which other molecules they will form complexes." In his presentation speech, Salo Gronowitz of the Royal Swedish Academy of Sciences said that the three chemists had "laid the foundation to what today is one of the most expansive chemical research areas, for which Cram has coined the term host-guest chemistry, while Lehn calls it supramolecular chemistry. Their research has been of enormous importance for the development of coordination chemistry, organic synthesis, analytical chemistry, bioinorganic and bioorganic chemistry; it is no longer science fiction to prepare supermolecules which are better and more versatile catalysts than the highly specialized enzymes."

The work of Pedersen, Cram, and Lehn has opened up many possibilities for future research. As Gronowitz suggested, it may soon be possible to create totally artificial enzymes with clear advantages over the natural substances that control the destinies of cells. Because enzymes are biological catalysts that govern virtually everything a cell can do or become, artificial equivalents that provide greater stability and selectivity hold great promise for medical and industrial applications. The laureates' work also makes possible the chemical separation of substances with greater precision than was possible before. It offers the hope of developing extremely sensitive chemicals that will be able to remove poisonous substances from contaminated soil, water, or air.

In 1947 Pedersen moved to Salem, New Jersey, and married Susan Ault, with whom he had two daughters. In 1969 he retired from Du Pont and pursued interests in fishing, gardening, bird study, and poetry. His wife died in 1983, and Pedersen himself died in 1989. He is remembered by his colleagues as an unassuming yet charming man who found great enjoyment in his work.

ABOUT: American Men and Women of Science, 1989; New York Times October 15, 1987; New York Times October 27, 1989; New Scientist October 22, 1987; Science October 30, 1987.

NORMAN F. RAMSEY

RAMSEY, NORMAN F.

(August 27, 1915–)
Nobel Prize for Physics, 1989
(shared with Hans G. Dehmelt and Wolfgang Paul)

The American physicist Norman Foster Ramsey Jr. was born in Washington, D.C. His mother had taught mathematics at the University of Kansas; his father, Brigadier-General Norman F. Ramsey Sr., was a West Point graduate serving in the Army Ordnance Corps. His father's assignments took Ramsey's family to Kansas, then to Paris, France, then to New Jersey, and back to Kansas. Ramsey flourished intellectually through these moves, skipping two grades and graduating from high school at age fifteen.

Since Ramsey was interested in science, he entered Columbia University in 1931 as an engineering major. Soon, though, he shifted to mathematics in search of "a deeper understanding of nature than what was expected of engineers." It was not until he graduated in 1935 that he "discovered that physics was a possible profession" and that it was the field he preferred.

Columbia offered Ramsey a fellowship to Cambridge University, in England, where he enrolled as a physics undergraduate. While earning his second bachelor's degree, he learned of the research being done by I. I. RABI and decided to return to Columbia to do his Ph.D. work with Rabi.

Rabi was studying the quantum-mechanical properties of atoms and molecules. Quantum mechanics asserts that atoms and molecules can exist only at certain discrete energy levels. They can only change energy levels by releasing or absorb-

ing a photon (a particle of light) with energy equal to the difference between the two states. That amount of energy is called a quantum.

Rabi was using a new method, the molecular beam, developed by OTTO STERN and Walter Gerlach, in his studies. A molecular beam is a thin stream of molecules or atoms. Atomic nuclei behave like tiny magnets; by passing a molecular beam through a magnetic field, physicists can make observations about the magnetic properties of the molecule or atom in the beam, such as its magnetic moment (strength) or its spin. Quantum mechanical spin is analogous to the property of rotating on an axis, like a top. Stern and Gerlach passed molecular beams through a magnetic field and found that, in addition to having discrete energy levels, atoms exist with only certain magnetic moments and spins, which they were able to measure.

Only a few months after Ramsey returned to Columbia, Rabi invented the molecular beam magnetic resonance method of studying molecules, which brought him the 1944 Nobel Prize for Physics. The technique improved on Stern's and Gerlach's method by passing a molecular beam through a strong static magnetic field while subjecting it to a second, rapidly rotating magnetic field. (The latter is often provided by radio waves or microwaves.) Tuning the rotating field so that its resonance frequency (its rate of vibration) matches that of the static one caused the electrons or atomic nuclei to change magnetic orientation in a detectable way. Because the resonance frequency depends upon the magnetic moment of the nucleus, Rabi could measure moments by measuring the frequency that made the nuclei change their orientation. Thanks to his timely arrival, Ramsey was the first graduate student to work in the new field of magnetic resonance, and in 1940 he was awarded a Ph.D. for his study of magnetic moments of molecules.

That same year, Ramsey married Elinor Stedman Jameson and moved to the University of Illinois, fully intending to spend his life there. World War II interrupted these plans. Within a few weeks, Ramsey had moved again to the Massachusetts Institute of Technology (MIT) Radiation Laboratory to head a radar research group. After two years he went to Washington, D.C., as a radar consultant to the secretary of war and then to Los Alamos, New Mexico, to work on the Manhattan Project, the United States atomic bomb project.

At the war's end, he returned to Columbia as an associate professor and to Rabi's molecular beam lab. One year later, Ramsey made yet another move, this time to Harvard University, where he has remained ever since. He promptly set up a molecular beam lab and took up the task of measuring magnetic moments more precisely. To do this, he would need to find a way to keep the static magnetic field extremely uniform over the length of the beam; any irregularities shifted and blurred the resonance frequency. Ramsey soon found he could not eliminate the irregularities with existing magnet technology. In 1949 he invented a new method that allowed a considerable increase in accuracy without the necessity of improving the static magnetic field.

In his new method, called the separated oscillatory field method, the molecular beam passes through two rotating magnetic fields, separated by a long region containing only a static magnetic field. If the two oscillating fields are tuned to the same frequency and are precisely in phase, the first one tips the spinning nuclei partly over, and the second one completes the tip. The advantage to this method, as Ramsey showed, is that small field irregularities in the long region between the oscillating fields have no effect on the measurement of the resonance frequency.

The separated oscillatory fields method was one of the inventions that led to Ramsey's 1989 Nobel Prize for Physics. It has been used by Ramsey and many others to make very accurate measurements of the properties of atoms and molecules. In addition, it led to the development of atomic clocks, which use the magnetic resonance frequencies of atoms as a standard for timekeeping. Since 1967, "one second is no longer based on the rotation of the earth or its movement around the sun, but is instead defined as the time interval during which the cesium atom makes a certain number of oscillations," Ingvar Lindgren of the Royal Swedish Academy of Sciences explained, when presenting Ramsey with the prize. Cesium clocks have a mar-

gin of error of one-thousandth of a second every 300 years, a millionfold improvement over older clocks.

Ramsey's Nobel Prize was also awarded for the atomic hydrogen maser (microwave amplification by stimulated emission of radiation), invented by Ramsey and his former student Daniel Kleppner in 1961. His maser exposes a trapped beam of hydrogen atoms to microwave radiation at a resonance frequency, stimulating the atoms to change their magnetic orientation and emit even more microwave radiation.

The hydrogen maser has been very successful both as an accurate clock and as a means of measuring fundamental properties of hydrogen atoms. Over fairly short times—several hours—it is 100 times more accurate than a cesium clock, although cesium clocks are more accurate over longer time spans.

Ramsey's inventions have proven invaluable to scientific research. For example, by comparing two hydrogen masers, one on the ground and one shot to a 6,000-mile altitude by a rocket, scientists were able to measure the tiny variations in their timekeeping predicted by ALBERT EINSTEIN's general theory of relativity.

Atomic clocks borne aloft by satellites allow navigators to determine their position on the earth's surface to within 10 meters. Atomic clocks were also essential for navigation in United States space missions.

Robert Pool of *Science* magazine has suggested that Ramsey's Nobel Prize is as much a lifetime achievement award as an honor for specific inventions. Ramsey has studied and measured a very wide variety of atomic and molecular properties; for example, he laid the foundation for the theories behind the development of nuclear magnetic resonance (NMR) and magnetic resonance imaging (MRI). Co-worker Daniel Kleppner has called him a "monumental figure in contemporary physics."

Ramsey has also played a major organizational role in American physics. In addition to founding and presiding over several of the nation's best respected institutions, he has served in executive positions for a wide range of organizations, including the American Physical Society, the American Institute of Physics, the American Association for the Advancement of Science, the National Research Council, and the United Chapters of Phi Beta Kappa. He was also the first Assistant Secretary General for Science for NATO.

Ramsey has been a member or head of many advisory panels. He headed the high energy physics panel of the President's Scientific Advisory Board in 1963 and has also advised the Air Force, the Defense Department, the Atomic Energy Commission, and the National Bureau of Standards.

Ramsey shared the 1989 Nobel Prize in Physics with HANS G. DEHMELT and WOLFGANG PAUL, both of whom have also developed high-precision techniques for studying the properties of atoms. In awarding the prize, Lindgren emphasized particularly the importance of the atomic clock and predicted that its continued development would soon lead to clocks 100,000 times more accurate. "This corresponds to an uncertainty of less than 1 second since the creation of the universe 15 billion years ago," he said.

"Do we need such accuracy?" Lindgren asked, answering that "navigation and communication in space require a growing degree of exactness. . . . The new technique may be even more important for testing very fundamental principles of physics. Further tests of quantum physics and relativity theory may force us to revise our assumptions about time and space or about the smallest building blocks of matter."

Ramsey has continued to experiment, write, and teach since his retirement from Harvard's Higgins Professorship in Physics in 1986. He married Ellie Welch after the death of his first wife in 1983. The couple, he says, has a "combined family of seven children and six grandchildren. We enjoy downhill and cross-country skiing, hiking, bicycling, and trekking as well as musical and cultural events."

Ramsey has received many honorary degrees and awards, including the Presidential Certificate of Merit (1950), the E. O. Lawrence Award (1960), the Davisson-Germer Prize (1974), the Columbia Award for Excellence in Science (1980), the Institute of Electrical and Electronics Engineers Medal of Honor (1984) and Centennial Medal (1987), the Rabi Prize (1985), the Rumford Premium (1985), the Compton Medal (1986), the Oersted Medal (1988), and the National Medal of Science (1988).

SELECTED WORKS: Experimental Nuclear Physics, 1953, with E. Segrè; Nuclear Moments, 1953; Quick Calculus, 1965, 1985, with D. Kleppner.

ABOUT: International Who's Who, 1990; New York Times October 13, 1989; Physics Today December 1989; Science October 20, 1989; Scientific American December 1989; U.S. News and World Report October 23, 1989; Washington Post October 13, 1989.

SAKMANN, BERT
(June 12, 1942–)
Nobel Prize for Physiology or Medicine, 1991
(shared with Erwin Neher)

The German physiologist Bert Sakmann was born and raised in Stuttgart. His father, Bertold Sakmann, was a theater director, and his mother,

BERT SAKMANN

the former Annemarie Schaefer, was a physiotherapist. He was trained as a physician at the universities of Tübingen and Munich and completed an internship in surgery, internal medicine, and gynecology at Munich's University Hospital in 1970.

While receiving the standard medical training, Sakmann also pursued an interest in basic research. During his medical internship he spent a year as a research assistant at the Max Planck Institute for Psychiatry in Munich, where he investigated the activity of the retina, the net of light-sensitive cells in the eye.

Like the rest of the nervous system, the retina functions electrically. Between the inside and the outside of nerve cells there exists an unequal distribution of ions, such as positively charged sodium, potassium, and calcium atoms and negatively charged chlorine atoms. In the 1940s and early 1950s the English physiologists ALAN HODGKIN and ANDREW HUXLEY established that these ions move across the nerve cell membrane (the cell's outer wall) in response to electrical, physical, or chemical stimulation from other cells. This movement in turn spreads an electric current along the membrane, resulting in a nerve impulse.

These ions do not move through passive holes in the nerve cell membrane, Hodgkin and Huxley hypothesized, but through gates or channels embedded in the membrane that can control the flow of specific ions and are themselves controlled by electrical stimulation or another form of stimulation.

By the mid-1970s scientists had put together a clear picture of ion channels. They appeared to be large protein molecules, or collections of molecules, with a hole in the middle that could be opened and closed. When the hole is open, ions can slip through the cell membrane. When it is closed, the channel is impenetrable.

Sakmann spent the years from 1971 through 1973 as a postdoctoral assistant in BERNARD KATZ's biophysics laboratory at University College in London. He then returned to Germany to take a position as assistant professor at the Max Planck Institute in Göttingen. There he shared laboratory space with ERWIN NEHER. In conversation, Sakmann later recalled, the two men agreed that ion channels represented "one of the most urgent problems in membrane biophysics." While a great deal had been deduced about their structure and function, all the research to date had involved indirect methods: no one had ever been able to isolate a single ion channel and study its individual properties.

At that time scientists studied ion channels by using a voltage clamp, which had been invented in the mid-1930s by K. C. Cole of Columbia University and refined by Hodgkin and Huxley. A voltage clamp is a device that "freezes" the electric field of a portion of the cell membrane at the level the experimenter chooses, so that the flow of selected ions at a given point can be measured at any time.

Voltage clamps, while very useful, have several drawbacks. First, the clamp controls a comparatively large area of cell membrane and therefore thousands of ion channels. Second, some ions are able to bypass the ion channels and leak through the cell membrane by way of pores. This flow creates additional electrical activity, or background noise, against which the activities of the channels must be studied.

Sakmann and Neher first solved these problems in 1976, using hollow glass tubes (pipettes) with ultrafine tips only a few microns (millionths of a meter) in diameter. When the pipette is pressed against a nerve cell membrane, the glass forms a strong, highly resistant seal. Instruments within the pipette respond only to the micron-sized patch of membrane surrounded by the pipette's wall. Such a small piece of membrane can contain only one or a few ion channels. By connecting the pipette to a voltage clamp, scientists can study the behavior of a single ion channel under various conditions.

Sakmann and Neher called their technique "patch clamping." At first there were a few problems, such as leakage between the pipette and the membrane, which led to bothersome levels of background noise. In 1980, however, Neher found a solution to this problem. He discovered that they could achieve the results they needed by applying suction to the pipette, using freshly made and polished pipettes for each experiment, and being scrupulously careful to avoid contaminating either the pipette or the cell surface. The resulting seal would be tremendously strong, both physically and electrically.

The refined patch-clamp technique was a scientific breakthrough. The seal is so strong that experimenters can tear the patch of membrane, ion channel and all, right out of the cell. They can then study the isolated channel or leave the pipette in place and study the inside of the cell. Since background noise has been almost entirely eliminated, they can measure the tiniest electric currents and observe the behavior of an individual ion channel with great clarity.

Frances Ashcroft of the University of Oxford has recalled that after they discovered patch clamping, Neher and Sakmann "opened their lab to the whole world, and the whole world went to Mecca." As other scientists learned the technique, it began to be applied more widely. Sakmann's and Neher's research on the acetylcholine receptor, which is located on a muscle and is activated by a nerve, had a revolutionary impact on the study of the nervous system and muscles.

But patch clamping also revealed that cells with no particular electrical activity—in the kidney, liver, blood, and elsewhere—also contain ion channels. The study of ion channels has shed light on the fertilization of eggs, the mechanics of muscle contraction, and the regulation of the heartbeat. It was scientists' use of patch clamping that led to the discovery that a defective chloride ion channel is the cause of the lethal inherited disease cystic fibrosis.

"Once we had developed these tools," Sakmann recalled, "the fun began." Sakmann has worked with several groups of scientists to prepare altered, genetically engineered forms of ion channels such as the acetylcholine receptor. Patch-clamp studies are then used to compare the natural with the engineered receptor in order to learn more about its functions. Sakmann's use of patch clamping to study mammalian brain cells has revealed secrets of the memory process. As he later explained, "The brain is the least understood organ, and what we have done [with patch clamping] is bring a little light into the zoo of channels within it."

Sakmann and Neher were awarded the 1991 Nobel Prize for Physiology or Medicine for their invention of the patch-clamp technique. They "conclusively established with their technique that ion channels do exist," the Nobel Assembly of the Karolinska Institute noted. "This new knowledge and this new analytical tool have during the past ten years revolutionized modern biology, facilitated research, and contributed to the understanding of the cellular mechanisms underlying several diseases."

The assembly emphasized the practical effects of the pair's prizewinning work. "Many . . . diseases [including cystic fibrosis, epilepsy, several cardiovascular diseases, and neuromuscular disorders] depend entirely or partially on a defect [in the] regulation of ion channels, and a number of drugs act directly on ion channels. Many pathological mechanisms have been clarified during the eighties through ion channel studies. . . . With the help of the technique of Neher and Sakmann, it is now possible to tailor-make drugs to achieve an optimal effect on particular ion channels," the assembly wrote. "Neher and Sakmann's contributions have meant a revolution for the field of cell biology."

Sakmann's wife Christianne, whom he married in 1970, is an ophthalmologist; they have three children. He is known as a scientist who is devoted to his family and has a good sense of humor. In his spare time he reads, plays tennis, and skis.

Sakmann was appointed director of the cell physiology department of the Göttingen Institute in 1985. In 1989 he moved to the Max Planck Institute for Medical Research in Heidelberg. His awards include the German Society for Physical Chemistry's Nernst Prize (1977), Great Britain's Feldberg Foundation Prize (1979), Israel's Magnes Foundation's Magnes Award (1981), Columbia University's Spencer Award (1983) and Louisa Gross-Horwitz Award (1986), and the Gairdner Foundation's International Research Award (1989).

WORKS BY: "The Patch Clamp Technique," with E. Neher, Scientific American March 1992.

ABOUT: Chemical and Engineering News October 14, 1991; New Scientist October 12, 1991; New York Times October 8, 1991; Science October 25, 1991; Washington Post October 8, 1991.

SCHWARTZ, MELVIN

(November 2, 1932–   )
Nobel Prize for Physics, 1988
(shared with Leon M. Lederman and Jack
    Steinberger)

The American physicist and entrepreneur Melvin Schwartz was born in New York City. He was the oldest child of Harry Schwartz, a laundryman, and Hannah (Shulman) Schwartz, a homemaker. He recalled that in the midst of the Great Depression, his parents "worked extraordinarily hard to give us economic stability, but at the same time they managed to instill in me two qualities which became the foundation of my personal and professional life. One is an unbounded sense of optimism; the other is a strong feeling as to the importance of using one's mind for the betterment of mankind."

MELVIN SCHWARTZ

At age twelve, Schwartz entered the Bronx High School of Science, where he served as news editor of the school paper and developed an interest in physics. He graduated in 1949. Schwartz wrote later of that point in his life, "The path to follow was fairly obvious. The Columbia [University] physics department at that time was unmatched by any in the world. Largely a product of the late Professor I. I. RABI, it was a department which was to provide the ambiance for six Nobel Prize pieces of work in widely diverse fields during the next thirteen years. And, in addition, it was the host for a period of time to another half dozen or so future Nobel laureates either as students or as postdoctoral researchers." In 1953, having completed his undergraduate degree in physics and mathematics, Schwartz entered the department's graduate program. That same year he also married Marilyn Fenster, with whom he eventually had three children: David, Diana, and Betty.

As a National Science and Quincy Ward Boese Fellow, Schwartz prepared his doctorate under the supervision of JACK STEINBERGER. Schwartz and Steinberger established a warm relationship. Schwartz described Steinberger as "my teacher, my mentor, and my closest colleague during my years at Columbia" and credited Steinberger with inspiring his love of particle physics. (Particle physics is the study of the atom and its parts, such as electrons, neutrons, and protons.) Not surprisingly, when he finished his doctorate in 1958, Schwartz joined Columbia's faculty. He became a full professor in 1963.

Schwartz was still an assistant professor, however, when he did his Nobel Prize–winning work between 1960 and 1962. At that time, scientists had long been aware of the existence of four fundamental forces that govern the physical interactions of matter: gravitation, electromagnetism, the strong nuclear force, and the weak nuclear force. The latter two forces operate only at the subatomic level: the strong force governs the interactions of protons and neutrons, and the weak force is effective in the interactions of less massive particles, such as electrons, which do not participate in the strong force.

Gravitation, the weakest of the four forces, does not play any significant role on the subatomic scale. The effects at short distances of electromagnetic and strong nuclear interactions can be investigated experimentally by the use of beams of particles, such as protons and electrons, accelerated in machines, such as cyclotrons and synchrotrons. Although the weak nuclear force was known to be responsible for one form of radioactivity, called beta decay, no one had gathered any information about the weak nuclear force by using the technique of colliding particle beams. One difficulty was that the weak force was masked by the much stronger electromagnetism and the strong nuclear force.

During a coffee-hour discussion in 1959, TSUNG-DAO LEE, a colleague of Schwartz's in the Columbia physics department, challenged his colleagues to come up with a way to observe and measure the weak force. That evening, Schwartz had a brainstorm—"Use neutrinos!" Neutrinos are particles that have no electrical charge and virtually no mass. They are therefore not affected by the electromagnetic force or the strong nuclear force. As Schwartz explained later, "Neutrinos do nothing but weak interactions."

Unfortunately, neutrinos, too, were difficult to study. Although billions upon billions of neutrinos pass through the earth daily, they almost never interact with other particles. Schwartz reasoned, however, that if enough neutrinos could be gathered in one place, the probability of interaction would rise. Therefore, if he could create a concentrated beam of neutrinos, he might be able to study uncontaminated weak force interactions.

Schwartz, Steinberger, and Lederman soon developed a technique for creating such a beam. They used Brookhaven National Laboratory's newly completed alternating gradient synchrotron to fire bursts of protons, at an energy of 15 billion electron volts, at a beryllium target. The impact at such a large energy level tore the nuclei of the beryllium atoms apart, creating a flood of subatomic particles. Among those particles were pions, which decay (break down) almost instantly into neutrinos and muons. (A muon is a particle similar to, but heavier than, an electron.)

The next task was to eliminate all the particles except the neutrinos. Schwartz and his colleagues

blocked the particles' path with a 10-ton wall of steel salvaged from a scrapped battleship. All the particles except the neutrinos were blocked by the steel; the neutrinos, which rarely interact with other particles, passed straight through. The result was a neutrino beam.

This new tool could be used for investigating the weak force. It also proved useful for investigating the neutrino itself, about which relatively little was known. Physicists, for example, had suggested that there might be two different kinds of neutrinos. That is, the neutrino formed from the decay of a pion might be different from the neutrino produced by beta decay. (In beta decay, a neutron decays into a proton, an electron, and a neutrino.) The two kinds of neutrinos were referred to as the muon type and the electron type, because the first—which resulted from pion decay—was always accompanied by a muon, and the second—which resulted from beta decay—was always accompanied by an electron. Schwartz and his colleagues realized that their neutrino beam was ideally suited to test this two-neutrino hypothesis because the neutrinos in the beam were all necessarily of the muon type—that is, they were all produced by the decay of pions.

To conduct the experiment, Schwartz, Steinberger, and Lederman built a 10-ton spark chamber containing ninety aluminum plates and focused the neutrino beam on it. (A spark chamber is a detection device in which particles are shot through neon gas, creating electric currents that cause the gas to glow. Different types of particles create different types of visible "trails" in the chamber.) Every time a neutrino collided with the nucleus of an aluminum atom, it would give off particles that could be identified by their distinctive trails. If the collisions yielded equal numbers of muons and electrons, the experimenters could conclude that the neutrinos associated with these particles did not differ. If the collisions yielded no electrons, however, the experimenters would have confirmed the two-neutrino hypothesis (according to which collisions from muon-type neutrinos should generate only muons).

During the eight months in which they conducted the experiment, approximately 100,000 billion neutrinos passed through the spark chamber. Fewer than 60 of those neutrinos collided with other particles. Significantly, however, every one of these collisions produced a muon rather than an electron. The scientists had confirmed the existence of two distinct kinds of neutrinos.

Gösta Ekspong of the Royal Swedish Academy of Sciences characterized this discovery as an "indispensable" contribution to the development of the standard model of particle physics. The standard model is a continually evolving theory describing the functions and behavior of all subatomic particles. With each new refinement to the standard model, physicists come one step closer to the development of a unified description of natural forces.

Yet in awarding Schwartz, Lederman, and Steinberger the 1988 Nobel Prize for Physics, Ekspong placed as much emphasis on the technique they devised as on the results they achieved with it. Indeed, in the years since Schwartz and his colleagues completed their experiment, neutrino beams have become a mainstay for studying fundamental interactions at laboratories throughout the world. As Ekspong stated, the three researchers had "started a bold new line of research, which gave rich fruit from the beginning."

Schwartz remained on the Columbia faculty until 1966, when he left to work at the newly constructed Stanford Linear Accelerator in California. He published a textbook, *Principles of Electrodynamics,* in 1972. Shortly afterward, "lured . . . by the new industrial revolution in 'Silicon Valley,'" Schwartz founded Digital Pathways, Inc., a company that develops and manufactures software that protects computer systems from outside tampering. In part out of commitment to his company, and in part out of frustration with the bureaucracy endemic to today's "big physics," Schwartz left Stanford in 1983 to turn his full attention to Digital Pathways, of which he was chairman and chief executive officer. In January 1991, he moved again, to become the associate director of high energy and nuclear physics at Brookhaven National Laboratory. He describes these changes in his life positively, saying, "Although it is difficult to predict the future I still have all the optimism that I had back when I first grew up in New York—life can be a marvelous adventure."

Schwartz belongs to the National Academy of Sciences and is a fellow of the American Physical Society, which awarded him its Hughes Prize in 1964.

SELECTED WORKS: Principles of Electrodynamics, 1972, 1985.

ABOUT: New Scientist October 29, 1988; New York Times October 20, 1988; Physics Today January, 1989; Science November 4, 1988; Who's Who in America, 1990.

SHARPE, WILLIAM F.
(June 16, 1934–)
Nobel Memorial Prize in Economic Sciences, 1990
(shared with Harry M. Markowitz and Merton H. Miller)

The American financial economist William Forsyth Sharpe was born in Boston, Massachu-

WILLIAM F. SHARPE

setts, to Russell Thornley and Evelyn Forsyth Maloy Sharpe. Both his parents were academic administrators.

When the United States entered World War II, his father's national guard unit was activated and the family moved first to Texas and then to California. Sharpe graduated from high school in Riverside, then enrolled at the University of California at Berkeley with the intention of earning a medical degree. "A year of the associated courses convinced me that my preferences lay elsewhere," Sharpe recalled later. He transferred to the University of California at Los Angeles and majored in business administration. This major required that he take a course in economics, a course that, Sharpe remembers, "had a major influence on my career. . . . I was greatly attracted to the rigor and relevance of microeconomic theory." Microeconomics is the study of the behavior of individual industries, companies, or other basic economic units.

Sharpe, a Phi Beta Kappa scholar, went on to earn B.A. and M.A. degrees from the University of California at Los Angeles (UCLA). In 1954 he married Roberta Ruth Branton, with whom he has two children, Jonathan Forsyth and Deborah Ann.

In the mid-1950s Sharpe interrupted his education to serve in the Army Quartermaster Corps. After two years he was discharged with the rank of captain, and he returned to UCLA. While pursuing his doctorate, Sharpe worked for the Rand Corporation, a research firm. As he tried to decide on a dissertation topic, his finance professor, J. Fred Watson, suggested he contact HARRY M. MARKOWITZ, who was also at Rand.

Markowitz was in the process of developing his ground-breaking portfolio theory. A portfolio is a single investor's collection of stocks, bonds, or other investments. Markowitz's theory stated that by diversifying—that is, by holding several types of securities from several types of firms—investors can reduce the risk that their investments will be adversely affected by an external influence.

With Markowitz's help, Sharpe earned his Ph.D. in 1961 and took a position on the finance faculty at the University of Washington's School of Business, where he continued the work he had begun with Markowitz.

Only a year later he submitted a paper, "Capital Asset Prices: A Theory of Market Equilibrium under Conditions of Risk," to the *Journal of Finance*. The paper, published in 1964, introduced his capital asset pricing model (CAPM), the work for which he shared the 1990 Nobel Memorial Prize in Economic Sciences.

Sharpe's CAPM derived directly from Markowitz's work. Markowitz had shown that investors should diversify their investments among several types of firms in order to maximize their potential gain; Sharpe began with the assumption that all investors would heed Markowitz's advice. Even the most diversified portfolio, Sharpe determined, carries some unavoidable risk: The value of the securities in the portfolio will rise and fall over time, with some securities fluctuating more than others do. There are always investors willing to purchase such high-risk securities, but only if the potential return is high—the riskier a stock, the better the potential return must be. It is up to each individual investor to determine how much risk to accept.

To facilitate investors' decisions, Sharpe developed a model that showed how to measure the risk of each individual security, based on its historical performance. Sharpe's model introduced the "beta" measure of risk. A particular stock's beta measure indicates that stock's riskiness, or how that stock has performed in relation to the entire market. In Sharpe's model, stocks that historically are about as risky as the overall market are assigned a beta of 1; those that carry a higher risk—whose prices have been rising and falling more quickly than has the market as a whole—are assigned higher beta values.

Sharpe's beta measure was rapidly adopted by financial markets and financial analysts. Today Sharpe's model is considered the standard for the investment industry and is used by corporate, institutional, and pension fund managers to plan and evaluate their investments.

Sharpe's model has also become "the backbone of modern price theory of financial markets," as Assar Lindbeck of the Royal Swedish Academy of Sciences noted when awarding Sharpe the Nobel Prize. Once a particular company's beta measure is determined, that company's value in comparison to the market can also be calculated. Today, the CAPM is the method of choice for pricing regulated public utilities. It is used by corporate managers to determine the price of the corporations they are considering taking over. It is also used by courts to determine the value of corporations that do not sell shares on the stock market.

Sharpe remained at the University of Washington until 1968, publishing books on the economics of computers and on computer programming as well as continuing to work on the CAPM. After two years at the University of California at Irvine, he joined the faculty of the Stanford Graduate School of Business in 1970. He was named Timken Professor of Finance in 1973.

During the 1970s Sharpe continued to study capital markets and also looked at the investment policies of pension funds. While at Stanford, he also served as a consultant to Merrill Lynch Pierce Fenner & Smith and Wells Fargo Investment Advisors, where his work included computing beta values for stocks and portfolios. Sharpe spent the academic year 1976–1977 at the National Bureau of Economic Research. He also wrote a textbook, *Investments,* first published in 1978.

In 1980 Sharpe was elected president of the American Finance Association. In the years that followed he helped establish a number of programs and seminars on economic theory, including a program on international investment management that was offered jointly by the Stanford Business School and the London Graduate School of Business.

In 1986, while on leave from the business school, Sharpe founded Sharpe-Russell Research, a research firm supported by several major pension funds and by the Frank Russell Company to help pensions, endowments, and foundations allocate assets for investments. In 1989 he became an emeritus member of the Stanford Business School faculty so that he could devote more time to research and consulting activities. This status, he has noted, permits him to "continue to participate in the intellectual life of the school [and] . . . provide assistance to (and learn from) a highly sophisticated group of clients."

The Royal Swedish Academy of Sciences awarded the 1990 Nobel Memorial Prize in Economic Sciences to Sharpe, Markowitz, and MERTON H. MILLER "for their pioneering work in the theory of financial economics." The announcement was applauded by economists because it was the first time the award was given purely for financial work rather than theoretical economics. FRANCO MODIGLIANI called the prize "the final seal of approval" because it recognized "for the first time that finance is a major area of economics."

Miller was awarded the prize for his work in corporate finance. He had shown that a company's value does not depend on its method of financing or its dividend policy; this led to a revolution in the way corporations finance acquisitions and other projects. The research conducted by Sharpe, Markowitz, and Miller has changed forever the way investment managers, stockbrokers, bankers, and millions of investors look at financial markets. "Each one of them gave one building block for a unified theory of financial economics," said Assar Lindbeck. "This theory would have been incomplete if any one of these pieces were missing."

Sharpe was divorced from his first wife in 1986 and married Kathryn Peck, who is a partner of and the administrator for the firm now known as William F. Sharpe Associates. Sharpe has written that he and his wife "enjoy sailing, opera, and Stanford football and basketball games, especially when the weather is good, the music well performed, and the opponents vanquished."

Sharpe is a member and past director of the American Economic Association and the Western Finance Association. He has served as a trustee of the Research Foundation of the Institute of Chartered Financial Analysts and as a member of the prize committee of the Council on Education and Research of the Institute of Chartered Financial Analysts. He also advises Nikko Securities' Institute of Investment Technology and the Institutional Portfolio Management Division of the Union Bank of Switzerland.

He has won the Financial Analysts' Federation Graham and Dodd Award for excellence in financial writing five times, as well as the Financial Analysts' Federation's Nicholas Molodovsky Award (1989), the Western Finance Association's Enduring Contribution Award (1989), and the Dow-Jones and American Assembly of Collegiate Schools of Business Award (1980).

ADDITIONAL WORKS: The Economics of Computers, 1969; Portfolio Theory and Capital Markets, 1970; BASIC: An Introduction to Computer Programming Using the BASIC Language, 1971; Introduction to Managerial Economics, 1973; Fundamentals of Investments, 1989, with Gordon J. Alexander.

ABOUT: Economist February 2, 1991; Forbes September 5, 1988; Los Angeles Times October 17, 1990; Newsweek October 29, 1990; New York Times October 17, 1990; Wall Street Journal October 17, 1990; Washington Post October 17, 1990; Who's Who in America, 1990.

SOLOW, ROBERT M.

(August 23, 1924–)

Nobel Memorial Prize in Economic Sciences, 1987

The American economist Robert Merton Solow (sō´ lō) was born in Brooklyn, New York. His parents were Milton Henry Solow, a fur buyer, and Hannah Gertrude (Sarney) Solow, a homemaker who raised Robert and his two sisters. Solow attended New York public schools and was an above-average student, though he has said he was "not very intellectual" until his last year of high school. "Then one of those teachers who make a difference taught me to read the great nineteenth-century French and Russian novelists and to take ideas seriously." On graduating in 1940, he accepted a scholarship to Harvard.

Solow was unsure of his academic goals, but, he wrote later, "Like many children of the Depression I was curious about what made society tick." At Harvard he studied sociology and anthropology under such eminent scholars as Talcott Parsons and Clyde Kluckhohn. He also took some beginning courses in economics, but he did not commit himself to that field.

In 1942, at the age of eighteen, he recognized that "there were more urgent and exciting matters than what I was doing." He joined the army to fight in World War II, serving in North Africa, Sicily, and Italy before his discharge in 1945. Solow credits those three years as a soldier, characterized as they were by "skill and mutual loyalty," with forming his character.

On returning to Harvard, Solow had to choose a major. He had recently married Barbara Muriel Lewis, now an economic historian who has taught at Boston University and Harvard. She suggested that the field of economics was interesting. "I had to do something right away," Solow recalled later, "so I decided I might as well do that." He discovered that economics satisfied a craving for analytical rigor that sociology had left unfulfilled. Nevertheless, he wrote later, he entered the field "almost casually. . . . By a piece of good luck, WASSILY LEONTIEF became my teacher, guide, and friend. I learned from him the spirit as well as the substance of modern economic theory."

After completing his B.A. in 1947, Solow continued his graduate studies at Harvard and developed an interest in statistics. His Ph.D. thesis, a probabilistic study of the distribution of income by size among families, received Harvard's Wells Prize, which offered, he has written, "publication in book form and $500 (in 1951 prices!) upon completion." Nevertheless, when Solow reread his work, he thought he could improve it. "But I never returned to that work and the thesis remains unpublished (and the check uncashed)."

Solow headed immediately to an assistant professorship in the economics department at the Massachusetts Institute of Technology (MIT), where he has remained ever since. Soon, though, his focus shifted again. "MIT hired me primarily to teach courses in statistics and econometrics. In

ROBERT M. SOLOW

small part of observed growth. Explaining what Solow termed the "residual," and which is generally understood to be largely technical change, had become a major activity of economists. Solow has shown that it was no accident that we often observe sustained economic growth and that much of this growth was due to technical change.

Solow also later collaborated with Samuelson and R. Dorfman in writing *Linear Programming and Economic Analysis.* That book, published in 1958, introduced a generation of young economists to postwar developments in the theory of economic growth.

Solow's work in growth theory, begun in these contributions and continued through the years, gave economists both a theoretical foundation and an empirical structure for examining the economic effect of technological change. He presented many of his ideas in his textbook *Growth Theory: An Exposition,* which Oxford University Press published in 1970. A second edition appeared in 1988.

Solow's ideas had major implications for the real-life actions of governments, such as the encouragement of higher education and research and development in order to stimulate economic growth. Such practical applicability is a hallmark of Solow's work. A proponent of the idea that governmental intervention in markets is essential to effective economic policy, Solow has demonstrated long-standing concern for human problems such as unemployment and for the practical effects of economic policy-making. Between 1961 and 1962 he served as senior staff economist on President Kennedy's Council of Economic Advisors, and he continued as a member of various advisory committees to the executive branch from 1963 to 1968. He was also a member of the board of directors of the Federal Reserve Bank of Boston between 1974 and 1980, becoming its chair in 1979. The 1973 article he co-wrote with Alan Binder, "Does Fiscal Policy Matter?" has become a standard in the field.

The *New York Times* has characterized Solow as "*the* economist's economist," noting that he "has had important things to say about almost every aspect of modern economics." His several books and more than 100 scholarly articles have addressed the full range of macroeconomic theory, analyzing markets, unemployment, the nature of inflation, the role of stocks, and the theory of capital and interest.

As a result of this diverse and influential work, Solow had long been spoken of as a candidate for a Nobel Prize. In awarding him the 1987 Nobel Memorial Prize in Economics, the Nobel committee particularly emphasized his contributions to growth theory. As Karl-Göran Mäler of the Royal Academy of Sciences noted in his presentation speech, Solow's "model of economic growth . . .

the beginning I fully intended to make my career along those lines. It did not turn out that way, probably for a geographical reason. I was given the office next to PAUL SAMUELSON's. . . . I suppose it was inevitable that I should drift back into 'straight' economics, where I discovered an instinctive macroeconomist struggling to get out."

Solow's most important and long-lasting contribution to straight economics was made in the 1950s. Considering the existing theories of economic growth, he concluded that "the story told by these models felt wrong." These economies implied that capitalist economies were very unstable, that they could slide off course easily, precipitously, and perhaps irrevocably. As Solow put it, "An expedition from Mars arriving on Earth having read this literature would have expected to find only the wreckage of a capitalism that had shaken itself to pieces long ago." Solow set himself to explain why "sustained, though disturbed, growth was not a rarity" in the world's economies.

In 1956 and 1957 Solow presented a new theory of economic growth in two articles that quickly became classics in growth theory. The equilibrium rate of growth of an economy is where the growth rates of capital and population are the same. One of Solow's classic papers showed that under plausible assumptions the growth path of an economy was in fact stable. In contrast to previous models, the Solow model contained a variable capital-labor ratio that would propel an economy that had strayed out of equilibrium back into its steady state. Also in contrast to previous models, the rate of interest affects the level of income but not its rate of growth. The second paper showed that the growth of the capital-labor ratio explained only a is not only of interest for specialists in growth theory but has become a unifying organizing principle in much of contemporary macroeconomics." Mäler also credited Solow's "empirical research of the growth process" with being "of fundamental importance for the development of economic science."

Solow has earned a reputation as a lucid writer and a witty and dedicated teacher. He has been an Institute Professor at MIT since 1974, and although he has lectured at universities around the world, he claims never to have wanted to leave his department. As he put it, "The MIT economics department has been a wonderful place to teach and work. It has provided me—and not only me—with sharp and delightful colleagues and with a long line of spectacular students. I estimate that if I had neglected the students I could have written 25 percent more scientific papers. The choice was easy to make and I do not regret it."

Solow has three children, John, Andrew, and Katherine. He considers his grandchildren and sailing his most important leisure interests.

In addition to the Nobel Prize, Solow has received the American Economic Association's John Bates Clark Medal (1961) and the Seidman Award in Political Economics (1983). He served as president of the Econometric Society (1964) and of the American Economic Association (1979), as vice president of the American Academy of Arts and Sciences (1970), and as a member of the Council of the National Academy of Sciences (1977–1980). He also belongs to the American Philosophical Society, the British Academy, and the Accademia dei Lincei in Rome.

ADDITIONAL WORKS: Capital Theory and the Rate of Return, 1963; The Nature and Sources of Unemployment in the U.S., 1964.

ABOUT: Blaug, M. Great Economists Since Keynes, 1985; New York Times October 22, 1987; Who's Who in America, 1990; Who's Who in Economics, 1990.

STEINBERGER, JACK
(May 25, 1921–   )
Nobel Prize for Physics, 1988
(shared with Leon M. Lederman and Melvin Schwartz)

The American physicist Jack Steinberger was born in Bad Kissingen, Germany. His father, Ludwig Steinberger, served as cantor and religious teacher to the town's small Jewish community, and his college-educated mother, Berta (May) Steinberger, supplemented the family's income by giving English and French lessons.

JACK STEINBERGER

In 1934, after the Nazis came to power, the Steinbergers arranged for Jack and his older brother to leave Germany. With the help of the American Jewish Charities, the boys were settled in the Chicago home of Barnett Faroll, a prosperous grain broker. In 1938 Faroll brought Steinberger's parents and younger brother to Chicago as well. The family acquired a delicatessen, from which they made a modest living.

After graduating from the highly regarded New Trier Township High School in the Chicago suburb of Winnetka, Steinberger was awarded a scholarship at the Armour Institute of Technology (now the Illinois Institute of Technology). His scholarship ended after two years, however, and Steinberger was forced to find work. He found a job washing equipment at a pharmaceutical laboratory for eighteen dollars a week. In the evenings, Steinberger studied chemistry at the University of Chicago; on weekends, he worked in the family store. This year of constant labor ended when a new scholarship from the University of Chicago allowed him to give up his day job. Steinberger completed his bachelor's degree in chemistry in 1942. Throughout his studies, he had taken just one course in physics.

His career focus changed when he enlisted in the army after the bombing of Pearl Harbor. Assigned by the army to the Massachusetts Institute of Technology Radiation Laboratory, he worked with outstanding physicists and took courses in physics. After the war, he returned to the University of Chicago for graduate work in physics. His primary interest was theory, but when he had trouble finding a topic for a doctoral thesis, his adviser, ENRICO FERMI, suggested that he pursue an experimental problem in particle physics. (Particle physics is the study of the atom and its parts, such as electrons, neutrons, and protons.) By the time he received his Ph.D. in 1948, Steinberger had found his niche as an experimental physicist.

Nevertheless, it took him a while to recognize his calling. He recalls deciding to "try theory again" at the Institute for Advanced Study in Princeton. After working there for a year and finding himself "no match" for the other young theoreticians, he left for the University of California at Berkeley. "There," he said later, "the experimental possibilities in the Radiation Laboratory . . . were so great that I reverted easily to my wild state, that is, experimentation." From this point on, Steinberger remained devoted to experimental physics, completing work that would bring him world renown and, eventually, the Nobel Prize.

In 1950 Steinberger moved to Columbia, where he joined an extraordinary faculty that was to garner six independent Nobel Prizes for work done between the late 1940s and the early 1960s. Steinberger's work at Columbia earned high praise; his former student MELVIN SCHWARTZ has called him "the best experimental physicist I have ever been associated with, and the best teacher." Steinberger became a full professor in 1954 and shortly thereafter began to experiment with the newly invented bubble chamber. His refinements to the bubble chamber, which is used to trace the motion of subatomic particles, are considered a significant contribution to experimental physics, though they are not directly related to the work that won him the Nobel Prize.

The experiment that did lead to Steinberger's Nobel Prize began in 1959 with a coffee-hour discussion led by TSUNG-DAO LEE, another Columbia physicist. At the time, scientists had long been aware of the existence of four fundamental forces that govern the physical interactions of matter: gravitation, electromagnetism, the strong nuclear force, and the weak nuclear force. The latter two forces operate only at the subatomic level: the strong force governs the interactions of protons and neutrons, and the weak force is effective in the interactions of less massive particles, such as electrons, which do not participate in the strong force.

Gravitation, the weakest of the four forces, does not play any significant role on the subatomic scale. The effects at short distances of electromagnetic and strong nuclear interactions can be experimentally investigated by the use of beams of particles, such as protons and electrons, accelerated in machines such as cyclotrons and synchrotrons. Although the weak nuclear force was known to be responsible for one form of radioactivity, called beta decay, no one had gathered any information about the weak nuclear force by using the technique of colliding particle beams. One difficulty was that the weak force was masked by the much stronger electromagnetism and the strong nuclear force.

In the course of his coffee-hour talk, Lee challenged his colleagues to devise an experiment in which the weak force could be observed and measured directly. Thinking about this challenge later that night, Schwartz—Steinberger's twenty-seven-year-old protégé—suddenly realized that the best promise for a solution lay in the neutrino.

Neutrinos are particles with no electrical charge and virtually no mass. They are therefore not affected by either the electromagnetic force or the strong force. They rarely interact with other particles—billions pass unnoticed through every square centimeter of the earth every day—but the rare neutrino interactions that do occur involve only the weak force. Schwartz realized that if enough neutrinos could be gathered in one place, the probability of interaction would rise. Therefore, if he could create a concentrated beam of neutrinos, he might be able to study uncontaminated weak force interactions.

Schwartz quickly teamed with Steinberger and a third Columbia physicist, LEON M. LEDERMAN, to test his idea. They used Brookhaven National Laboratory's newly completed alternating gradient synchrotron to fire bursts of protons, at an energy of 15 billion electron volts, at a beryllium target. The impact at such a large energy level tore the nuclei of the beryllium atoms apart, creating a flood of subatomic particles. Among those particles were pions, which decay (break down) almost instantly into neutrinos and muons. (A muon is a particle similar to, but heavier than, an electron.)

The next task was to eliminate all the particles except the neutrinos. Steinberger and his colleagues blocked the particles' path with a 10-ton wall of steel salvaged from a scrapped battleship. All the particles except the neutrinos were blocked by the steel; the neutrinos, which rarely interact with other particles, passed straight through. The result was a neutrino beam.

This new tool could be used for investigating the weak force. It also proved useful for investigating the neutrino itself, about which relatively little was known. Physicists, for example, had suggested that there might be two kinds of neutrinos. That is, the neutrino formed from the decay of a pion might be different from the neutrino produced by beta decay. (In beta decay, a neutron decays into a proton, an electron, and a neutrino.) The two kinds of neutrinos were referred to as the muon type and the electron type, because the first—which resulted from pion decay—was always accompanied by a muon, and the second—which resulted from beta decay—was always accompanied by an electron. Steinberger and his colleagues realized that their neutrino beam was ideally suited to test this two-neutrino hypothesis, because the neutrinos in the beam were all necessarily of the muon type—that is, they were all produced by the decay of pions.

To conduct the experiment, Steinberger, Schwartz, and Lederman built a 10-ton spark chamber containing ninety aluminum plates and focused the neutrino beam on it. (A spark chamber is a detection device in which particles are shot through neon gas, creating electric currents that cause the gas to glow. Different types of particles create different types of visible "trails" in the chamber.) Every time a neutrino collided with the nucleus of an aluminum atom, it would give off particles that could be identified by their distinctive trails. If the collisions yielded equal numbers of muons and electrons, the experimenters could conclude that the neutrinos associated with these particles did not differ. If the collisions yielded no electrons, however, the experimenters would have confirmed the two-neutrino hypothesis (according to which collisions from muon-type neutrinos should generate only muons).

During the eight months in which they conducted the experiment, approximately 100,000 billion neutrinos passed through the spark chamber. Fewer than 60 of those neutrinos collided with other particles. Significantly, however, every one of these collisions produced a muon rather than an electron. The scientists had confirmed the existence of two distinct kinds of neutrinos.

The neutron-beam experiment provoked a flurry of theoretical and experimental work that helped develop the standard model of particle physics. The standard model is a continually evolving theory describing the functions and behavior of all subatomic particles. With each new refinement to the standard model, physicists come one step closer to the development of a unified description of natural forces.

In awarding Steinberger, Schwartz, and Lederman the 1988 Nobel Prize for Physics, Gösta Ekspong of the Royal Swedish Academy of Sciences placed as much emphasis on the technique they devised as on the results they achieved with it. Indeed, in the years since Steinberger and his colleagues completed their experiment, high-energy neutrino beams have become a mainstay for studying fundamental interactions at accelerators throughout the world. As Ekspong stated, the three researchers had "started a bold new line of research, which gave rich fruit from the beginning."

Since completing his Nobel Prize–winning experiment, Steinberger has continued to explore subatomic physics. In 1968 he moved from Columbia to CERN (the European Center for Nuclear Research) in Geneva, Switzerland, to become the director responsible for experimental research in particle physics. Although officially retired since 1986, Steinberger has continued to act as spokesperson for ALEPH, one of four major experiments taking place at CERN's large electron positron collider. He also holds a professorship at the Scuola Normale Superiore in Pisa.

Steinberger has two children, Joseph and Richard, from his marriage to Joan Beauregard, from whom he was divorced in 1962. He has been married since 1962 to Cynthia Alff, a biologist and former student, with whom he has two more children, Julia and John.

Steinberger is a member of the National Academy of Sciences, the American Academy of Arts and Sciences, and the Heidelberg Academy of Sciences. President Ronald Reagan awarded him the United States National Medal of Science (1988), and he has received an honorary doctorate from the Illinois Institute of Technology (1989).

ABOUT: New Scientist October 29, 1988; New York Times October 20, 1988; Physics Today January, 1989; Science November 4, 1988; Who's Who in America, 1990.

TAYLOR, RICHARD E.

(November 2, 1929–)
Nobel Prize for Physics, 1990
(shared with Jerome I. Friedman and Henry W. Kendall)

The Canadian physicist Richard Edward Taylor was born in Medicine Hat, then a small town, in southwestern Alberta. His father was the son of Scottish and Irish homesteaders. His mother was American, the daughter of Norwegian immigrants to the United States who moved to Alberta's prairie land shortly after World War I.

The beginning of World War II brought many changes to Medicine Hat, including a Royal Air Force training school, a prisoner-of-war camp, and a military research facility. According to Taylor, these changes "transformed our town and widened the horizons of the young people there." The ten-year-old had opportunities to meet highly educated, sophisticated people and enjoy new cultural experiences. "The first live symphonic music I ever heard was played by German prisoners of war," he remembered. "I developed an interest in explosives and blew three fingers off my left hand just before hostilities ended in Europe. The atomic bomb that ended the war later that summer made me intensely aware of physicists and physics."

Until the early 1900s physicists believed that atoms were the fundamental particles of matter and could not be broken down into smaller con-

RICHARD E. TAYLOR

Stanford News Service

stituents. However, that image of the atom became outdated in 1911, when ERNEST RUTHERFORD formulated the concept of the atomic nucleus, describing it as a very small, positively charged region located in the center of the atom and orbited by negatively charged electrons. In 1919 he discovered that within the nucleus there is a positively charged particle called the proton. In 1932 JAMES CHADWICK discovered a second particle within the nucleus—a noncharged particle called the neutron. From these discoveries, scientists concluded that the atom was made up of three fundamental particles: the proton and the neutron, which are located in the atom's nucleus and collectively called nucleons, and the electron, which orbits the nucleus.

Further study of the atom showed that this conclusion was incorrect; researchers continued to find more subatomic particles in addition to those three. As the number of "elementary" particles climbed into the hundreds, physicists became convinced that there must be some smaller, fundamental substance that serves as a building block for all these particles.

During the 1950s physicists began using a technique called electron scattering to study the structure and behavior of atoms. Electron scattering involves bombarding atoms with high-speed electrons and observing the motion, or "scattering," of the electrons as they emerge from collisions with target atoms. If the electrons hit atomic constituents, they emerge at an angle; if they hit nothing, they pass straight through. The higher the speed of the bombarding electrons, the farther into the target atoms they penetrate and the more information can be obtained from their behavior. Some

high-speed collisions, called inelastic scattering, are strong enough to break apart the target atoms and scatter and reveal their subatomic particles.

In 1950 Taylor completed a baccalaureate program in mathematics and physics at the University of Alberta in Edmonton, Canada. He earned a master's degree, also from the University of Alberta, in 1952. Taylor later explained that he "was not an outstanding student . . . [but] did reasonably well in mathematics and science thanks to some talented and dedicated teachers."

While attending the University of Alberta, Taylor met and married Rita Bonneau. When his studies were completed, he and his wife moved to California, where he began doctoral studies at Stanford University. He later remembered that "the first two years at Stanford were exciting beyond description—the physics department at Stanford included FELIX BLOCH, Leonard Schiff, WILLIS E. LAMB JR., ROBERT HOFSTADTER, and W. K. H. (Pief) Panofsky. . . . I had to work hard to keep up with my fellow students, but learning physics was great fun in those surroundings." After two years Taylor began working in Stanford's High Energy Physics Laboratory with its new linear accelerator. In high-energy physics, researchers use particle accelerators to speed the particles used in scattering experiments. A linear accelerator is a type of particle accelerator that accelerates the bombarding particles in a straight line. Other types of accelerators, such as cyclotrons, speed particles by pushing them around a circular path.

In 1958 Taylor was invited by the École Normale Supérieure in Paris to join a group of physicists working on a new linear accelerator under construction in Orsay. He spent the next three years in France helping to construct the accelerator and participating in electron-scattering experiments.

In 1961 Taylor, his wife, and their one-year-old son, Ted, returned to the United States. Taylor joined the staff of the Lawrence Berkeley Laboratory in California but left that position after less than a year to return to Stanford, where he participated in the design of the Stanford Linear Accelerator Center (SLAC), which was then under construction. The SLAC was to house a 2-mile-long particle accelerator partially buried under the hills near the Stanford campus. It was designed to enable researchers to perform scattering experiments at energies far greater than previously possible.

Taylor received his Ph.D. from Stanford in 1962. In 1963 he began working with Pief Panofsky, scientists from the California Institute of Technology (Caltech), and two colleagues from the Massachusetts Institute of Technology (MIT), JEROME I. FRIEDMAN and HENRY W. KENDALL, to develop specifications for the SLAC's electron-scattering apparatus. In 1964 he was placed in charge of the design team responsible for building End Station A, one of the SLAC's two experimental facilities that would be used by researchers to monitor the results of scattering experiments conducted at the SLAC. For the next ten years Taylor helped design and build the monitoring equipment and participated in a number of scattering experiments. He became an associate professor of Physics at the SLAC in 1968 and became a full professor in 1970.

While Taylor was working on his Ph.D., MURRAY GELL-MANN of Caltech had devised a way to categorize and group the hundreds of subatomic particles that had been discovered. He theorized a model of these particles, picturing them as clusters of even smaller particles, which he called quarks, choosing the name from a passage in James Joyce's *Finnegans Wake*. (Essentially the same model was proposed independently by physicist George Zweig.) Six types of quarks, Gell-Mann theorized, make up the fundamental components of many subatomic particles. Just as atoms are characterized and classified by the number of electrons and protons they have, subatomic particles can be characterized by the number and types of quarks they have. Gell-Mann's model was widely accepted as a useful way to classify particles, but because no one was able to observe anything as small as quarks in experiments, some physicists thought of them not as real particles but as "mathematical quantities" useful for modeling particle behavior.

Taylor, Friedman, and Kendall changed all that. The three physicists confirmed Gell-Mann's theory, using the new state-of-the-art SLAC. In a series of experiments from 1967 to 1973 they were able to observe the first traces of quarks. Their experiments were called deep inelastic scattering experiments: *deep* was a reference to how far into the nucleus of the atom they were able to penetrate, and *inelastic* meant that the bombarding electrons were forceful enough to shatter the components of the nucleus. Taylor and his colleagues sent beams of electrons traveling at nearly the speed of light—faster than ever before possible—toward targets of liquid hydrogen or deuterium. At this speed, they saw something new. The electrons were hitting some hard particles inside the nucleons, particles that scattered the electrons at large angles relative to their original direction. These particles could only be Gell-Mann's quarks. Along with the quarks, the three physicists also identified particles called gluons, electrically neutral particles that bind quarks together. As the Royal Swedish Academy of Scientists noted when it awarded the 1990 Nobel Prize for Physics to Taylor, Friedman,

and Kendall, "All matter on earth, including our human bodies, consists to more than 99 percent of quarks with associated gluons. The little that remains is electrons."

Taylor and his colleagues received the 1990 Nobel Prize for providing the first evidence that quarks are indeed actual particles that form the fundamental constituents of protons and neutrons. The academy, in announcing the award, described this new discovery as "a repetition, at a deeper level, of one of the most dramatic events in the history of physics, the discovery of the nucleus of the atom." When accepting the prize, Taylor credited their achievement to the SLAC. He said, "We were given a rare opportunity to look a bit deeper into the way things are in the realm of the very small" and commented that Panofsky's creation of the SLAC was the true achievement.

From 1982 until 1986 he served as associate director for research at the SLAC. Taylor retired from this position in 1986 to devote more of his time to research. Taylor is a member of the American Physics Society and the Canadian Association of Physicists, and his many awards include a 1971 Guggenheim Fellowship that enabled him to spend a sabbatical year at the European Center for Nuclear Research (CERN). He received an honorary doctorate from the Université de Paris-Sud in 1980 and was awarded the Alexander von Humboldt Award in 1981. In 1989 Taylor, Friedman, and Kendall shared the W. K. H. Panofsky Prize from the American Physical Society.

ABOUT: American Men and Women of Science, 1989–90; Los Angeles Times October 18, 1990; Newsweek October 29, 1990; New York Times October 18, 1990; Science October 26, 1990; Science News October 27, 1990.

THOMAS, E. DONNALL

(March 15, 1920–)
Nobel Prize for Physiology or Medicine, 1990
(shared with Joseph E. Murray)

The American physician Edward Donnall Thomas was born in Mart, Texas. His father, Edward E. Thomas, was a doctor, and his mother, the former Angie Hill, was a schoolteacher. In his small Texas village, Thomas recalls, "my high school class consisted of about fifteen people. I was not an outstanding student even in this small group."

Thomas entered the University of Texas at Austin in 1937, graduating with a B.A. in 1941. He stayed at Austin for another two years, earning his master's degree in 1943, and then enrolled in the University of Texas Medical Branch at Galveston. After six months he transferred to Harvard Medical School, earning an M.D. in 1946. He per-

E. DONNALL THOMAS

formed his internship and residency in Boston at Peter Bent Brigham Hospital (now Brigham and Women's Hospital) and began to specialize in blood diseases. From 1948 to 1950 he served as a physician in the United States Army; then he worked for a year as a postdoctoral fellow at Massachusetts Institute of Technology (MIT).

At MIT Thomas researched new treatments for leukemia. Leukemia is a cancer of the body's blood-forming tissues—an uncontrolled growth of the white blood cells, which are produced in the bone marrow. At that time leukemia was the most incurable form of cancer. In other types of cancer, the diseased cells are frequently located in a single lump—a tumor—which a surgeon can remove. In leukemia, though, the diseased cells are spread throughout the body; there is no way to cut the cancer out.

One of the consequences of World War II was increased research on the effects of exposure to radiation such as X rays. It soon became clear that radiation is fatal in part because it kills blood-producing cells, such as those in the bone marrow. Perhaps, scientists thought, they could cure leukemia by using X rays to kill cancerous white blood cells throughout a patient's body. However, a patient cannot survive without white blood cells, because white blood cells play a crucial role in the body's immune system—its ability to resist disease.

During the early 1950s scientists showed that they could save the lives of irradiated mice by transplanting them with bone marrow from normal mice to reconstitute their immune systems. However, these experiments worked only because they used inbred strains of mice. All the mice from a given inbred strain are as genetically similar as identical twins. A long history of disasters had proved that in outbred species (such as humans), transplants of tissues or organs between different individuals were invariably rejected. The only exception was for identical twins, who are biochemically alike.

The mouse experiments piqued Thomas's scientific interest. In 1955 he moved to New York to teach medicine at Columbia University's College of Physicians and Surgeons and to take the position of physician-in-chief at the Mary Imogene Bassett Hospital in Cooperstown. One of his colleagues at the hospital, Joseph Ferrebee, was also interested in transplantation. "We decided to begin studies of marrow grafting in outbred species," mostly dogs, Thomas recalled, "and to begin cautious exploration of marrow infusion in human patients in need of a marrow graft because of disease or its treatment." The latter reference was to kidney grafts, which were being tried by JOSEPH E. MURRAY, among others. One approach surgeons were considering was to perform a bone marrow transplant together with a kidney transplant, essentially altering the patient's immune system to recognize the transplanted organ.

All these attempts using individuals other than identical twins were failures. Thomas performed the first marrow graft between identical twins in 1956, but not even that operation could be counted as a success because the patient's leukemia recurred. With other grafts, the body rejected the transplanted material. In this case the bone marrow, being more or less a transplanted immune system, was lethally rejecting the rest of the body. This was called graft-versus-host disease (GVHD). "The many failures of . . . marrow grafting in human patients caused most investigators to abandon such studies in the 1960s," Thomas recalled.

Thomas did not abandon his research. He and his co-workers had a few experimental successes with donor and recipient dogs that came from the same litter. In 1963 Thomas became a professor at the University of Washington Medical School in Seattle and continued to work on marrow grafts. His team began experimenting with drugs that suppress the immune system to reduce transplant rejection and GVHD, similar to the work Murray was then doing with kidney transplants.

Meanwhile, JEAN DAUSSET and his associates had been studying human genetic factors called histocompatibility antigens (HLA) that determine transplant rejection or acceptance. There are millions of varieties of HLA in the human population, so it is extremely difficult to find a donor who matches a patient's HLA type, except for close relatives such as brothers or sisters. Dausset and others showed that HLA-matched siblings can exchange skin grafts and suggested that this might work for other organs as well.

By 1968 Thomas and his co-workers were ready to take up Dausset's challenge. In November of that year the immunologist Robert Good performed the first successful bone marrow transplant between nonidentical but HLA-matched siblings to save an immunologically deficient infant. In March 1969 Thomas's team transplanted matched bone marrow into an adult leukemia patient, a much more difficult operation. Over the course of the 1970s Thomas and others developed complete procedures for treating leukemia patients: radiation and chemotherapy to reduce the cancer and cripple the immune system so the graft would not be rejected, tissue typing to ensure a compatible graft, immunosuppressive drugs to control GVHD, and elaborate medical care after the operation. Like people with acquired immune deficiency syndrome (AIDS), bone marrow recipients have severely suppressed immune systems and suffer from a variety of unusual infections that require new forms of treatment. By the late 1970s many leukemia patients were truly being cured by these methods.

Thomas and Murray shared the 1990 Nobel Prize for Physiology or Medicine "for their discoveries concerning organ and cell transplantation in the treatment of human disease." "I'm very surprised to win the Nobel Prize," Thomas said. "I really didn't think I would ever get it, because our work is so clinical. Most of the prizes recently have gone to basic scientists." Thomas's and Murray's work certainly had direct, practical effects: By 1987, 20,000 bone marrow transplants had been performed, and the survival rate for certain forms of leukemia is now almost 90 percent.

Bone marrow transplants are also used to treat certain inherited blood diseases, such as sickle cell anemia, and to help people whose bone marrow has been accidentally destroyed by exposure to radiation. The need to treat radiation exposure, itself a consequence of World War II, was one of Thomas's original incentives to investigate bone marrow transplantation. As he pointed out, "In an atomic age, with reactor accidents, not to mention stupidities with bombs, somebody is going to get more radiation than is good for him."

Thomas married Dorothy Martin, a fellow student at the University of Texas, in 1942. She has devoted herself to managing Thomas's research programs and writing scientific papers. The transplant surgeon George Santos has said that if Thomas is the father of bone marrow transplants, "then Dottie Thomas is the mother." The Thomases have two sons and a daughter.

Thomas's colleagues describe him as exact and methodical, with a dry wit. Outside the laboratory,

he enjoys big-game hunting. He is a member of the National Academy of Sciences, the Académie Royale de Médicine de Belgique, the Swiss Society of Hematology, and numerous medical and scientific societies. His many awards include an honorary doctorate from the University of Cagliari in Sardinia (1981), the Karl Landsteiner Memorial Award (1987), the Terry Fox Award (1990), the Gairdner Foundation International Award (1990), and the National Science Medal (1990).

ABOUT: The Chimera August 1990; Los Angeles Times October 9, 1990; New York Times October 9, 1990; Science October 19, 1990; Science News October 3, 1990; Time October 22, 1990; U.S. News and World Report October 22, 1990; Washington Post October 9, 1990; Who's Who in America, 1991.

TONEGAWA, SUSUMU
(September 5, 1939–)
Nobel Prize for Physiology or Medicine, 1987

The Japanese immunologist Susumu Tonegawa (tō nä gä wä) was born in Nagoya, Japan, to Tsutomu and Miyoko (Masuko) Tonegawa. He was the second of four children. His father, Tsutomu, was an engineer employed by a textile company that required him to move every few years from one rural town to another. Although Susumu and his siblings enjoyed "the space and freedom of the countryside," he and his elder brother were eventually sent to live with their uncle in Tokyo to take advantage of the capital's superior schools.

Tonegawa attended the distinguished Hibiya high school, where he became interested in chemistry. Upon graduation, he applied to the chemistry department of the University of Kyoto. He failed the entrance examination once, but he succeeded on his second attempt and was admitted in 1959.

During his senior year, Tonegawa "became fascinated by the then blossoming science of molecular biology" after reading papers by the French biologists FRANÇOIS JACOB and JACQUES MONOD. Molecular biology is the study of the large molecules that perform biological functions. These molecules include proteins, which are made of chains of amino acids and which provide much of the substance of living organisms, and DNA and RNA, which are nucleic acids composed of chains of subunits known as bases.

A gene, the unit of heredity, is a sequence of bases in a piece of DNA. The order and type of bases in a gene constitutes a code (known as the genetic code) that contains information about some feature of the organism. The cell can decode this information to produce a chain of amino acids, making a useful protein. Jacob's and Monod's research in the late 1950s and early 1960s concerned the question of how bacteria and bacteriophages

SUSUMU TONEGAWA

(which infect bacterial cells as viruses infect human cells) control which genes are decoded into protein. Their pioneering work inspired Tonegawa to enter the relatively new field of molecular genetics.

After receiving his B.S. degree in 1963, Tonegawa chose to remain at the University of Kyoto to begin graduate studies in molecular biology. He worked for two months under Itaru Watanabe at the university's Institute for Virus Research. At that point, Watanabe took him aside and suggested that he would be better off studying at better-equipped institutions overseas.

Shortly thereafter, Tonegawa enrolled at the University of California at San Diego, where he studied bacteriophages in the laboratory of Masaki Hayashi. Tonegawa received his Ph.D. in 1968, and in early 1969 he began to work under RENATO DULBECCO at the nearby Salk Institute. He studied simian virus 40 (SV40), a mammalian virus important in genetic engineering, with the aim of finding out how its genes replicate themselves when the virus reproduces.

Tonegawa's United States visa was due to expire at the end of 1970, and he would therefore be forced to leave the country for at least two years. Dulbecco, traveling in Europe, visited NIELS K. JERNE at the newly established Basel Institute of Immunology in Switzerland and suggested that Tonegawa go there.

Tonegawa moved to the institute in early 1971. At first he tried to continue his work on SV40, but he soon realized, as he wrote later, "that this was not a subject that aroused great interest in an institute almost entirely staffed by immunologists nor one that allowed me to take full advantage of my many talented colleagues." (Up to this point, Tonegawa had been researching genetic replication in viruses. Immunologists, on the other hand, study how a body resists infection from viruses or bacteria.) He therefore decided to abandon his previous research and to learn immunology instead, taking advantage of the expertise that surrounded him.

At the time Tonegawa arrived at the institute, immunologists were struggling with the problem of the origin of antibody diversity. When an organism is infected, it manufactures special proteins, called antibodies, to fight the invader. Each antibody has a molecular structure that enables it to bind to, and destroy, one specific compound (called the antigen for that antibody). The work of KARL LANDSTEINER had shown that an organism is capable of fighting millions of different antigens. In order to do so, however, the organism must be able to manufacture millions of structurally distinct antibodies, an ability that puzzled immunologists. How could one organism contain genetic information on so many different antibody structures?

During the late 1960s and early 1970s, there were two competing explanations for antibody diversity. Some researchers believed that the specific genetic blueprint for every possible antibody was part of the genetic code contained in the germ cells, which transmit genetic information from one generation to the next. This was called the germ line theory. Others thought that an organism's genes couldn't possibly hold that much information. They theorized that the germ cells carry only general information about the structure of antibodies and that the diversification of antibodies takes place later, in the soma (body) cells. In other words, as immune system cells develop in the offspring, their genes mutate to provide blueprints for millions of different antibodies. This was called the somatic mutation theory.

"I felt from the beginning that I could contribute to resolving this question by applying the recently invented techniques of molecular biology," Tonegawa wrote later. In his first experiment, he attempted to count the number of antibody genes a germ cell carries. Tonegawa later admitted, "it turned out to be nearly impossible to make a convincing interpretation of the data obtained in these early studies." He therefore decided to try a different approach.

The work of RODNEY R. PORTER and GERALD M. EDELMAN in the 1950s and 1960s had outlined the general structure of an antibody molecule. Each antibody is made up of two polypeptides—that is, two long chains of amino acids. Because one chain has a greater molecular weight than the other, the two chains are referred to as *light* and *heavy*. The active site of the antibody molecule—the part of the molecule that binds to the corresponding antigen—includes elements from both the heavy and light chains.

The work of Porter and Edelman had shown that each chain could be divided into a constant (or C) region, which was the same for all antibodies of a given general class, and a variable (or V) region, which was distinct for each individual antibody. In 1965 William Dreyer of the California Institute of Technology and J. C. Bennett of the University of Alabama School of Medicine had suggested that each chain was encoded by two genes, one for the C region and the other for the V region. This "two genes, one polypeptide chain" theory was accepted by most immunologists. Molecular biologists, however, found it objectionable because in all other cases that had been studied, a single polypeptide in an organism could be accounted for by a single gene. Why, then, should antibodies be an exception? "My personal reaction to the model when I learned of it in the early 1970s was also that of skepticism," Tonegawa said later. "However, at the same time I thought that the model might be testable if one were to use restriction enzymes."

Restriction enzymes, which had recently been discovered by WERNER ARBER, DANIEL NATHANS, and HAMILTON O. SMITH, cut DNA at specific sites. Cutting a gene with restriction enzymes produces a distinctive pattern of DNA fragments—in effect, a "fingerprint" for that gene. Tonegawa and his postdoctoral assistant Nobumichi Hozumi used restriction enzymes to break up two samples of DNA: one from embryonic mouse cells and one from antibody-producing cells of an adult mouse. They found that a particular segment of DNA from the adult mouse corresponded to *two separate* segments of DNA in the mouse embryo. These two segments of the embryonic DNA clearly represented two different genes—a V gene and a C gene—that would later join together as the mouse developed.

Tonegawa now collaborated with WALTER GILBERT and his associate Allan Maxam of Harvard University, who had developed a method for determining the precise structure of a piece of DNA. To their surprise, they found that the segment of DNA that they had identified as the light-chain V gene was not a complete gene. Instead, it was a gene segment—a portion of a gene—that only coded for part of the length of the V region. The remainder of the V region was coded for by a separate segment of DNA, which they labeled the joining (or J) segment. The immunologists Thomas J. Kindt and J. Donald Capra have called this "the key experiment in the modern era of molecular immunology."

"If the germ line cell carries multiple copies of different V and J gene segments," Tonegawa explained in his Nobel lecture, "the number of com-

plete V 'genes' that can be generated by random joinings between these two types of gene segments would be much greater than the total number of the inherited gene segments." Further work by Tonegawa and others proved that heavy-chain V regions require a third gene segment, called diversity (or D), in addition to V and J. They found that although the joining of the V-J or V-D-J segments was carefully controlled, errors or mutations could cause additional combinations to occur, giving the completed V regions an additional source of variability.

In addition, it was later shown that mutations occur in the V gene segment, especially while the immune response to a particular antigen is being refined. "In the beginning of the 1980s I began to feel that the great mystery of antibody diversity had been solved, at least in its outlines," Tonegawa wrote later. Other immunologists agreed: DNA recombination and mutation could generate perhaps 10 billion different kinds of antibodies, more than enough to solve the diversity problem.

In 1981, at the invitation of SALVADOR LURIA, Tonegawa moved back to the United States to take a professorship at the Center for Cancer Research at the Massachusetts Institute of Technology. There he played a major role in explaining the function of the receptors on T cells, another important component of the immune system.

Tonegawa was awarded the 1987 Nobel Prize for Physiology or Medicine "for the elucidation of the unique capacity of the immune system to produce [an] enormous diversity of antibodies." Hans Wigzell of the Karolinska Institute, himself an immunologist, characterized Tonegawa as "the great molecular biologist in immunology" and noted that "if you are given the Nobel Prize alone, what higher tribute can you be paid?" (Indeed, since 1960, only three other people have won nonshared Nobel Prizes for Physiology or Medicine.)

Tonegawa is described by his colleagues as "an aggressive, driven, and brilliant researcher" who works long hours (especially at night) and tends not to socialize. He was married in 1985 to Mayumi Yoshinari, a former television reporter with whom he has a son, Hidde. Tonegawa has retained his Japanese citizenship, but he has been scathing in his criticism of the scientific research system in Japan and has never returned to work in his native country.

In addition to the Nobel Prize, Tonegawa's numerous awards include the Avery Landsteiner Prize (1981), the Gairdner Foundation International Award (1983), the Bunkakunsho Order of Culture from the Emperor of Japan (1984), the Robert Koch Prize (1986), and the Lasker Prize (1987). He is an honorary member of the American Association of Immunologists and the Scandinavian Society for Immunology and a foreign member of the United States National Academy of Sciences.

SELECTED WORKS: "The Molecules of the Immune System," Scientific American October 1985.

ABOUT: New Scientist October 15, 1987; New York Times September 22, 1987; New York Times October 13, 1987; Science October 23, 1987; Who's Who in America, 1990; Who's Who, 1990.

UNITED NATIONS PEACEKEEPING FORCES
(founded June 1948)
Nobel Prize for Peace, 1988

The United Nations (UN) peacekeeping forces originated in 1948 when the UN Security Council sent observers to monitor a truce between Israel and the surrounding Arab states. Since that time, the UN peacekeeping forces have been involved in eighteen operations around the world, helping to maintain or reestablish peace in areas that have been the scene of armed conflict. The forces consist of two distinct groups: unarmed observers, who are employed to gather information and monitor activities; and lightly armed military forces, who are employed to separate hostile parties and maintain security.

Many of the conflicts in which the UN peacekeeping forces have intervened are the direct result of the fall of the British empire. From the mid-nineteenth until the early twentieth century, Great Britain had been the world's greatest military and political power. Large parts of Africa, Asia, and the Middle East were under British control. After World War I, however, British influence in the world began to weaken, declining even further during the years of the Great Depression. In the two decades after the end of World War II, Britain granted independence to most of the nations in what had been its empire. The withdrawal of British control left power vacuums in many regions of the world, precipitating a number of regional conflicts that continue to the present day.

In 1922 the land of Palestine was placed under British control by the League of Nations, an international organization founded at the end of World War I. The League of Nations hoped that, under the guiding hand of Great Britain, Palestine would emerge as an independent, self-governing nation. Britain, however, found it impossible to settle the continuing conflict between Arabs and Jews, both of whom had historical claims to the land. The problem escalated after World War II, when Jewish immigration to Palestine increased drastically.

In 1947 the United Nations—successor to the League of Nations—proposed a partition plan by which the land of Palestine would be divided into an Arab state and a Jewish state. Despite protests from the Palestinian Arabs, this plan was implemented on May 14, 1948, when Great Britain withdrew from Palestine. Israel, the Jewish state, declared its independence and was almost immediately attacked by the armies of five surrounding Arab states: Lebanon, Syria, Iraq, Transjordan (now Jordan), and Egypt. After several weeks of fighting, the UN was able to persuade the disputing countries to declare a truce.

In order to make sure that the truce would hold, the UN Security Council sent a group of observers to the area. Originally, the observers consisted of a few soldiers and members of the UN Secretariat. The logistics of their operation were largely improvised and their ability to communicate with one another was limited. They were, however, able to provide reliable reports to the United Nations of any violations of the truce agreement. By 1949 this ad hoc group of observers had evolved into an official body called the United Nations Truce Supervision Organization (UNTSO). The UNTSO remains active today, with observers stationed in Israel, Egypt, Jordan, Lebanon, and Syria.

While Israel and its Arab neighbors were quarreling over the future of Palestine, India and Pakistan were fighting for control of the tiny province of Kashmir. India had been under British rule since the eighteenth century. On August 15, 1947, Great Britain withdrew from India, leaving behind two independent states: the Muslim state of Pakistan and the Hindu state of India. Kashmir, whose leadership was Hindu but whose population was primarily Muslim, was claimed by both countries. The armed conflict over Kashmir ended in July 1948, when the United Nations succeeded in arranging a cease-fire. In 1949, inspired by the success of its observer group in the Middle East, the UN Security Council sent a similar group—the United Nations Military Observer Group in India and Pakistan (UNMOGIP)—to monitor the cease-fire. The dispute remains unsettled, but the cease-fire holds and a small observer force remains in the area today.

Meanwhile, the troubles in the Middle East continued. The Suez Canal, controlled by Great Britain since 1875, was suddenly nationalized by Egypt in 1956. Britain, France, and Israel attacked Egypt in retaliation. Worldwide opinion condemned the invasion. The UN Security Council realized that unarmed military observers would not be able to handle this conflict, which had spiraled into a major international crisis. It therefore sent an armed peacekeeping force to separate the combatants. The new force, called the First United Nations Emergency Force (UNEF I) supervised the withdrawal of foreign troops from Egyptian territory. The force also served as a buffer along the Egyptian-Israeli border and in the Gaza strip (a narrow band of land situated between the two countries, bordering on the Mediterranean Sea). By the summer of 1957, UNEF I had proven its ability to maintain stability in the region.

The use of armed forces to make peace was an unprecedented step for the United Nations, and it was taken only after significant debate and reflection. In 1956 UN secretary-general DAG HAMMARSKJÖLD defined a set of principles to guide the use of peacekeeping forces—principles that are still followed today. Under Hammarskjöld's guidelines, a UN peacekeeping force may not intervene in a conflict without the permission of the disputing parties; it must achieve its goals by means of negotiation and persuasion rather than violence; it may take orders only from the UN Security Council; and it must be supported financially by all the member nations of the United Nations.

Since the time when Hammarskjöld first articulated these guidelines, UN peacekeeping forces—both observer groups and military troops—have played a significant role in ending conflicts and maintaining stability in trouble spots all over the world. In 1960, for example, when Belgium granted independence to the Congo (now Zaire), Belgians living in the former colony responded with violent protests. Belgium sent in troops to quell the uprisings, but the Congo government, seeking to preserve its independence, considered this an unwelcome invasion. A UN peacekeeping force was dispatched to supervise the withdrawal of Belgian forces and to prevent civil war in the country.

Also in 1960, the island of Cyprus, which had long been the object of disputes between Greece and Turkey, officially declared its independence. Although its new constitution was carefully designed to allow Greek Cypriots and Turkish Cypriots to share power equally, the country soon erupted into civil war. In 1964 a UN peacekeeping force was sent to Cyprus, where, for a decade, it prevented war between the ethnic groups.

In 1967, after the Six-Day War, which pitted Egypt, Syria, and Jordan against Israel, a UN peacekeeping force was assigned to monitor the truce agreement between the countries. In 1974, after an attack on Israel by Egypt, Jordan, and Syria, another peacekeeping force was installed in the Golan Heights, on the western border of Syria, to maintain a buffer zone between Israeli and Syrian forces.

In the 1970s the Palestine Liberation Organization (PLO)—a coalition of Palestinian groups whose goal is to liberate their homeland from what they view as an illegitimate Israeli occupation—

began a series of terrorist acts against Israel. In 1978 Israel retaliated against a PLO raid by invading Lebanon, which was then a PLO stronghold. Following this invasion, the UN established the United Nations Interim Force in Lebanon (UNIFIL), an unusually large peacekeeping force whose duties included monitoring Israeli troop withdrawal, maintaining peace among Lebanon's warring ethnic factions, and helping the Lebanese government reestablish its authority. UNIFIL did succeed in having the Israeli troops withdraw, although the conflicts continue.

In 1988, at the conclusion of an eight-year war between Iran and Iraq, the United Nations installed a peacekeeping force along the border between the two countries to observe the withdrawal of troops and to monitor any violations of the cease-fire agreement.

Shortly thereafter, the UN peacekeeping forces received the 1988 Nobel Prize for Peace. In presenting the award, Egil Aarvik of the Norwegian Nobel Committee called the UN forces "a tangible expression of the world community's will to solve conflicts by peaceful means." He explained, "The technological development of weapons systems has resulted in the peaceful resolution of conflicts becoming the only realistic possibility. Nuclear weapons have made the concept of wielding total power an absurdity. In conflict situations it is therefore vitally necessary that there are openings where real negotiations can be initiated."

Aarvik pointed out that despite the acknowledged success of the UN peacekeeping forces, "confidence in the United Nations has otherwise been a variable factor. The United Nations has for many been seen as a body without power or effectiveness. . . . This year's peace prize is a recognition and homage to one organ of the United Nations. But it ought to be understood as a serious comment on the fact that we must, united and with our whole hearts, invest in the United Nations."

UN secretary-general Javier Pérez de Cuéllar accepted the prize on behalf of the peacekeeping forces. In his Nobel lecture, he pointed out that despite regional conflicts in many parts of the world—conflicts in which the United States and the Soviet Union, with their immense nuclear arsenals and broad political interests, might easily have become involved—the UN had played a significant role in preventing serious confrontations between East and West. At the time Pérez de Cuéllar accepted the award, there were already signs that the Soviet Union would abdicate its position as a world superpower, and the prospect of a third world war looked increasingly unlikely. Nevertheless, he said, "the community of nations . . . [is] now encountering a new generation of global problems which can only be faced effectively through an unprecedented degree of international cooperation." He suggested that the notion of peacekeeping—"the use of soldiers as a catalyst for peace rather than as the instruments of war"—may be the key to resolving international disputes in the future. To be successful, however, a peace-keeping operation "must have a workable and realistic mandate fully supported by the international community." He urged the countries of the world to support the UN peacekeeping activities both logistically and financially.

The annual cost for the UN peacekeeping operation continues to rise. In 1988, considering the imminent deployment of forces in other areas, such as southern Africa, the western Sahara, and Cambodia, Pérez de Cuéllar calculated that the cost could reach $1.5 billion a year. In a news conference in December 1988, he expressed his fear that the Nobel Prize might turn out to be "a posthumous award" for the UN peacekeeping forces unless governments show greater willingness to pay for them in the future. Financing the peacekeeping forces has been a longstanding problem for the UN, partly because member nations have tended to withhold portions of their annual dues for various political reasons. Also, despite Dag Hammarskjöld's directive that the cost of the peace-keeping forces be shared by all UN members, many governments have maintained that the forces should be paid for only by interested parties.

Today's UN peacekeeping forces, made up of military personnel from fifty-eight countries from every continent, are made available by the Security Council upon request. They are most often dispatched to areas where a cease-fire has been established but a formal peace treaty has not yet been drawn. They are generally placed in a buffer zone between the disputing parties so that if hostilities resume, the combatants will confront the UN troops first.

UN soldiers wear the military uniforms of their own nations, but they also wear distinctive blue caps or helmets that identify them as members of the peacekeeping force. They carry light defensive weapons, which they use only when necessary for self-protection. (Members of observer groups carry no weapons at all.) As of 1988, 764 soldiers had died while serving in the UN peacekeeping forces.

Since winning the Nobel Prize in 1988, the UN peacekeeping forces have been involved in several additional operations. In December 1988 a force was sent to Angola to monitor the departure of occupying Cuban troops. In April 1989 another force was sent to Namibia to help the former South African colony make the transition to independence. In September 1989 a force was sent to Central America to patrol the borders around Nicaragua, whose government—under the control of the left-wing Sandinista party—had been offering military assistance to leftist insurgents in neighboring El Salvador. By halting the flow of Nicaraguan guerrillas to El Salvador, and by disarming members of the contras (Nicaraguan rebels who opposed the Sandinista government), the UN force hoped to prevent further fighting in both countries.

Most recently, in April 1991, after a coalition of international military forces led by the United States compelled Iraq to withdraw from its violent annexation of Kuwait, a UN peacekeeping force was sent to the area to supervise troop withdrawal, monitor Iraq's adherence to the cease-fire agreement, and serve as a buffer along the Iraq-Kuwait border.

SELECTED PUBLICATIONS: On the Front Lines: The United Nations' Role in Preventing and Containing Conflict, 1984; The Blue Helmets, 1985.

PERIODICALS: Issues Before the General Assembly of the United Nations (annual); United Nations Chronicle (monthly).

ABOUT: Fabian, L. Soldiers Without Enemies, 1971; New York Times December 11, 1988; San Francisco Chronicle October 25, 1989; U.N. Chronicle December 1988; U.N. Chronicle June 1989; Urquhart, B. A Life in Peace and War, 1969; U.S. News and World Report October 10, 1988; von Horn, C. Soldiering for Peace, 1966.

VARMUS, HAROLD E.

(December 18, 1939–)
Nobel Prize for Physiology or Medicine, 1989
(shared with J. Michael Bishop)

The American virologist Harold Eliot Varmus was born in Oceanside, New York. His father, Frank Varmus, was a doctor, and his mother, Beatrice (Barasch) Varmus, was a social worker. Both parents were first-generation Americans, descendants of eastern European immigrants. Varmus and his younger sister grew up in Freeport, New York, attending public schools. "The most decisive turn in my intellectual history came in the fall of 1957, when I entered Amherst College intending to prepare for medical school," Varmus recalled. "The evident intensity and pleasure of academic life there challenged my presumptions about my future as a physician, and my course of study drifted from science to philosophy and finally to English literature." Graduating from Amherst in English in 1961, he entered the graduate program at Harvard University. But soon, "I decided I wanted to have more to do with contemporary life than I would as a student of seven-

HAROLD E. VARMUS

teenth-century English prose." He left Harvard in 1962 with an M.A. and entered the Columbia College of Physicians and Surgeons.

Though he began his medical training with an interest in psychiatry, Varmus was quickly attracted to basic medical research and a career in academic medicine. He received his M.D. in 1966 and spent two years as an intern and resident at Columbia-Presbyterian Hospital before moving to the United States National Institutes of Health to work with the biochemist Ira Pastan. "Perhaps because his wife was a poet," Varmus later suggested, "Ira Pastan agreed to take me into his laboratory, despite my lack of scientific credentials." Pastan had just begun studying the mechanics of protein production in the cell in the bacterium *E. coli*. Varmus, in preparation, read the seminal papers on the subject by FRANÇOIS JACOB and JACQUES MONOD. "I knew then that, one way or another, my life was about to change," Varmus recalled.

Jacob's and Monod's work was one of the first great achievements of the new science of molecular biology. Molecular biology is the study of the large molecules that perform biological functions. Following JAMES D. WATSON's and FRANCIS CRICK's 1954 discovery of the structure of DNA, molecular biologists had established (among other things) that genes, the units of heredity, are made of the nucleic acid DNA and that the genetic information encoded in DNA is transcribed into the nucleic acid RNA. RNA is in turn decoded to make the proteins on which life depends. Jacob's and Monod's discoveries concerned how bacteria and bacteriophages (which infect bacterial cells as viruses infect human cells) control when genes are "turned on" and encoded into protein.

Working with bacterial genes taught Varmus basic scientific method and "ultimately shaped the way I later thought about the problems of detecting single genes in more complex, eukaryotic cells" (those from higher organisms such as mammals), Varmus recalled. He was excited by the prospect of applying these methods "to eukaryotic organisms, particularly in a way that might be informative about human disease. . . . I knew enough about viruses and their association with tumors in animals to understand that they might provide a relatively simple entry into a problem as complex as cancer. In fact, for anyone interested in the genetic basis of cancer, viruses seemed to be the only game in town."

Cancer is uncontrolled cell growth. Rather than reproducing normal cells, a cancerous cell produces transformed cells. A mass of transformed cells is called a tumor. A virus can cause cancer by invading a cell's reproductive machinery, forcing it to make more viruses instead of more cells. For example, a virus composed of DNA would introduce its DNA in place of the cell's, and the cell's reproductive center would reproduce the foreign DNA.

The original example of a virus that causes tumors was that discovered by PEYTON ROUS and known as Rous sarcoma virus (RSV). Remarkably, RSV was made of RNA, and not DNA. Since it is DNA that carries genetic information, and controls cell growth, scientists were not sure how an RNA-based virus was able to alter cell growth. "What surprised and beckoned me," Varmus wrote, "were two rather simple but heretical hypotheses that described curious ways the genes of RNA tumor viruses might mingle with [the DNA] of host cells."

In 1964 HOWARD M. TEMIN had proposed the provirus hypothesis: that the regular process of transcription is reversed and RNA from the virus is copied into DNA—a process for which there was at the time no precedent—and this DNA both somehow induces cancers and produces copies of the original RNA virus. In 1970 Temin and DAVID BALTIMORE independently announced the discovery of the enzyme reverse transcriptase, which copies RNA into DNA; this provided substantial support for the provirus hypothesis and gave other workers an invaluable tool for studying RSV and its relatives.

The other hypothesis (not contradictory to the provirus hypothesis) had been proposed by Robert J. Huebner and George J. Todaro of the National Cancer Institute in 1969. The virogene-oncogene hypothesis suggested that the DNA of normal cells contains silent (inactive) cancer-causing genes, called oncogenes, descended from virus infections in their ancestors, that remain silent until they are activated by carcinogens—such as asbestos—to produce new cancers.

Varmus decided to study tumor viruses at the University of California at San Francisco, where J. MICHAEL BISHOP and the microbiologists Leon Levintow and Warren Levinson had just begun to work with RSV. Varmus started working with Bishop in 1970 as a postdoctoral fellow and joined the faculty in 1972.

In 1970 the virologist G. Steven Martin of the University of California, Berkeley, showed that a certain RSV gene, named *src* (for sarcoma), determined the virus's ability to cause cancers; genes with this property are called oncogenes. The virologist Peter K. Vogt of the University of Southern California soon discovered a mutant of the RSV virus in which the *src* gene was left out, or deleted (*src*⁻). Varmus and Bishop reasoned that if DNA from "normal" *src* virus (*src*⁺) was hybridized (matched up) with *src*⁻ RNA, the only DNA left unhybridized would be that for *src* itself. In this way, they could isolate the *src* gene. Dominique Stehelin, a postdoctoral fellow in their laboratory, eventually performed the work, and in 1976 Varmus and Bishop reported the isolation of part of an *src* gene. They then developed an *src* gene "probe" that could locate the *src* gene. Stehelin used the probe and discovered *src*-like genes in normal chicken DNA, as had been predicted by Huebner's and Todaro's virogene-oncogene hypothesis.

When Varmus and his colleagues inserted the *src* probe into DNA from other species, however, they saw startling results. Stehelin found *src* genes in a number of other birds, even those more distantly related to the chicken, and another postdoctoral fellow, Deborah Specter, even found *src*-like sequences in mammals. These findings led the group to conclude that the cancer-causing gene did not result from a viral infection but was a normal, cellular gene carried by the host. Bishop and his associates suggested that cellular oncogenes are present in all the animals because they have some normal, necessary function in animal cells and probably "normally influenced those processes gone awry in tumorigenesis, control of cell growth or development."

The discovery of cellular oncogenes caused great excitement and controversy in the scientific community. By 1981 evidence from numerous laboratories confirmed the conclusions Bishop and his co-workers had formed.

Bishop and Varmus were awarded the 1989 Nobel Prize in Physiology or Medicine for their discoveries. Erling Norrby of the Karolinska Institute stated when presenting the Nobel Prizes, "Through your discovery of the cellular origin of retroviral oncogenes you set in motion an avalanche of research on factors that govern the normal growth of cells. This research has given us a new perspective on one of the most fundamental phenomena in biology and as a consequence also new insights into the complex group of diseases that we call cancer."

When the award was announced, Dominique Stehelin, by then a researcher at the Pasteur Institute, complained that this narrowly worded citation could refer only to the 1976 *src* experiments for which he claimed to have done "all the work from A to Z." Some other French scientists and government officials joined in his protest.

In 1969 Varmus married Constance Louise Casey, a poet and award-winning journalist; they have two sons. David Baltimore has called Varmus and Bishop "the quintessential medical scientists" and has cited Varmus for his tendency "to take a very long-range perspective. . . . [He] can see what it would mean if his experiments are successful, and he carries them out very methodically." Varmus maintains interests in literature and the arts, as well as backpacking, skiing, and other outdoor sports.

Varmus is a member of the National Academy of Sciences, the American Academy of Arts and Sciences, and numerous other scientific societies. His awards include California Scientist of the Year (1982), the Albert Lasker Basic Medical Research Award (1982), the Passano Foundation Award (1983), the Armand Hammer Cancer Prize (1984), the Gairdner Foundation International Award (1984), the Alfred P. Sloan Prize (1984), and the American College of Physicians Award (1987).

SELECTED WORKS: Molecular Biology of Tumor Viruses, 1982, 1985.

ABOUT: American Men and Women of Science, 1989; New York Times October 10, 1989; Science October 20, 1989; Washington Post October 10, 1989; Who's Who in America, 1989.